STEV

BIC

STEVE BAUER ON BICYCLING

by Steve Bauer
with Gerald Donaldson

Macmillan of Canada
A Division of Canada Publishing Corporation
Toronto, Ontario, Canada

Canadian Cataloguing in Publication Data

Bauer, Steve, 1959–
  Steve Bauer on bicycling

Bibliography: p.
Includes index.
ISBN 0-7715-9458-5

1. Cycling. I. Donaldson, Gerald. II. Title.
GV1041.B39 1989   796.6   C89-094680-9

Cover and text design: David Shaw
Illustrations: FULL SPECTRUM ART INC., Toronto

Gear Chart on p. 95 from *The Penguin Bicycle Handbook: How to maintain and repair your bicycle*, by Rob van der Plas (Penguin Books, 1983) copyright © Rob van der Plas, 1983, pp. 256-7. Reproduced by permission of Penguin Books Ltd.

Printed in Canada

Macmillan of Canada
A Division of Canada Publishing Corporation
Toronto, Ontario, Canada

Contents

My Cycling Life

My first experience on a bicycle came at quite an early age and you might say I've been cycling ever since. That first bicycle had 18-inch wheels, yet it was too big for me and I had to climb onto it from the porch of our house. When I pushed off and was finally able to wobble once around the house without anyone's help it was a big day at the Bauers.

That first ride was about five years after I was born, on June 12, 1959, in Fenwick, Ontario, a small town not far from Niagara Falls. All my early cycling adventures took place near there in the towns and open country-side where I was an average all-Canadian boy.

After I'd outgrown that first bike my parents got me one of those three-speed, stick-shift models, with the high handlebars and the banana seats and the little bars on the back to support you while you're doing wheelies. I did lots of them and that bike was loads of fun, similar to the BMX bikes kids have now. With its knobby tires it was also related to today's mountain bikes, and we used to ride them in the forest and the fields, as well as up and down the road. I used to organize makeshift races with my friends who lived down the street, and we had a ball competing and generally raising heck.

Eventually we grew out of those bicycles, and I traded mine in and bought my first racer. It was called a Hirondell Monufrance though I don't know if it really was a French bike, but it had an impressive name and some Simplex components. It wasn't a lugged frame but was welded together at the joints, and though not really a high-quality bicycle, I got a lot of miles out of it.

With my friends and schoolmates I used to ride up and down the streets in Fenwick and nearby Pelham, after classes or in the evenings, stopping at the local snack shops and some-times, according to my parents, get-ting into too much trouble. But we logged a lot of distance on our bikes and always had small competitions among ourselves, doing laps around the schoolyard or in the local parking lots. Another favorite riding place was the cemetery in Fonthill, which had some nice small roads and some challenging corners we used to race through like crazy. Maybe that loca-tion among the tombstones should have made us think about the dangers of what we were doing, but we never slowed down and always had a good time.

A few years later, while I was still in high school, I was having trouble deciding what I would do with my time in the summer. I had played a lot of organized baseball as a kid and now was really too old to play in the sandlot leagues. I either had to go on to the seniors or take up another sport. I'd played soccer for one summer but wasn't really that keen on it, maybe because I wasn't very talented.

My mother had been reading articles in the local papers about the St. Catharines Cycling Club, about how Karen Strong, Tim and Lister Farrar, Gord Singleton and others were doing well in bicycle racing. Since I spent so much time on my bike, my mother suggested we contact the club and I go out with them and maybe watch a race.

We did that and I went to see a race in Delhi, Ontario, which was quite a coincidence because that community has a lot of Belgian expatriates who are cycling enthusiasts, and I would later live and race in Belgium. As I watched that first race I was really impressed and found it tremendously exciting. I managed to try riding one of the racing bikes, which had a very fast, hard and quick-handling feel that I'd never experienced before. I was hooked.

So I borrowed a racing bike and went out training with the St. Catharines club. I was quite strong then and in good shape, so they thought I should get my junior racing license, which I did in midsummer of 1975, and I had some success relatively early on. I went to a fairly high-caliber competition in London, Ontario, where I had my first win, a 100-kilometer road race in Springbank Park. I think it was only the third race I'd entered as a licensed junior rider, so that gave me a lot of confidence.

Here I was in such an exciting sport and apparently I had enough ability to be competitive. It was all the incentive I needed to continue racing.

I had more success in junior 'B' class competitions, and the next big step was racing in the 1976 Canadian National Championships, which were held on the track in Montreal. It was wonderfully exciting to walk into the Montreal velodrome, and I remember getting a rush of adrenaline just looking at that big-banked track and realizing the Olympics had just taken place there. Then, to get up on that beautiful track and actually race around it was the experience of a lifetime for someone so new and naive about cycling.

I became a member of the Canadian National Team, and we rode in the Junior World Championships in Vienna in 1977. That was the farthest I'd ever been away from home, and let me tell you I was a wide-eyed boy. In the individual pursuit I placed thirteenth; our team pursuit placing was seventh, and in the eyes of the National Team coaches I had enough talent to also ride in the Senior World Championships in Venezuela the same year. My cycling ability was really taking me out into the world and I was very happy about that.

On the National Team at that time were Jocelyn Lovell, Ron Hayman, Hugh Walton and me riding in the four-man team pursuit. Jocelyn was also riding the kilometer, Gord Singleton was riding the sprint, Karen Strong was in the women's road race and pursuit. So I was in good company, on the same team with people I admired, and I learned a lot very quickly.

Associating with those dedicated athletes was a real motivation for me, and I began to realize that I could compete internationally at the highest level and maybe go on to achieve something big. It was a huge challenge for me at the time, but I decided that here was an opportunity to devote myself to a sport that I really enjoyed. If I made the commitment I could continue to pursue it for some time, learning and improving under the guidance of the Canadian National Team and riding internationally.

From that point on I decided to take up cycling full time. While I finished high school and attended the University of Waterloo, cycling became my "career," though we were still amateurs and riding under the constraints of a very tight budget. The lack of money was more incentive to go chasing some American dollars by winning races. With team members such as Hugh Walton I went to the United States to challenge the big names, people like John Howard, the Stetna brothers, and other American riders who had performed well internationally. We earned our keep and won races, which put some money in our pockets so we were able to travel further. In the summer of '78 we traveled a great deal south of the border, doing all the major races and preparing ourselves for the bigger international events later in the season.

This pattern continued for me through the early 80s, and my success in the States gained me a place on an American-based team sponsored by the American Manufacturing Foundation (AMF). I trained in Florida in the winter of 1981 and went on that year to win the National Prestige series as the best short-circuit rider in the United States. Then Fred Mengoni took me under his wing and personally sponsored me. Fred is a wealthy, Italian-born American cycling enthusiast, and with the support of him and AMF I was able to pursue racing full-time as an amateur and do the best races in the United States. Meanwhile, I continued riding with the Canadian National Team, getting the international experience that you really have to have to compete on even terms with the cycling elite in Europe. I was a very fortunate rider and really had the best of both worlds.

Fred Mengoni was very instrumental in directing my career, and in the winter of 1983-84 he contacted Greg LeMond and arranged for me to train with him. Fred, who knew how the real racing world worked in Europe, had been telling me that I had to train more, train longer, and he thought Greg would be a good example for me. Greg LeMond was one of the first non-Europeans to make it big as a professional in Europe and had just won the 1983 World Championship. That winter I stayed in one of Fred's condominiums in Sacramento, California, and learned how to train like a pro. I was very impressed by Greg's dedication and discipline. And knowing that he was World Champion made me realize what the benefits could be. Besides that, we became good friends, and later, teammates.

My training paid off that summer of 1984 at the Olympics in Los Angeles. In the 190-kilometer men's individual road race I finished just a bike length behind Alexi Grewal of the U.S., and my silver medal was Canada's first Olympic cycling medal in 76 years.

I turned professional immediately after the Olympics so that I could compete in the 1984 World Championship in Barcelona. I made that decision because I felt I now had a direction; I knew how to train like a pro, how to go that extra distance and prepare myself for the most difficult races in the world.

After my performance in Barcelona I knew I had made the right decision. It gave me a huge boost of confidence, showing me I could compete with famous pros like Sean Kelly, Bernard Hinault and all the big names I had admired for so long. I managed to beat all but two of the top 118 international professionals in Barcelona, and my bronze medal there helped me sign on with one of the best teams in bicycle racing.

At this time Greg was negotiating a contract with L'Equipe La Vie Claire of France, owned by a wealthy entrepreneur, Bernard Tapie, who had one of cycling's top coaches in Paul Koechli. Greg had talked to them about me and recommended to me that I should try to sign up with La Vie Claire. I talked with Paul in August just before the World Championships and he said he was interested. But he was also interested in some other young riders.

Then, the day before the race in Barcelona, Bernard Tapie and Paul came to me and offered me a contract. When I placed third in the World Championship the next day—their star rider, Bernard Hinault, dropped out of the race from heat exhaustion—I think it helped convince them that my value as a profes-

sional rider might be higher than they'd first thought. And I, too, was convinced that I was mentally and physically ready to tackle racing in Europe. It helped that I started my first pro season on an excellent team with a great sponsor, the best possible direction from Paul Koechli and some of the world's finest teammates, including Greg LeMond and Bernard Hinault.

In the fall of 1984 I married Elayne and her coming with me to Europe was also very, very important for me. I don't think I could have done it alone, going to live in Belgium, experiencing culture shock and adapting to a whole new way of life. Elayne, who'd been the girl next door in Fenwick, was a little bit anxious about the move, but her being there all the time for me was a vital factor in my settling in to the the life of a professional bicycle racer. For most foreigners coming to race in Europe, wives are very instrumental in their careers. With Elayne's help my career has gone rather well.

In my first pro season I had some good results, the most prominent being in the Tour de France, where I finished tenth overall and wore the White Jersey (for the best-placed "neo pro" of the Tour) for 16 days. But beyond the good results I've had in racing, the most vivid memories for me are emotional and physical, which is really what cycling is all about.

Professional racing can be very relaxed at times, but at critical moments in the race and near the finish it can be so incredibly intense, and the concentration can be so very strong and directed that you feel as if you'll drown in adrenaline. Much of racing is just a blur, but I remember the times that you're riding so close, the peloton (the main bunch of racers) is moving so quickly down narrow roads and down descents, you're really on the edge of control—right on the very limit because the bikes are so close together.

You're wheel to wheel, shoulder to shoulder, and if the race is at a critical point you need to be in front before a particular turn or a hill. Everyone is really fighting for position and not giving an inch. You're right on the edge of the road. At times you have to brake extremely hard. Your reaction time must be instantaneous or else you'll be tumbling off the road or into another rider. Besides concentrating on your basic survival, you have to keep a clear head and be ready for anything.

There might be a lull in the action for a while when everyone is riding along fairly calmly, and boom! The race takes off again. There's attacking left and right, and bang! The focus changes from talking to your buddy beside you to racing at 60 kilometers an hour, fighting a crosswind that wants to throw you in the ditch. It's entirely unpredictable—and that keeps it exciting.

There are so many variables: weather, wind, race tactics, the course—you may be racing over roads you've never seen before and you've no idea what's around the next bend. You must remain alert for whatever might be coming up: gravel in the corners, a sudden narrowing of the road, a shift in the wind, a sudden shower, who might be attacking, who might be controlling the race, who

looks strong, who doesn't look strong, how far the race has to go. . . . So many possibilities to consider, to stay on top of things and concentrate on trying to be the best on any given day.

These types of pressures within the race are sometimes very, very powerful, and the state of alertness might be compared to a Formula One driver where the concentration has to be so intense on every corner and the precision so very exact that your head aches. That's not all that hurts, because with all those considerations you're still giving that mighty physical output, racing under your own power, to meet the challenge of being the first to the finish.

We race in some appalling weather, among the worst being a very cold rain where you have to put on extra clothes (rain coats, winter gloves, booties), but still you're cold, wet, miserable and easily discouraged. You're racing under conditions that your body just does not like, but you still must give your maximum performance.

The best cure for that is to win, and the feeling of elation can start before you actually cross the line. One of the most memorable moments for me is when you're so close to the finish and so far in front that you know without a doubt that you're the winner. The adrenaline pours through your aching body and you feel almost invincible. You're tireless, you have that unbeatable advantage, you feel so good that there's no pain left anymore. Though getting to that point may have been incredibly difficult, the output of energy enormously exhausting and the concentration absolutely withering, when you arrive at that place in the race all is forgotten.

Crossing the line in first place, knowing you've accomplished your dream,...that rush of good feeling you've wished for for so long is now yours and you can cherish it for a few short moments—that's what I remember best.

I've won my share of major events, and those experiences are wonderful motivators to keep me pushing for more success. Another method I use to elevate my overall level of performance is to pursue specific goals within a race. One of my goals had always been to wear the Yellow Jersey, symbolic of the leading rider in the Tour de France. But the highlight of the 1988 Tour for me was getting the Yellow Jersey back after I'd won it in the first stage. Winning it the first time was a big bonus, something that had eluded me for four years. But getting it back after one week was something really special.

There was a hill near the end of the stage that day and the Colombian Luis Herrara, one of the best climbers in the business, was attacking. He split the group just over the top and I went with them. We were 15 or 20 strong and going away, and the Yellow Jersey wasn't there—the rider wearing it was somewhere back in the pack—and I got this surge of ela-

tion and felt I could get that Jersey back. I really attacked the group and made the descent flat out to keep in front. It was terrifying and I wasn't even thinking about winning the race. I just wanted to keep the distance between me and the guy wearing the Yellow Jersey at the maximum. I was so confident that this was my day. It was. I got the Yellow Jersey back and wore it for five days in all.

Wearing the Yellow Jersey means you're not just part of the race, you're the focus of the race. Everyone's attention is on you. This is the biggest, most publicized cycling event in the world, and here you are with the Jersey that shows you're number one so far along the road. It's an honor and you feel a responsibility to do your absolute best to defend it, which is harder than ever to do because you know that you're in the limelight and everyone is out to catch you. But it gives you an extra surge of energy, a psychological boost that helps you perform at your best. It gave me the determination to give my best performance ever and helped me finish fourth overall in the Tour.

They say that the Yellow Jersey gives you wings, and it certainly makes for a powerful feeling. But similar rewards and pleasures are there for any cyclist. All you have to do is to pedal your bike.

PART ONE

Let's Go Cycling

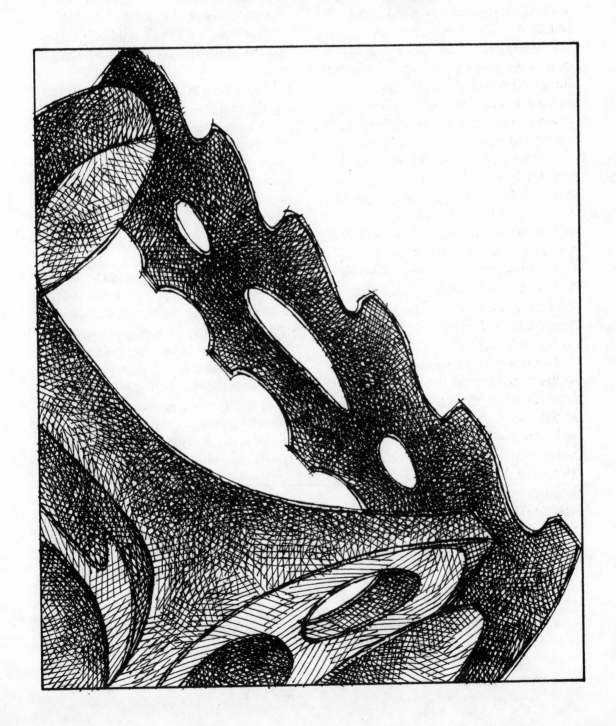

Pedal Power

The Joys of Cycling

I ride a bicycle to make my living, but even if I didn't ride for that reason I would cycle anyway—just for the fun of it. The sheer pleasure of riding is still a great motivator for me, and it's been that way since my first time on a bike. The feeling of accomplishment, the sense of freedom and the adventure of it all are still there. It was child's play way back then. Now that it's my job, I'm still having that kind of fun.

Sure, the fun factor tends to fade when I'm climbing an alp in a mountain stage of the Tour de France, but it's still a great thrill and challenge to come freewheeling down the other side with the wind in my face—especially if I'm in the lead! Life as a professional bike racer has its ups and downs and is often really hard work, but for me, it's always a labor of love.

You don't have to race your bike to enjoy cycling. One of the sport's biggest bonuses, and a major reason for its wide-ranging popularity, is that it's so accessible—anyone can do it. Unlike tennis, golf or skiing, you don't need access to exclusive clubs or special facilities to enjoy yourself as a recreational cyclist. Nor do you need to be a particularly physical type, as in football, or need special skills, as in skating, in order to cycle well. Kids can learn to ride shortly after they develop enough coordination and sense of balance to walk. Then it can become the sport for a lifetime where age is no barrier.

Beyond that, the physical and psychological benefits of cycling can contribute to a more productive, satisfying and longer life.

The bicycle is tailor-made for these life-style-conscious days, when so many people are concerned with health and fitness. Cycling's inherent sense of fun and its stress-free nature make it one of the easiest and most enjoyable ways to become fit and stay that way—painlessly. Pedaling, one of the best cardiovascular activities and a terrific method for burning off calories, gives you all the positive benefits without the bodily wear and tear, and boredom, of running several miles or bouncing around in an aerobics workout.

When cycling becomes part of your life-style, you can combine its practical use, as a means of transport, with your fitness regimen. Bicycle commuters have the best of both worlds: keeping fit while beating the traffic and the pressures of the clock. Instead of having to set aside extra time for a workout, you get it on your way to and from work, or running errands, or going shopping. All of this riding can be done with a clear social conscience, too, because bikes don't pollute the environment or contribute to the din of urban noise. Plus they're much easier to park than cars and they're a lot cheaper to buy and run. Bikes can play a leading utilitarian role in your daily routine, but the possibilities extend far beyond that.

You can use your bike to explore

life, and enrich it. Cycling is almost as natural an activity as walking. In fact, you could call it walking with a little mechanical assistance. You supply the motive power, you set the pace, and you reap the rewards. Unlike riding in a motorized vehicle, sitting in the saddle puts you in touch with nature, and yourself. Some of my best moments on a bike have come during leisurely training runs in the countryside when I can appreciate the landscape and listen to the birds. Problems and stress seem to evaporate, things are easier to put into perspective, and the world seems a better place.

It's by no means a holiday for me riding in events like the Giro d'Italia or the Tour de Suisse during the racing season, but cycle touring is a great way to travel. Exploring and sight-seeing trips on bicycles put you right into the landscape, exposed to the elements, and there's no better way to really get to know a new environment intimately. Bike explorations give you a sense of pioneering freedom not to be found in other means of travel. You feel in charge of your own destiny, and the challenge and adventure of long-distance touring, making your own way over new terrain and choosing your own forks in the road, is immensely satisfying.

The sport of cycling caters to all tastes, and many branches of it are devoted to less-leisurely pursuits on bicycles. If you're competitive by nature, there's no better way to test yourself, to probe your limits, than to take up the challenge of bike racing, even at the most amateur level. It may not look like much fun when you watch a race close up, all those grimacing faces, the grunts, groans and gasping for breath in a crowd of whirring sprockets and spinning wheels, but believe me it's a tremendous thrill.

Most of my cycling is done at speed, and that turns the act of pedaling into a whole new ball game. You just can't beat the thrill of going fast, the euphoria that comes from being intoxicated by your own velocity. And it's a natural high, created partly by the chemicals (endorphins) the body produces during vigorous exercise. The sensation is intensified even more by the knowledge that you are providing the power for your pleasure, not artificially, but through the simple, basic act of pedaling your bike.

With so much going for it, you'd wonder why the whole world doesn't cycle. In fact, a surprisingly large portion of the planet's population does. And judging by the ever larger crowds of enthusiasts I see in my travels, the converts to life on two wheels are multiplying by leaps and bounds. If you aren't one of us yet, I hope you will be after reading this book.

When you do join the rank and file of bicycle enthusiasts, you'll find that you become part of a tradition with a fascinating history.

A Short History of Cycling

Back in the cradle of civilization it seems likely that the idea of putting two wheels in tandem and riding on them occurred shortly after the invention of the wheel. Somebody probably looked at a chariot or cart and considered the possibilities of replacing horsepower with manpower. Judging by their artistic depictions of bikelike contraptions, the ancient Egyptians, Etruscans and Babylonians were on the right track. Whether the concept ever got off the drawing board, we don't know, but some of the illustrations of gods and men astride reasonable facsimiles of bicycles are more than 3,000 years old.

After that earliest period of two-wheeled thinking, there is a lengthy gap until the great tinkerer and inventor Leonardo da Vinci (1452-1519) turned his hand to the concept and included a fair approximation of a bicycle among his drawings. A church built in Stoke Poges, Buckinghamshire, England, in 1637 has a stained-glass window featuring a cyclist of sorts. The rider is a naked cherub who seems to be enjoying himself immensely, tooting a long trumpet as he straddles a spoke-wheeled device with elaborate curlicues on the handlebars.

Some historians think the unclad Stoke Poges horn-tooter is riding a glorified hobby horse, a single-wheeled toy with the head of a horse favored by kids of the Middle Ages. And in fact, the forerunners of bicycles are direct descendants of the hobby horse and were really toys for adults. (Come to think of it, they still are.)

Down through the years there was a lot of give and take while cycling took shape, and there is some argument among historians over precise dates, but here's a quick rundown of the agreed milestones in the evolution of the bicycle:

1791: The Comte de Sivrac added a second wheel and a saddle to a hobby horse, and his invention caught on with fashionable young

An early hobby-horse, heavy and cumbersome, was propelled by the rider pushing his feet along the ground. Its wooden or steel-rimmed wheels gave a well-deserved name to its descendants: bone-shakers.

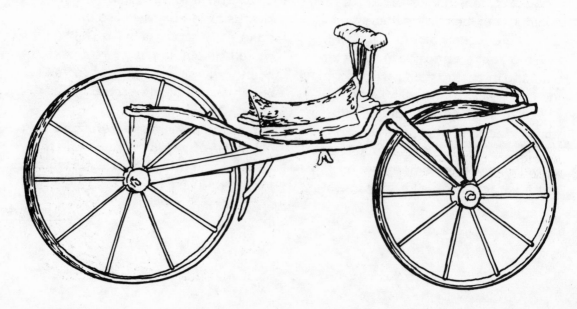

people who scooted merrily along the boulevards of Paris on their foot-powered cycles. The French called the wooden machines *celeriferes* (to carry fast) or *velocipedes* (fast feet), though they weren't particularly speedy and would travel only as fast as the rider could move his feet along the ground. Nor would they turn easily because the front wheel was fixed.

1817: The Comte's concept was improved upon by Baron von Drais, a German who added a steerable front wheel. The growing band of two-wheeled enthusiasts, still mainly in France, could now include more elaborate maneuvers to their repertoire of cycling tricks, and they rewarded the baron by christening his device the Draisene.

1818-20: Variations on the Draisene/ hobby horse were exported to Britain and North America, though in the latter case the fixation with real horses and the lack of many smooth-surfaced roads tended to restrict the spread of the new fad. But the British hopped onto the dandy horse, as they called it, with great enthusiasm and

were largely responsible for bikes as we know them today. The major breakthroughs came from innovative carpenters, blacksmiths, coopers and wheelwrights, who turned their talents to the more efficient use of leg power on two wheels.

1839-40: Kirkpatrick Macmillan, a Scottish blacksmith, hammered out an idea incorporating long levers, which worked like pedals to pull long arms, or treadles, which turned the axle of the rear wheel—something like the long arms used on the wheels of steam engines. Macmillan also was involved in the first recorded cycling accident when he knocked a Glaswegian child down while test-driving his invention. He was fined five shillings.

1861: The credit for the next biking breakthrough goes back to France where a father and son, Pierre and Ernest Michaux, attached pedals to the front wheels of a Draisene. The

A primitive set of pedals and treadle-arms connected to the front hub propelled this designer's dream at a rather grinding pace.

Michaux family marketed their invention, and by 1867 their 300 employees were cranking out five new machines a day. The Michaux company hired professional riders to help develop and publicize their products.

1868: Michaux staged the first known bicycle race, a track event, which was run over 1,200 meters at the St. Cloud park near Paris. It was won by an Englishman named James Moore riding a Michaux. A year later Moore rode another Michaux velocipede to win the first recorded road race, a 123-kilometer event from Paris to Rouen where the field of more than 200 riders included five women. Moore's winning time was just over ten hours and the last finisher took twice that long. The next developments in cycling revolved around the quest for more speed—and comfort.

1871-76: In England, velocipedes were called bone-shakers, because of the rough ride caused by iron strips mounted on wooden-spoked wheels. James Starley, who also invented an adjustable candlestick and a weird-looking quadricycle, developed a bone-shaker with a very large front wheel, in effect a higher gear that produced more speed. He called his contraption the Ordinary, but it was soon nicknamed the Penny Farthing, the front wheel being large like a British penny and the rear smaller like a farthing. Starley ironed out the kinks in the Ordinary's rough ride by using wire spokes in the wheels and adding solid rubber tires.

1879: Starley and his contemporaries were unable to solve the stability problems encountered by an Ordinary rider perched high over a front wheel, sometimes seven feet off the ground. Finally, H.J. Lawson, another British inventor, designed the Safety, a machine with more equally sized wheels, the rear one being driven by a chain turned from centrally mounted pedals. Lawson called his Safety a *bicyclette*, or small bicycle, borrowing the word from France, where it was in common use.

1885-87: John Kemp Starley, nephew of James, developed the Rover safety bicycle, an improvement on Lawson's design. The Rover evolved quickly into what closely resembles today's bicycle, with wheels of equal diameter, a diamond-shaped frame, curved front forks and handlebars for steering. The Rover suffered only from the want of better tires to become a thoroughly efficient machine.

1887: John Boyd Dunlop, a Scottish veterinary working in Dublin, cobbled up inflatable tires from rubber sheets and strips of linen and clamped them onto the wheels of his son's bike. Dr. Dunlop's pneumatic tires soon became all the rage, and the idea was imported to France by the brothers Michelin, who developed tires that could be removed from the wheels to repair punctures. The Dunlop and Michelin rubber companies went into production to supply the increasing demand for tires, both for the bicycle and its greatest rival, the newly invented motorcar.

1890-99: The development of the Safety bicycle propelled cycling through several phases of popularity. At first it was regarded as an eccentric pastime for the athletically adventurous. Then it became a fashionable novelty favored by the idle rich, and large crowds gathered in the parks of London, Paris and New York to watch high society cavort on two wheels. Bicycles became socially acceptable and were mass produced so they were more affordable. In 1895, two million bikes were sold in the U.S. where prices dropped from $100 to $30 in a short time. Two years later there were 830 bike manufacturers in England. The fad was taken up by the middle classes, who used bicycles as a practical means of transport, as well as for leisure pursuits. The League of American Wheelmen (LAW) flourished and membership in the Cyclists' Touring Club (CTC) in England went from 16,343 in 1895 to 60,449 in 1899. Cyclists banded together, partly to celebrate the joys of their sport and partly to present a united front against increasing anti-bike hostilities.

1900: By the turn of the century the bike boom leveled off, and cycling had become less of a craze and more of a fact of life in most Western societies. But it wasn't always a smooth ride for cyclists. They had continual run-ins with farmers whose horses tended to bolt near bikes, and equestrians viewed cyclists as their natural enemies for much the same reason. The proliferation of the horseless carriage caused further hostilities with the proponents of pedal power and mechanical horsepower fighting over their rights to the roads. Certain companies in the bike business aban-

doned it in favor of cars, among them Peugeot in France, Morris in England, Daimler, Benz and Opel in Germany, and Ford in America. The Wright brothers, proprietors of another American cycle shop, got sidetracked from two-wheeled travel on the ground by the vision of taking to the skies with their new invention, the airplane.

Doctors, at first, took a dim view of cycling, maintaining it caused all manner of ills, including such physical deformities as bent spines and elongated legs. Women cyclists, who wore decadent costumes like bloomers for easier maneuverability, were at first regarded as vulgar misfits and, with their cycling menfolk—who dressed in breeches and stockings or knickerbockers, as they were called in the States—were sometimes refused service in respectable places of business. But cyclists persisted and eventually became more accepted. Bicycles became, in their own modest way, vehicles of social change.

The popularity of the cycling movement ebbed and flowed over the years. In the U.S., Henry Ford's gas-powered, mass-produced products relegated bikes to the backseat of public opinion for several decades. In England the aristocrats grew tired of their bikes and looked down their noses at the commoners who used them for everyday life. But the upper-class twits were outnumbered, and cycling flourished in Britain and continental Europe, where bikes became more and more highly developed. Following World War II the Europeans became car crazy, like the North Americans who thought cycling was for kids, though the typical bikes were cumbersome, heavy, balloon-tired devices that required some strength to handle.

En route to their present status, bicycles have functioned at all levels of society and have even seen service as machines of war. Cycling soldiers fought in both World Wars and several lesser ones, and recently the North Vietnamese army fared quite well on their bicycles against much better-equipped forces. Many Third World countries have adopted cycling wholesale, using bicycles as beasts of burden and as the prime means of transport; approximately 80 percent of all personal travel in China is via the bicycle.

In less-industrialized societies the bike is indispensable for practical reasons. But as soon as technology takes over, there's more leisure time and people look for ways to fill it. The current bike boom in our part of the world came about when people got tired of riding around in their cars. They sought pleasurable new pastimes, improved health and fitness and found them all in cycling.

The trend started in the 1970s, mainly in the U.S. where the bike—particularly the "European racer"—came into fashion, and the phenomenon has spread to all affluent societies. By the mid 1970s the U.S. branched out on a new venture—mountain bikes, which are now in the forefront and taking cycling into an exciting new era.

Some countries, like Holland where 80 percent of the inhabitants own bicycles, have long been cycle-minded, and in Western Europe, Japan and North America, bicycles outsell cars. More than 100 million Americans call themselves cyclists; in Canada approximately one-third of the total population cycles, and every second household has at least one bicycle.

The new popularity has led to an international manufacturing competition, resulting in tremendous improvements in sophistication and quality, as well as several exciting new variations on the basic bicycle structure. Cyclists have never had it so good.

Some Cycling Feats

I promote my own line of Steve Bauer bikes through racing, and I guess that makes me part of a tradition, too, because, from the earliest days, feats on bicycles have played a large part in the spread of the popularity of cycling.

Besides racing against their own kind, cyclists have pitted themselves against the clock, and other means of transport. In 1895 a cyclist outran a racehorse over a measured mile, in a time of 95 seconds. Four years later an American named Charles Murphy rode behind a train on a specially prepared length of track. He clocked a mile in 57.8 seconds and was known thereafter as Mile-a-Minute Murphy. It was six years before a racing car could better his pace.

Mile-a-Minute Murphy was taking advantage of an early form of motor-pacing, one of the methods I use for training. By following closely behind a vehicle, a rider can break away from the restrictions imposed by air resistance. Murphy's average speed was just over 63 miles an hour. The current record, a highly technological feat that was achieved on a bicycle traveling behind a specially designed windbreak attached to a streamlined racing car in Utah, is more than 150 miles an hour.

Aerodynamically designed, human-powered devices operated by cycling mechanisms are always setting new speed records it seems, but one of the most remarkable bike-power achievements is the flight of the Gossamer Albatross. In 1979, a cyclist, Bryan Allen, pedaled the motorless lightweight aircraft across the English Channel.

From the beginning, certain adventurous people have taken the idea of bicycle touring to great lengths. In 1884 Thomas Stevens, a pioneering—and very hardy—rider, took his Ordinary (or highwheeler, as the Americans called them) from California to Massachusetts. During his epic journey he had to outrun a pack of coyotes and dodge bullets from drunken cowboys. Twelve years later a woman, Margaret Valentine, completed another trans-American trek, and in this century the intrepid Irish lady, Dervla Murphy, has cycled to some of the most remote corners of the world.

Endurance competitions were all the rage at the end of the last century and the beginning of this one. In 1883

a British cyclist, J.H. Adams, pedaled an Ordinary for 24 hours, covering a distance of 242.5 miles. Not content with cycling just once around the clock, the English invented six-day bicycle races, and for a while these events were nearly as big as base-ball in the United States. In 1897 the record for a six-day race was set by Charles W. Miller, who toured around a track inside New York's Madison Square Garden for 144 hours, logging 2,088.35 miles for an average of 14.5 miles an hour. In the next few years winning distances increased to nearly 3,000 miles, and the riders became public figures, who were well paid for their pains. One of the greatest six-day riders was a Canadian, Torchy Peden, who won nearly 40 of the 144-hour marathons before these "races to nowhere," as they were called, petered out in pop-ularity in the New World.

In Europe, however, bike racing, especially road racing, has been big news from day one. In fact, the big-gest race of them all was first organ-ized to make news. Following the success of the first recorded road race, in 1869, French cycling enthusiasts staged several annual point-to-point events, mainly from Paris to other cities. They were often organized and promoted by newspa-pers intent on increasing readership. In 1903 the editor of the *L'Auto*, Henri Desgrange, a former professional bike racer, decided to promote his publication with a race that covered much of the country. He called it the Tour de France.

Nowadays, events like the Tour de France capture the public imagina-tion as never before, and increasing media coverage of cycling competition is bringing it to a huge worldwide audience. The top riders have become household names, and people like Fausto Coppi (Italy), Jacques Anquetil (France), and Eddy Merckx (Belgium) were heroes of the postwar decades whose fame spread far beyond the borders of their own countries.

As a young Canadian racer I was inspired by riders like Jocelyn Lovell, and when I went to Europe I had the good fortune to be able to help two of my teammates, Bernard Hinault and Greg LeMond, win the Tour de France. I, too, have had my share of success, and for me, part of the reward of being ranked one of the best racers in the world is understanding that my accomplishments will help motivate others—especially recreational cyclists. This works both ways, and knowing that my success will inspire others helps me push harder so that I can further promote the sport I love.

In major international competition fitness is a prime factor in being able to stay at the front of the peloton. And the pursuit of fitness is a main reason cycling has so many new converts.

The Road to Fitness

A big bonus in bicycle riding is that fitness comes with the territory. You don't have to go out of your way to find it, because the very act of pedaling sets the wheels in motion to improve physical fitness. And you get to sit down on the job!

You don't see any overweight people in my line of work, nor do many dedicated recreational cyclists carry spare tires around their waists. That's because weight control is another natural byproduct of cycling: the energy you expend in the saddle consumes calories, between 300 and 800 an hour, depending on the gear you're in, the speed you're traveling, the effort you put out, and other factors. Also, when you become hooked on cycling you tend to become more diet conscious. You realize that you need the proper foods to feed your two-wheel habit and you watch what you eat.

Cycling, cross-country skiing, swimming and running, are rated the best aerobic sports to improve cardiovascular (heart/lung) endurance, a main component of physical fitness. Aerobic exercise is energetic activity that elevates the heart rate to a certain level and keeps it there for a period of time. The heart, as everyone knows these days, is just a big muscle, and to stay in top-notch condition it needs a regular workout. This effort also makes the lungs expand and increases their efficiency in processing oxygen, the key factor in providing energy for the muscles in the body to work. Pumping along on a bicycle is one of the easiest, most accessible ways of doing your body these favors.

The trend among fitness enthusiasts these days is to combine various forms of exercise in what is called cross-training, and cycling is the favorite common denominator. You can ride your bicycle to your tennis or squash game or to the fitness club to get a nicely rounded workout. And inclement weather needn't interfere with your fitness regimen. Your bike converts easily into an exercise bike, so that you can ride out winter's storms in the comfort of your home.

Besides giving you a cardiovascular workout, cycling also improves overall muscle strength, tone and endurance. This effect is seen mainly in the lower body, but that's where most of our major muscles are. And when those muscles are used regularly, cholesterol and blood-pressure levels are reduced, contributing to a reservoir of fitness that gives you better resistance to disease and improved overall health. Beyond that, as most people know from experience, a state of fitness gives you extra energy and stamina to simply enjoy life more. In short, it makes you feel good.

It also improves your mental outlook.

A bicycle can be a powerful stress-management tool, and those with extra-heavy workloads and hectic lives can help maintain mental equilibrium by literally riding away from their pressures and anxieties. After a hard day at the office, a bike becomes a getaway vehicle par excellence, and it's not surprising that many shrinks are confirmed bike nuts. These are the people who keep telling us we need to relax and unwind, we need more play in our adult lives, and we should have rewarding hobbies; we can increase our self-esteem through the satisfaction and well-being of being physically fit. We can practice what they preach by cycling.

It should be obvious by now that becoming a committed cyclist is a good thing. But the nonbelievers may still need more persuasion.

The Cycling Life Style

Bicycles are engineering masterpieces, the most efficient machines for harnessing human energy yet invented. Using the same amount of energy, you cover eight times as much ground on a bike as you do when walking.

Bicycles outperform automobiles in urban areas—as you may have noticed while sitting in your car stuck in a traffic jam. Many studies have proven that bicycles are the fastest mode of transport, including all forms of public transit, in short journeys in major metropolitan areas. This is

especially true during rush hours, but the proliferation of bicycle couriers (all of them bike nuts, it seems) shows that cycling works at any time in big cities.

As practical vehicles, bicycles leave cars behind in several ways. Scientists have calculated that a car consumes 96 percent more energy to convey one passenger over the same distance as a bike, and it needs gas to do it. But bikes don't burn up resources, nor do they pollute the environment with noxious emissions or noise. They cause much less wear and tear on the roads, and they use up far less space than cars. And when you arrive at your destination on a bike, you don't have to search for a parking space—nor do you have to pay for it.

When it comes to comparing costs, bikes come out way ahead. A good bike bought by an adult should last a lifetime. Even the best bike costs a fraction of what it takes to buy a new car. Since bikes are more economical and reliable than any car, their operating and maintenance costs are minimal. Add the cost of insuring a car—which will buy a very good bike, or several if you're a younger driver— and it's no contest.

Never before have cyclists gotten more for their money. The bike boom and the resulting competition among manufacturers has brought down the prices, while product quality has improved immeasurably. And today's bike buyers can benefit from another cycling phenomenon: the dedication and expertise of the people in the bike business. Surely no other sport has such passionate devotees retailing its equipment. The staff in the better bike shops are keen enthusiasts who make it their business to keep up with what's going on in the field. And when their day's work is done, they can be found out on the road cycling.

Of course, there are negative aspects to the cycling life. Many of the hassles involve fighting over rights on the road with motor vehicles, an ancient struggle that continues to this day. Also, when you ride your bike, especially when you ride it fast, you need lots of oxygen. And while bikes don't contribute to air pollution the way internal-combustion

engines do, their riders suffer from having to inhale others' exhaust fumes. One sure cure for the problem would be to have the world convert to cycle power. Until then we'll just have to try to choose cycling routes away from the worst pollution.

Weather is less of a problem. When it gets really bad you can seek shelter, but the latest cycle clothing will handle just about anything the weatherman throws at you. We racers have garments to cover the full spectrum of nature's nastiness and must ride through whatever meteorological variations come our way: sweltering heat, bone-chilling cold, teeming rain, even sleet and snow— sometimes all of it in one event. You won't have to suffer through those extremes as a recreational cyclist, but be assured that we professionals in the field are helping you in the long run by testing clothing—and bikes—in all weather conditions.

I spend several hours of nearly every day of the year on a bike, but if you're a recreational cyclist you need to fit it into what may be an already busy routine. One of the best ways, as I've pointed out, is to use cycling for regular transportation. When you add a carrier to your bike you can use it to do your shopping, go to the post office, or run errands. You can even hitch a trailer to your bike for increased carrying capacity.

You can take your holidays on your bike, and for the ultimate in cycling togetherness, you might investigate the purchase of a tandem bike to ride with your favorite companion. As new parents, Elayne and I are now interested in child carriers for our bicycles. However, I recommend safety helmets for children and discourage riding with them on busy streets. Parks or quiet bike paths would be the best. I'll talk more about safety throughout the book. My Steve Bauer line of bikes includes models for children and we look forward to the time when we can cycle together as a family. When that day comes, the sport will have come full cycle for me.

All About Bikes

Types of Bicycles

There are more varieties of the basic bicycle on the market today than ever before. The main reason for this is the trend to using bikes for specific purposes: commuting, touring, fitness and so on. Beyond that, cyclists tend to be an upwardly mobile group, mastering one level of the sport, then seeking further challenges down the road and going to more expensive bikes. Entire families are cycling these days, and the adult riders want nothing but the best for their children.

Manufacturers are responding to the demand by building ranges of specialty bikes, available in varying degrees of quality and sophistication geared to the needs and skill levels of the riders. That's why Steve Bauer Bicycles sells over two-dozen models. This great variety is good news for cycle shoppers who know exactly what they want, but the profusion of bike types can be intimidating to novice bike hunters. The trick is to find exactly the bike you need.

The treasure hunt is made much easier when you divide bikes into two main categories. Using a certain amount of poetic/cycling license, I conveniently group them under the two broad labels of mountain bikes, and road bikes.

Mountain Bikes

Mountain bikes are the newest branch of the family and the easiest to categorize. They were invented for off-road travel, but they're everywhere these days and are being modified for specific uses. In my line of bikes we have mountain models for sports fitness, city, touring and competition purposes.

Also known as all-terrain bikes, or ATBs, mountain bikes evolved in the hills around San Francisco less than 15 years ago and now account for nearly half of all bikes sold in North America. Like that other Californian innovation, the personal computer, mountain bikes are user-friendly, and their easy-to-ride, go-anywhere virtues account for their popularity.

They're strongly built and have 15, 18 or 21 gears, sometimes wider, mattress-type saddles, flat handlebars, powerful brakes and fat tires. The bikes come with tire-tread patterns that are knobby with pronounced lugs for negotiating rough terrain, but smoother, narrower tires convert mountain bikes into effective road machines.

Mountain bikes are:
- easy to operate and handle because of their straightforward design, upright riding position and fingertip controls,

- less intimidating for novices because of their upright riding position and sturdy, uncomplicated look,
- favored by people with back problems who prefer the upright riding position,
- comfortable riding over shorter distances because of their wider tires, padded saddles and softer springing,
- rugged, reliable and relatively maintenance-free, including having less puncture-prone tires,
- versatile and easily adaptable to a variety of uses beyond climbing steep hills.

Mountain bikes are not:
- as comfortable for longer rides because the upright seating position doesn't allow the rider many position changes,
- as fast or easy to pedal and energy-efficient as road bikes, because they weigh more and their fat tires create greater rolling resistance,
- as nimble and maneuverable in tight situations on roads.

Road Bikes

Road bikes is the general term used to describe the rest of the field. Again, allowing a certain amount of latitude because of their cross-over capabilities, they can be broken down into three main subdivisions: basic bikes, sport bikes and racing bikes.

Basic Bikes

The traditional upright, heavy models like the ones our ancestors rode are harder to find these days but they still have their aficionados. These sturdy, no-nonsense machines have flat handlebars, wide tires and saddles. Usually they come equipped with coaster brakes (on the pedals), though some have caliper brakes. Most have fenders, mudguards and chainguards, and sometimes they come with luggage carriers. Gearing is usually limited to one, two, three or five speeds.

Sometimes these bikes are called coasters, and the elderly, but elegant English roadster fits into the category. So does the American cruiser, a direct descendant of the fat-framed, balloon-tired bikes of yesteryear U.S.A.

Basic bikes are:
- solid, no-nonsense utilitarian transportation,
- uncomplicated to operate and maintain,
- strong and reliable.

Basic bikes are not:
- easy to pedal, because of their weight and lack of gears,
- as adaptable to specific purposes,
- as much fun in the long run.

Sports Bikes

This middle-of-the-road grouping encompasses a whole range of bikes evolved from what used to be called the English racer or the 10-speed. Like them, modern sports road bikes have drop handlebars, thinner frames and tires, narrow saddles and caliper brakes on each wheel. Though they usually don't come with fenders, they can be equipped with them. Pedals with toe clips or some method of fixing shoes to the pedals are usually standard equipment, and most sports bikes come with at least 10 derailleur gears; 14, 16, 18, even 21 speeds are available, though 12 gears are the most common.

While sports bikes share a common denominator of basic configuration, they have been developed into the following subdivisions of purpose-built machines: fitness and training, commuting and city travel, and long- and short-distance touring, as well as bikes intended for general-purpose riding and recreation.

Each of those subdivisions has a range of models, built for entry-level use through to the deluxe top-of-the-line machines, so that the sports bikes grouping contains the greatest variety.

Sports bikes are:
- light in weight, and energy efficient because of the aerodynamic riding position,
- easy to pedal for the same reasons, with the added advantage of lots of gears,
- more comfortable and less tiring over long distances, because the drop handlebars allow a variety of riding positions,
- easy to handle and maneuver in tight situations,
- versatile and adaptable to a wide variety of uses.

Sports bikes are not:
- as easy to master for beginners, because they demand more input from the rider,
- as maintenance-free, because of their more complicated construction.

Racing Bikes

Racing bikes share similar characteristics with sports bikes, but are lighter, more sophisticated and refined. Sometimes called pro bikes, these are the top-of-the-line, state-of-the-art models designed for competition, but also widely used for recreational riding. Replacing their fragile tubular tires with more durable clincher-type rubber makes racers more suitable for everyday use.

Like sports cars, racing bikes are performance-oriented and are built for speed, maneuverability and more responsive handling. They're sensitive thoroughbreds and can provide all the thrills of the chase for more experienced cyclists. They're not made for comfort and demand more from the rider, but they deliver the most excitement.

Real racing bikes are closest to my heart, the epitomy of the sport of cycling. The best of them are works of art, beautiful enough to hang up on your wall like a piece of prized—and expensive—sculpture. And I know people who do that.

Racing bikes are:
- the most fun you can have on two wheels—but they can also be a source of a great deal of self-inflicted suffering!
- the best-handling, most nimble and energy-efficient,
- the most challenging and satisfying for the skilled rider.

Racing bikes are not:
- the easiest bikes to master,
- as comfortable to ride,
- as easy to maintain or keep—they're the most likely to be stolen.

Ladies' Bicycles

These days women and men generally ride the same bikes, the anatomical size differences accommodated simply by fitting the bike to the person. But some women prefer the traditional ladies' style of bike, which eliminates the top horizontal tube and has twin downward tubes instead, or a still-different arrangement of tubing called a mixte frame. You just step into them and they can be ridden while wearing a skirt or long coat. The absence of the top tube also makes these bikes of interest to very short people and to older folk who may not be agile enough to throw their leg over the top tube when mounting. One of my line of bikes, a high-fashion model, is built for women and named after Elayne, my wife.

Children's Bicycles

Many companies also make junior models, for children ten years and older, and most manufacturers cater to the younger cyclist. The best kids' bikes are essentially adultlike vehicles carefully sized to suit smaller people, using the same components and methods of construction in a scaled-down composition, without sacrificing quality.

Other Bike Types

Besides those general categories described so far, the wonderful world of cycling includes other offshoots of road and mountain machines, as well as certain contraptions that come from somewhere out in left field.

From the racing world come track bikes, ultralight machines with no brakes and only a single fixed gear, which are intended for use on wooden or concrete oval tracks (called velodromes—see Track Events). Some serious cyclists use them, fitted with brakes, for workouts on the roads. Triathlon bikes are racing bikes adapted for the sport, which combines swimming, running and cycling. Other racing derivatives are the time-trial bikes, those strange-looking aerodynamically contrived devices with solid wheels, which are smaller in the front than the back.

BMX bikes are first cousins to mountain bikes, but also distantly related to motorcycles, the type used to race in motocross (MX) events. They have smaller-diameter wheels, with arms instead of spokes, and have flat or high-rise handlebars; many people think this latter type is unsafe. Sometimes called choppers, they're popular mainly with kids, but in some parts of the world BMXs have reached cult status and experts can perform elaborate aerial stunts on their machines.

Other types with smaller wheels include shopping bikes, which come equipped with carriers. Folding bikes are another branch of the bike family

A modern tricycle: lightweight, functional, if still not all that common. They come in 10- and 12-speed models as well.

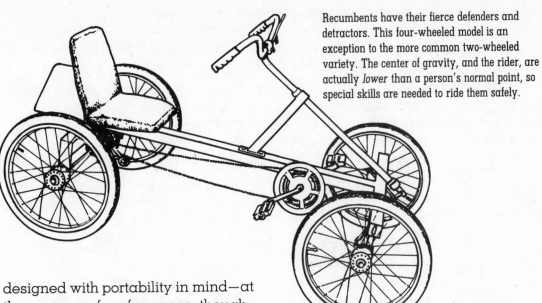

Recumbents have their fierce defenders and detractors. This four-wheeled model is an exception to the more common two-wheeled variety. The center of gravity, and the rider, are actually *lower* than a person's normal point, so special skills are needed to ride them safely.

designed with portability in mind—at the expense of performance, though the better ones ride quite well. Folding bikes, which fit into the trunk of a car and can be treated like a piece of luggage on a plane, also pack away easily in the home when not in use. One award-winning English design folds up into a suitcase-sized package (110 x 55 x 48 centimeters) and weighs just 10 kilos (22 pounds).

Tandem bikes have been around from the beginning, and they remain a great way to share cycling pleasures with someone you're close to. If you're not close when you start, you will be after a tandem ride, because operating one of these bikes calls for close cooperation. Tandems are long-legged, fast and efficient on the open road, but awkward in heavier traffic.

Unicycles represent the opposite end of the cycling spectrum from tandems, providing a solitary experience in a delicate balancing act.

More practical results can be had with recumbents, those cycling curiosities that let you lie down on the job. You ride them from a reclining position, with your feet forward, and the improved aerodynamics makes for more energy-efficient cycling.

With folding bicycles, the key to compactness is small wheels. The frame has reinforced hingepoints, so the whole bicycle can be carried in a bag the size of a medium suitcase.

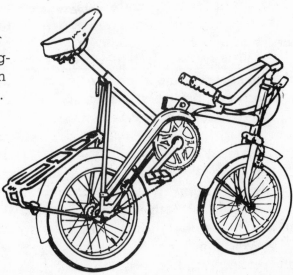

When recumbents are enclosed with bodywork, they're called Human Powered Vehicles, or HPVs, and some of these are capable of law-breaking speeds.

Once in a while you might see a quadricycle, but three-wheeled bikes are much more common; in fact, tricycles are more popular than ever. Once confined to kids and considered just a stepping stone to the real thing (bicycles), they are increasingly used by older people who prefer the stability. Adult tricycles are available in elaborate models that come with extra gears and plenty of carrying space for shopping expeditions.

That just about covers all the bases in types of bicycles. Now that we've seen the wide scope of their variety, let's look at what they have in common.

Bicycle Anatomy

Basically, bicycles are all put together the same way, but their dimensional variations, quality of materials, methods of construction, and attention to detail can make for completely different machines. Most casual riders don't care about the intimate details of bike building, but any cyclist can benefit from knowing more about what makes a bike tick. It adds to the appreciation of the sport, and it's useful to know a thing or two about a bike's nuts and bolts when you're buying a new one.

The anatomy of a bicycle can be broken down into two main elements: the frame and the components. The frame is the most vital part of a bike and all the components are attached to it.

The Frame

The frame is the heart and soul of a bike, affecting how it rides and handles, how durable it is—and how much it costs. The most important characteristics of the frame are its mathematics, particularly geometry, its composition and method of construction.

The typical frame is made from metal tubing forming two triangles fitted together to form a sort of diamond shape. Each part of this diamond-shaped frame has a name: the top tube, which has the saddle at one end and the handlebars at the other; the head tube, which holds the handlebars and front forks; the down tube, from the head tube down to the bottom bracket; the bottom bracket shell, where the pedals and axle are attached; and the seat tube, from the top tube down to the bottom bracket shell. The rear triangle of the diamond frame shares the seat tube; the other sides of the triangle are the chain stays, which are twin tubes of a smaller diameter running back from the bottom bracket shell to the rear, with dropouts into which the rear wheel fits; and the seat stays, which are smaller diameter twin tubes from

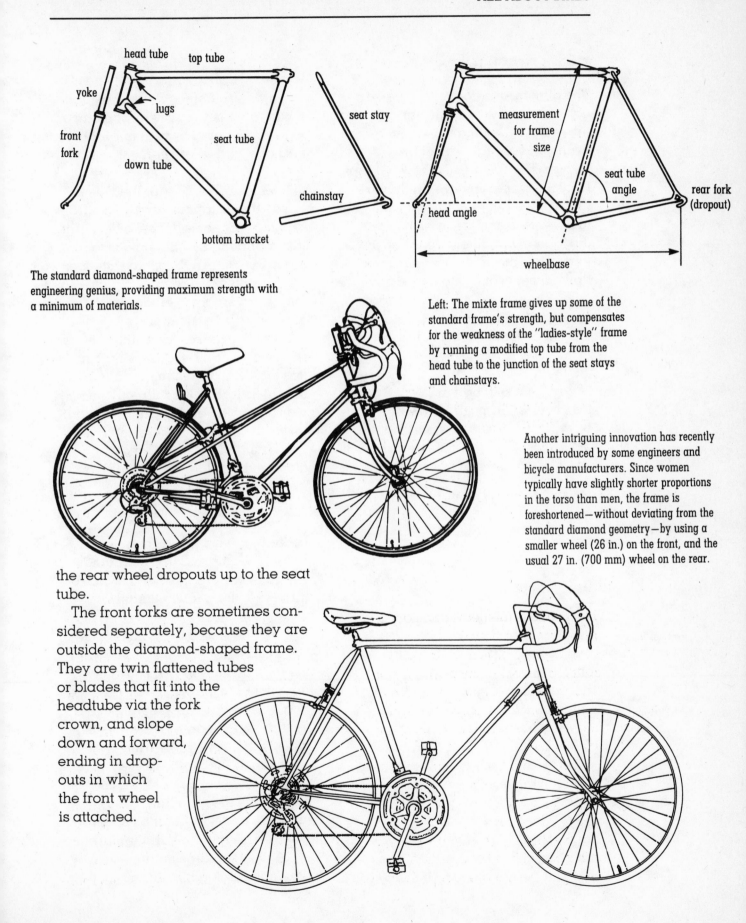

The standard diamond-shaped frame represents engineering genius, providing maximum strength with a minimum of materials.

Left: The mixte frame gives up some of the standard frame's strength, but compensates for the weakness of the "ladies-style" frame by running a modified top tube from the head tube to the junction of the seat stays and chainstays.

Another intriguing innovation has recently been introduced by some engineers and bicycle manufacturers. Since women typically have slightly shorter proportions in the torso than men, the frame is foreshortened—without deviating from the standard diamond geometry—by using a smaller wheel (26 in.) on the front, and the usual 27 in. (700 mm) wheel on the rear.

the rear wheel dropouts up to the seat tube.

The front forks are sometimes considered separately, because they are outside the diamond-shaped frame. They are twin flattened tubes or blades that fit into the headtube via the fork crown, and slope down and forward, ending in dropouts in which the front wheel is attached.

Frame Mathematics

The dimensions, angles of intersection and geometry of the various tubes shape the character of the frame and are the crux of bike design. They determine how the bike fits you (a topic I'll cover in the Bike Fit section), but most importantly, the tube lengths and the angles where the tubes meet differ according to the purpose of the bike. The most important elements of frame math are: wheelbase, head-tube angle/fork rake, seat-tube angle, chainstay length, bottom-bracket height and frame size.

Note: The bike world in North America is currently stuck somewhere between the metric system and the old English/American imperial system of weights and measures. In giv-ing the specifications for my line of bikes we use both systems, but lean toward the metric system, sometimes with the imperial system in brackets, so that's what I'll do here.

Wheelbase: The shorter the wheelbase—the distance between the front and rear dropouts (wheel axles)—the faster and more nimble the bike. Racing bikes, for instance, have steeper angles and more compact frames so that the overall wheelbase is shorter—101 centimeters (40 inches) or less. This makes for a stiffer, more responsive ride because the frame has less flex, and more pedaling energy is transmitted directly into forward motion. Touring and mountain bikes, in contrast, have wheelbases of 109 centimeters (43 inches) or more, making for greater stability, load-bearing capacity and a smoother ride—they tend to "buck" less when going over bumpy roads, because the frame has more give. Sport bikes make a tradeoff somewhere in between, while basic bikes have even longer wheelbases.

Head-Tube Angle/Fork Rake: The head-tube angle works closely with the rake of the front forks to affect directional stability. The steeper the angle formed by the meeting of the top tube and head tube—which is usually the same as the angle between the seat tube and top tube—and the steeper the forks, the more responsive the handling, but the twitchier and harsher the ride. A steep angle means a shorter turning radius, but requires more control by the rider. Racing bikes can have

A difference of just 3 or 4 degrees makes a significant difference in the bicycle's ride, responsiveness, and comfort. A steeper head-tube angle, with corresponding steepness in the seat-tube angle, increases rigidity; a shallower angle increases flexibility and leisurely handling.

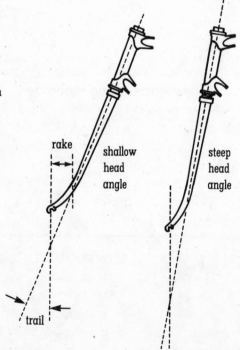

head-tube angles of up to 75 degrees and very slight fork rake, sport bikes have 73 degrees and a higher fork rake, while mountain bikes have head-tube angles of less than 70 degrees and forks with a pronounced bend in them of up to 7 centimeters (3 inches).

Chainstay Length: The shorter the distance from the bottom bracket to the rear dropout (rear axle), the quicker the bike feels under acceleration and the easier it feels in climbing. The point of the shorter chainstay is to locate the rider's body more directly over the rear wheel, but the performance improvement comes at the expense of stability and enough clearance for fenders. Thus racing bikes have chainstays of 41 centimeters (16 inches) or less, touring and mountain bikes have 45 centimeters (18 inches) or more.

Frame Materials

The lighter the better is the most fundamental fact of bike design, so the best frame tubing is as light as possible without sacrificing strength. The materials used to build frames include steel, steel alloys, aluminum, carbon fiber and exotic metals. Here's a rundown of their characteristics.

Steel: Ordinary mild carbon steel makes for ordinary, inexpensive frames that are heavy, rough riding and sluggish in the handling department. It is also prone to rust and corrosion if not heavily sealed with gobs of paint.

Bottom Bracket Height: The farther away the bottom bracket is from the ground the more clearance there is for the pedals, all the better to race around corners when the rider is leaning acutely to one side. So racing bikes for criterium events, which have lots of cornering, have bottom-bracket heights of about 28 centimeters (11 inches). Mountain bikes are higher still—in order to clear obstacles—up to nearly 30 centimeters (almost a foot). But the higher center of gravity results in less stability, so touring bikes have bottom-bracket heights of around 25 centimeters (10 inches).

Frame Size: The frame size is the length of the seat tube, and most adult bikes are manufactured in frame sizes of 48, 53, 58 and 64 centimeters (19, 21, 23 and 25 inches). More on that in the Bike Fit section.

Steel Alloys: Most frames these days are built from steel, in which small percentages of chrome and molybdenum or manganese and molybdenum are mixed in to create what is called high-strength or high-tensile steel. Alloy tubing is strong, responsive, fairly light and durable, and becomes even more so when it is butted. "Butted" means the walls are thinner in the middle than at the end, where the most stress is, and double-butted—thicker at each end—tubing is best. The majority of amateur and professional racing bikes are made with this type of tubing. It is still the best compromise for weight, rigidity, durability and cost. Our racing team

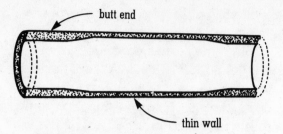

The thinner walls in high quality tubing make for lighter frames. The joints, however, must be strengthened by thickening the 4 or 5 cm. (2 or 3 inches) at each end. Lugs are specially brazed reinforcements at the joints; their intricate design has itself become a hallmark of the finer hand-made frames.

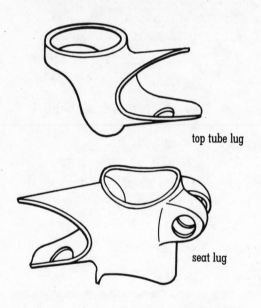

top tube lug

seat lug

uses these types of frames most of the time.

Aluminum: Besides being light in weight, aluminum frames tend to absorb vibration better than steel, resulting in a somewhat smoother ride. They also tend to flex more easily, and aluminum tubing for larger bike frames is sometimes oversized for greater rigidity.

Aluminum costs about the same as steel alloy and is more resistant to corrosion. However, it may not be as strong in the long run because it can be prone to metal fatigue over time. We see fewer aluminum frames in the pro ranks than you might think, but all the best cyclo-cross racers in the world use aluminum allen-type frames.

Carbon Fiber: Made by glueing together layers of exotic synthetic fibers, carbon fiber is used to make space rockets and high-tech racing cars. In bike frames, this makes for extra strength, rigidity and durability combined with light weight. It also makes for extra cost, which is why carbon-fiber frames, sometimes called composites, are not yet widely used in recreational bicycles. I use a carbon-fiber/Kevlar frame for mountain stages and some one-day races that have a lot of climbing.

Exotic Metals: Titanium frames have all the best qualities of other materials but cost a bundle. Magnesium shares many of the properties of aluminum, but is not as strong. It is relatively inexpensive but even more prone to corrosion than steel.

Some frame makers use a combination of materials to make better use of the virtues of the varying materials. Most frames have manufacturers' stickers on them to identify the type and grade of material used.

One way to test or compare the stiffness of different frames is to hold a bike by the handlebars and seat, lean it slightly away from you, and push gently on the pedal—in the six-o'clock position—with your foot. You will feel that some frames have more flex than others.

Frame Construction

Improved methods of construction mean that it's now possible to manufacture frames in quantity that are closer to the ideal of the custom-made, hand-built frame long prized by racers and keen cyclists. The methods used vary with the types of frame material, and the key factor is how the tubes are fitted together.

Mild steel frame tubing—the cheapest has seams along its length—is sometimes just welded together at the joints. Higher-quality, thicker-alloy tubing can also be welded, and smooth, even workmanship is the sign of a job well done. The most common method to link frame tubes is by means of lugs. To avoid weakening the frame material, brazing, which is bonding together at lower temperatures with the aid of another metal such as brass, is used to make connections inside the lugs. The best-quality lugs are short and elaborate in design for greater strength.

Many bike manufacturers, my own company included, use frames built by outside specialists. To assure the optimum frame quality according to purpose and price, we use different frames for different types of bikes within our line. Always, the overriding factor in our frame selection is the best possible workmanship, with attention to detail. Everything has to line up precisely and fit together tightly, because frames are the backbones of bikes. And the finishing touch, the paint job, should reflect the quality. If it looks goods, as the old saying goes, chances are it is good. Then, with exactly the right components, you've got a proper bicycle.

The Components

Everything besides the frame on a bike comes under the heading of components, and they're all attached to the frame. As with frames, components on most lines of bikes are made by specialist manufacturers, and the brand names of the best ones are familiar buzz words in the bike world. You often hear bike nuts dropping names like Shimano, SunTour and Sakae (from Japan), Huret (France) and Campagnolo (Italy), and the competition among component makers is fierce, which means better quality for the consumer.

The main components, in order of their importance, are: the wheels, drive train, brakes, steering system and saddle.

Wheels

Wheels, consisting of tires, rims, spokes and hubs, must be strong to accommodate your weight and the bike's, light to make pedaling easier, rigid to transmit power to the road, flexible to give you a smooth ride, and true-running (not wobbly) to be efficient. The emphasis on these requirements will vary according to whether a bike is for touring/all-terrain purposes (stronger, wider, heavier wheels), or sports/racing (sensitive, lighter, narrower wheels). The essential tradeoff is that narrower, lighter versions give a harsher ride while performing better.

Tires

The main choice here is between clinchers and tubular tires. Clinchers, sometimes called wired-ons, are constructed like ordinary car tires, with a rubber cover and an inner tube secured to the rim by a bead, which holds the inflated tire in place. Clinchers are the cheaper of the two, more puncture-resistant, and easier to repair at home, but a small hassle on the road. Today, some manufacturers have developed clinchers almost equal to tubulars in performance, and a lot of professional teams are racing with them.

Also known as tubs or sew-ups, tubular tires are glued to the rim and have the inner tube sewn inside the rubber cover. They go like the wind, but you're more likely to get a flat on tubs in the long run. They are much harder to repair, as the tire must be opened, the tube repaired and the tire resewn (see Tube Repair). My top-of-the-line racing bikes come with tubulars, but we provide clinchers, available in lightweight versions these days, on our non-racing models. Having two sets of wheels, clincher and tubular versions, is one way to get the best of both worlds on a touring or sports bike.

Tires are sized according to their diameter and cross-sectional width in millimeters or inches. The most common European diameter is 700 mm, though the precise diameter of a so-called 700 tire is actually 680 mm. In the U.S. and England the most common diameter is 685 mm (27 inches), while mountain bikes are usually 660 mm (26 inches) or less. Tire widths can be less than 28 mm (1 inch) for racers and over 50 mm (2 inches) for mountain bike tires, which also have more pronounced tread patterns.

Tires can be inflated to various pressures, and the recommended number of pounds per square inch (psi) is usually marked on the sidewalls. Higher pressure means higher performance, but a harsher ride. In general, narrower tires are rated to take higher pressures. Bikes carrying heavier loads, as in baggage and heavier people, might need higher pressures and more durable tires.

Rims and Hubs

Rims are made of steel, aluminum or alloys, and alloys are generally considered to be the most desirable. Steel is heavier, aluminum less durable, while alloy rims are resilient and tend to give the brakes a better grip in wet conditions. Chrome-plated rims are not a good idea, because the brakes will not grip them as well in wet weather. Rims are sized to match tire dimensions, but you need different rims for clinchers and tubulars.

Hubs are made of steel or alloy, and again alloy is better, being both lighter and stronger. The hubs contain an axle that runs on ball bearings, and the spokes are attached to flanges on the hub. The rear hub accommodates the gearing mechanism; it's on the inside in basic bikes and on the outside in multispeed bikes. Hubs come in two varieties, sealed or unsealed; the latter need to be greased periodically. Hubs are fixed to the dropouts by either axle nuts or quick-release levers. The latter system makes it much easier to remove the wheels, particularly the front one, which means you should lock up your front wheel when you park your bike.

Spokes

The best spokes are made of stainless steel. They are important to give the wheel its proper tension and keep it running true; they must be tightened individually. Spokes are laced from the hub flanges to the rim in patterns according to the purpose of the bike.

Racing bikes have the simplest lacing patterns and the fewest spokes.

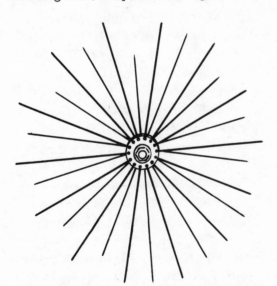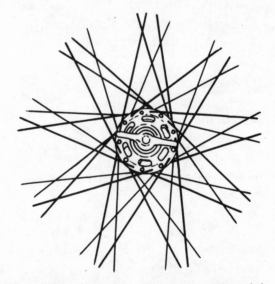

Spokes, properly tensioned and balanced, are what keep the rim stiff and running true. Wheels may be laced in a radial pattern, or in 2-cross, 3-cross, and 4-cross patterns (the number refers to the number of other spokes any particular spoke crosses in its span from hub to rim), each pattern giving the wheel, progressively, more load-bearing capacity. Spokes may snap with age—or with accidents—so it's a good idea to practice replacing broken spokes before leaving on a long tour. You must remove the wheel and tire, then thread the spoke through from hub to rim. If you have to bend the spoke, be careful not to crimp it. Tighten the screw through the hole in the rim, and put tape or a rubber band over the ends of the spokes to protect the tube.

Our team, and most racers, use 32-spoke wheels normally, but for rough road races, such as Paris-Roubaix, we use 36-spoke wheels. Touring wheels might have 42 spokes or more, interwoven in a more complex pattern. This "weave" makes the wheels heavier, but they have more lateral stability while carrying heavier loads and they absorb more road shock, which provides a smoother ride.

Spokes come in different thicknesses, or gauges—14, 15 and 16 gauge are the most common—but the most sophisticated types are butted, like frame tubes; that is, they have a thinner gauge in the middle than at the ends.

The Drive Train

To transmit pedal power into forward locomotion on a bicycle requires the use of an arrangement of components called the drive train. On a basic bike with a single gear this simply means pedals turning a front sprocket, which moves the rear wheel by means of a chain attached to a sprocket on the rear hub. Other basic bikes with up to five speeds have most of the gearing action contained inside the rear hub. More complicated, but much more flexible for cycling purposes, is the drive train for multispeed bikes.

Let's start with the crankset (or chainset), which is attached to the bottom bracket of the frame. The crankset consists of the pedals connected by cranks to one, two or three front chainrings (or chainwheels). The chainrings are connected by a chain to the freewheel on the hub of the rear wheel. The freewheel has sets of sprockets or cogs—five, six or seven of them. When they are allied to three chainrings on the crankset, this can mean up to 21 gears for a cyclist to play with. The number of teeth in the freewheel and crankset account for the different gear ratios available.

In order to engage those gears, front and rear derailleurs (from the French word meaning to de-rail) must be brought into play. One of these devices at the front moves the chain to the different chainrings and another at the rear moves the chain to the different freewheel cogs or sprockets. The derailleur is moved by cables attached to shift levers mounted on the frame or handlebars.

To demystify derailleurs and better understand how they work, you

If you can't afford the pricey, free-standing repair stands that bicycle shops use, just hang your bicycle from the rafters or beams in a basement or garage, to make repair and adjustments much easier.

might change gears while the wheels of your bike are off the ground—put it on a bike stand or hang it from the ceiling of your basement or garage. Turn the pedals with one hand, shift the derailleur with the other, and watch them in action.

The act of changing gears has been greatly improved by the relatively recent invention of indexed shifting. Before Shimano came up with the concept about three years ago, the rear derailleur in particular would not always move the chain exactly over the freewheel cogs, and you then had to fiddle it into place by adjusting the cable tension slightly. Indexed, or click, shifting works like changing gears in a car. You move the gear lever and it slots into place precisely, producing an audible click. Indexed shifting places the chain exactly where it should be and takes all the chance out of shifting. Our racing team has been using indexed shifting for the past three years, and I think it's the greatest improvement in recent bike history.

Drive-train components are usually assembled as a complete system from a single specialist manufacturer. But the bike buyer does have certain options in choosing drive-train components, and here's what to look for:

Pedals: Serious cyclists want their feet fixed to the pedals, to keep the foot in place during both the up and down strokes. This can be done by means of the traditional toe clips and straps, or the new pedal/shoe system. Toe clips and straps require some bending down to adjust, but the new method is simpler; it works like

ski boots on skis and simply clips a cleat on the sole of the shoe to the pedal. Mountain bike riders need to have their feet freer in rough country, and so their pedals are of the open, platform type.

Cranks: Cranks vary in length from 155 mm to 180 mm (6 to 7 inches), with 170 mm (6.75 inches) the norm. As a general rule, shorter people need shorter cranks, and racing cranks are longer. I use 172.5 for everything, time trials and mountains included.

Cranksets: Aluminum alloys or steel are the materials used, the latter on cheaper bikes. Detachable chainrings give more gearing options, should your requirements change after you buy your bike. For wider ranges of gears, as on mountain or touring bikes, three chainrings are better than the two preferred for competition purposes.

Freewheels: A six- and seven-speed freewheel requires a wider hub and

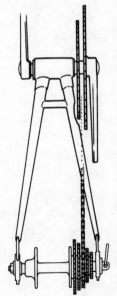

On a five-speed bike, the chain should align perfectly when it is on the chainring and the middle cog on the gear block. With a 10-speed, the chain runs at a small angle from the center gear to either chainring, and at greater angles the further you shift up or down. A greater angle means more wear on chainrings and chain; therefore you should choose a gear block that has the gears you will use most often in the central positions.

wheel to accommodate it. Also, the more speeds on the freewheel the more stress on the chain and chainrings, because the chain must work at a greater angle when engaged in the more extreme gears.

Chain: The chain is the hardest working part of your bike. Fortunately, though they're made up of a multitude of interconnected links, chains are uniformly very strong, even on cheaper bikes, and they're inexpensive to replace. Kept properly cleaned and lubricated, a chain should last at least 2500 kilometers (1,550 miles).

Derailleurs: They should be lightweight, sophisticated, fast and smooth shifting; also strong and reliable. The more of those qualities a derailleur has, the more expensive it will be. Their complexity and capacity is also a function of a bike's gearing.

Shift Levers: Levers can be mounted in several locations. Racers and serious riders prefer them on the down tube where the cable distance is shortest and shifting is quicker. A mountain bike usually has the shift lever on the handlebars, which allows shifting without taking your hands off the bars. Shifters mounted on the stem of the handlebars are less convenient and are usually found on cheaper bikes. Cyclo-cross riders and some riders in the rough Paris-Roubaix road race mount the levers on the end of the handlebars.

Less expensive derailleurs move more or less horizontally, with the jockey wheels taking up the slack in the chain as you shift from a larger gear to a smaller one. More expensive derailleurs are constructed so that they move diagonally, paralleling the edges of the gears, and thus maintaining equal chain tension at all times, and ensuring more responsive shifting.

chain on smallest cog chain on largest cog

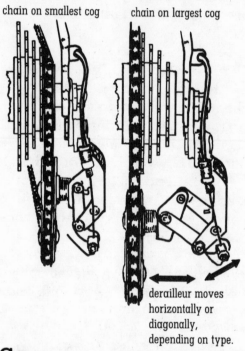

derailleur moves horizontally or diagonally, depending on type.

Gears

The number of gears on a bike is usually determined by the manufacturers, who outfit bikes with gearing best-suited for the bike's intended purpose. This is a good thing for those not very mathematically inclined, because the full story of gears is a complicated one. But gears are really there to make the act of cycling more efficient and to tailor the exertion required to suit the rider's style and preference. So, the more you know about them the better they'll serve you. It's also useful to know how to change the freewheel to adapt your bike's gearing to specific terrain.

Gears are intended to keep the rate of pedaling, or cadence, at the optimum number of revolutions per minute, according to your degree of fitness. This varies from about 60 strokes a minute to upward of 120 for very fit racers. It's easy enough to maintain your cadence over flat terrain, but more difficult when you climb a hill. When you shift to a lower gear on a hill you can maintain your normal cadence without extra effort—at least theoretically!

Gearing is a function of the number of teeth on the chainring and the freewheel. The more teeth on the front chainring, the higher the gear. The more teeth on a freewheel sprocket, the lower the gear. The chainrings on one of my racing bikes have 53 and 42 teeth, while the six sprockets on the freewheel range from 12 to 21 teeth. One of my touring bikes, which needs more pulling power, has three chainrings of 50, 45 and 28 teeth respectively (50 x 45 x 28), and a six-speed freewheel range of 14 to 30.

Gears are commonly referred to according to the number of teeth involved. Thus a gear using 53 on the front and 13 on the back is called a 53 by 13. Gear ratios are arrived at mathematically by dividing the number of back teeth (on the freewheel) into the front teeth (chainring). Thus, 53 divided by 13 equals a ratio of 4.08.

In the English-speaking world gear ratios are usually expressed in gear numbers, a system that began back in the days of the Ordinary bicycle when the large front wheel was the only gear and was measured in inches. Thus a 54-inch diameter wheel was a 54-inch gear. Today, gear numbers are calculated by multiplying the ratio by the wheel diameter in inches. Thus the gear number for a 53 x 13 on a 27-inch wheel is (53 ÷ 13) x 27, or 110 inches. The higher gear numbers are higher gears, and the lower numbers are lower gears, so that more than 100

inches is a top gear for high speed, 70 is a normal speed, and 40 or below are for climbing. The metric system is ignored in this method, but 700 mm wheels are close enough to 27- and 26-inch versions that the same numbers apply.

Another system of comparing gears, the one used in Europe and favored by racers, measures gears according to what is called development, which is the distance traveled with one revolution of the crank. The formula for establishing development, which uses metric measurement, begins with the same calculation as for the number system: chainring divided by back sprocket; but those figures are then multiplied by the wheel diameter and then by 3.14 (in other words, by the wheel circumference). Thus, the development of a 700-mm wheel (actually .680 of a meter) using front and rear teeth of 53 and 13, would be (53 ÷ 13) x .680 x 3.14, or 8.70 meters.

The nice thing about the development method is that it's directly related to distance traveled over the ground, and so allows you to calculate speed if you wish. The simple formula: development (the distance traveled with one revolution of the crank) multiplied by cadence (the number of revolutions of the crank per minute), multiplied again by 60 (min./hr.) and divided by 1,000 (m./km.) will tell you how fast you are traveling in kph. For example, that 53 x 13 combination gave a gear number of 4.08. A good brisk cadence is 90 revolutions per minute. Thus, 4.08 x 90 x 60/1000 yields a speed of 22 kilometers per hour. In multispeed gear arrangements, there is a certain amount of duplication, so that you get identical ratios with different gear combinations. For instance, a 42 x 12 front/back combination gives you the same ratio as a 53 x 15 combination. That's why a 14-speed bicycle might have only eight different gears for practical use. The amount of duplication depends on your choice of gearing, which in turn depends on the type of riding you do, the pattern of shifting you prefer, and the range of gears you require (see the Cadence and Gear Selection sections).

The primary considerations in choosing the ranges of gears on your bike are where and how you ride. Road racers, and very fit riders, prefer close ratios and higher gears (for example, 12-13-14-15-16 on the freewheel gear cluster, and 48-52 on the chainring). Commuting and city bikes need more middle gears (maybe 13-15-18-21-24), while touring and mountain bikes need more lower gears (say, 14-28 on the back, 36-48 on the front). Manufacturers cater to these requirements by outfitting bikes with gear ratio packages according to the intended use of the bike.

Before your eyes glaze over at all this, remember that the basic idea behind all these gear options is to make it possible for you to ride at a level of exertion and speed that fits your particular needs. Even if you don't understand the principles of physics behind the calculations, you should choose the gear combinations that allow you to ride at a pace that feels comfortable.

I'll talk more about using gears and shifting later on, but now it's time to stop—and look at brakes.

Brakes

The two most common types of brakes are center pull and side pull. Both work by squeezing calipers (or arms), which have brake shoes on them, against the rims of the wheels. The calipers are kept apart by a spring until the brake levers on the handlebars are squeezed. Center-pull brakes operate by pulling a centrally mounted yoke connected to each caliper. Side-pull brakes are simpler and direct, eliminating the yoke with a side-mounted cable directly on the calipers.

Both types will stop a bike equally well. Center pulls, with their extra hardware, are slightly less responsive, and racers tend to favor side pulls because of their compactness, rigidity and more sensitive feel. Center pulls are often used on touring and general-purpose bikes.

Cantilever brakes work like center pulls but eliminate the central yoke and calipers. Instead, cantilevers have twin cables attached directly to brake arms, which hold the shoes. The cantilever arrangement generates more leverage and thus they have more stopping power than center pulls or side pulls and are used in mountain and heavy-duty touring bikes.

Brakes levers are designed for either flat or drop handlebars. The levers used on mountain and commuting bikes, are flatter. Those intended for drop handlebars are more rounded in shape and contoured, so as to allow a variety of grips for the hands, including resting them on the hoods of the levers. Levers come in a variety of lengths to fit different hand sizes. The practice of providing an extra set of "safety" levers mounted under the handlebars has been found to be unsafe.

The Steering System

The components of the steering system include the handlebars, stem and headset. The headset, consisting of two sets of ball-bearing races, or grooves, at each end of the head tube of the frame, allows the forks to turn. The core of the steering system, it takes a tremendous beating from road shock and must be strongly built, durable and kept well-adjusted to allow smooth turning.

The stem connects the handlebars to the head tube and is vitally important to obtaining the correct riding position. It rests inside the top end of the fork yoke, which itself fits inside the head tube. Stems come in different sizes, according to the size of the bike frame, and can be extended up or down in the head tube to suit the dimensions of individual riders. The stem also allows the handlebars to be moved into a variety of positions, and can be changed to suit the position of any rider.

Like stems, handlebars are most commonly made of aluminum alloy, with steel sometimes used for moun-

Brake blocks, which are fitted into the brake shoes, come into contact with the rim and are vitally important. Rubber blocks work best on the thinner alloy rims of racing bikes but are much less effective in wet weather. Leather blocks are intended for steel rims only and are much less efficient than rubber. The best blocks are made of synthetic materials, which grip steel or alloy in any conditions.

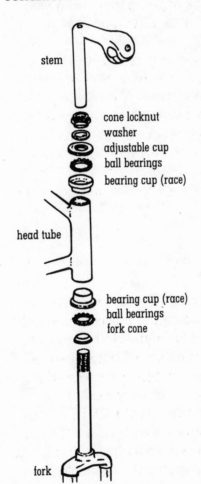

stem

cone locknut
washer
adjustable cup
ball bearings
bearing cup (race)

head tube

bearing cup (race)
ball bearings
fork cone

fork

An exploded view of the headset. Different models have minor variations in the configuration of the locknuts and bearing races, but the main principle, with moveable bearings taking the load, is the same. If disassembling parts such as this seems intimidating, give yourself lots of room and simply lay out the parts spatially as in the exploded diagram. Then when it comes time to put it all together again, it's quite easy and rapid.

tain bikes where extra strength is important. Those bikes, too, feature wider flat handlebars for greater leverage and the upright seating position better suited to off-road adventures. Most road bikes have handlebars with varying degrees of drop and width tailored to accommodate the riding positions used in different situations. Racers use narrower handlebars with a deeper drop, while tourers prefer wider bars with less drop.

The finishing touch on handlebars are the grips—rubber on flat types, while drops are wrapped in tape or coverings for comfort. The hollow ends of drops are also fitted with plugs to prevent injuries in a fall. Most road bikes come with pretaped handlebars, but various tapes and colors are available, as well as padded wrappings, for personal customizing.

The Saddle

The saddle places you in the most intimate contact with your bike and must be chosen with care. Leather saddles are favored by the purists because they fit like a glove—after being broken in, but this transition period is the main knock against leather. Plastic saddles are lightweight and durable but cause heat and sweat buildup. A popular compromise is a saddle comprised of a plastic base, a sandwich of foam padding and a leather cover.

Racing-type saddles are narrower for easier leg movement; touring saddles are wider because riders tend to sit back more. Mountain bike, or mattress-type saddles have more padding at critical points of contact and sometimes have springs underneath, like an inner-spring mattress. Some manufacturers also cater to the wider pelvic anatomy of women and provide specially contoured saddles. I like to use a racing saddle on my home bike so as to have the same feel as I get on my racing bike.

Saddles are attached to the frame by the seat post, which should allow minute adjustments of the saddle in every direction. This is important to set you in the correct riding position (see Bike Fit).

Now that we've seen what goes into making a bike, let's go and buy one.

A Bike Buyer's Guide

Bicycle Shops

Because of the wide selection of bikes on the market, the varied technology, the different brands, models, price ranges and the importance of backup service, where you buy your bike is nearly as important as the type you buy.

The best place to look for a new bike is in a specialty bicycle shop or in the bike sections of sports stores and department stores where bikes aren't treated as just another commodity. In a bike shop your chances of getting personal service by knowledgeable, attentive and interested staff is usually better. But some sports and department stores have long traditions of serving bike customers equally well. One such is Canadian Tire stores in Canada, where Steve Bauer bicycles are sold.

Bike retailers' reputations are known to experienced cyclists, and if you're a newcomer to the sport, or just interested in getting a new bike, ask around. Talk to cyclists, find out what shops they patronize, and why. Based on their recommendations you should go shopping for bike shops. Visit different retail outlets, browse around, talk to the sales staff, pick up brochures and form your own opinions. Here's what to look for:

- *Ambience*: Bikes and accessories should be well displayed and organized so that you don't have to wade through a maze of stuff. A clientele of obvious cycling enthusiasts is a positive sign. Posters, bulletin boards, club notices, local bike-event information and the like are good indicators of a keen, concerned and involved bike shop.
- *Selection*: A broad range of bikes covering the full spectrum of types in all price ranges is best if you're not sure what type you're looking for. If you know what you want, certain shops specialize in mountain bikes, others cater to the road-racing fraternity, others to family cycling. Still others concentrate on the upper or lower end of the market, pricewise. Better bike shops also stock a full line of spares, components and accessories.
- *Staff*: Ideally, the person you buy your bike from should be a cycling enthusiast; when they make particular recommendations they should be speaking from experience. Most bike-shop owners and staff are super-keen cyclists who do what they do out of sheer love for the sport. They should be good listeners, as well as good talkers, so they can line you up with exactly the bike to suit your requirements. If you're a novice they should speak your language, not in jargon (though my Cyclespeak section will help you sort out some of the necessary words), and they should not try to pressure you into buying something you don't want or need.

- *Service*: The best bike shops should have a policy of allowing test drives to help the bike buyer make a decision on a new bike. They have personnel skilled in properly adjusting and fitting the bike to the rider. They have skilled mechanics and technicians who assemble new bikes and service used ones—preferably on the premises. They offer free tuneups on new bikes, comprehensive warranties, and complete after-purchase service and maintainance.

Once you've chosen a bike shop it's a good idea to prearrange an appointment with a salesperson with whom you feel compatible, so that they can spend some time with you, helping you choose your bike. Try to avoid rush hours in the bike shop, which are mainly during weekends, especially in the peak cycling season of the summer. Pick a staff member who specializes in the type of bike or area of cycling you're interested in. The right person will be able to translate all the technicalities into the right bike for your budget and needs.

Choosing a Bike

Once you've got a general overview of the various types of bikes, as outlined in the previous section, here's a checklist of requirements to help you zero in on the best new bike for you:

- *Skill level*: High-performance machines can be intimidating at first, and novice riders will pay extra money for performance they won't use. Don't buy too far beyond your capabilities, but a bit more bike than you can handle is all right because you'll eventually improve your skills to match the bike's potential.
- *Fitness level*: Outright racing bikes, with closely spaced, higher gears, aren't suitable for moderately fit riders. If fitness is your goal, a sports/fitness machine with mid-range gearing is a good choice; for instance, one of my best-selling sports/fitness road bikes has a chainring of 52x42 and a freewheel ranging from 13 to 24. For casual riding, pick a painless-to-pedal, lower-geared touring or mountain bike. And remember you can ask your retailer for a different gear block (freewheel) if you have specific requirements.
- *Terrain*: If you're going to be cycling most often in a hilly area, it follows that you need more lower gears. Similarly, a serious all-terrain bike is wasted in an urban environment miles away from any rough country. Choose a bike best suited to your local conditions.
- *Use*: For open-road riding over longer distances, racing, sports or touring bikes are best. Those planning to ride with a club or in a group should pick similar machines; mountain bikes won't keep up with road bikes on pavement, and vice versa for off-road use. Commuters should pick a city bike, either an ATB or road type.

- *Frequency*: If you only plan to be a Sunday rider there's no point in buying a top-of-the-line, purpose-built special. Conversely, a cheaper bike will be disappointing day in, day out, and on longer trips. The more you use a bike, the further up-market you should go.

- *Personality*: If you're a competitive type, look for a racing bike that will let you exercise your urges best. For the upwardly mobile and/or conspicuous consumer, an expensive model has more prestige. Rough riders need sturdier bikes, while those who take care of their possessions might prefer a more fragile exotic machine.

- *Weight*: A key factor in bike choice is the weight/performance ratio: the lighter the bike, the faster. Real racers weigh in at around 10 kilos (22 pounds) or less. Lightweights range around 11 to 12 kilos (24 to 26 pounds), middleweights are 13 or 14 kilos (28 to 31 pounds) and heavyweights— anything over 15 kilos (33 pounds)—are hard pedaling and not really much fun.

- *Looks*: Don't be blinded by science when choosing your bike, but consider the appearance factor. You have to live with a bike's aesthetics as well as its performance. A good bike is a work of art and it should look it, including the paint job. Pick a bike you admire visually and you'll magnify the pleasures of cycling.

- *Feel*: Test drive your potential bike (if the shop permits, and like any reputable car dealer, they should) and gauge its compatibility. If you've never ridden with drop bars before, expect it to feel a little strange, but when you ride the right bike you'll feel it responding beneath you. Complete oneness with a bike comes over time, but you can sense if you and the bike are suitable companions very quickly. If it doesn't feel right, don't buy it. Try another.

- *Budget*: If you're cost-conscious keep an eye out for sales, particularly in winter clearouts before the new spring lines come in. Don't spend a bundle unnecessarily, because you can often get a good quality example of the type of bike you want within the lower price ranges.

Value for Money

In the world of reputable bike retailing, you get what you pay for. The more it costs, the better the bike. The sky's the limit when it comes to handmade bikes, but generally speaking, there are four price categories in production bikes (the following prices are only rough indicators and subject to change—likely increases—as time goes by):

- *Inexpensive (below $500)*: These bikes are heavier, made of lower grades of materials and have less-sophisticated components. The workmanship will be of lower quality, and you won't find a serious racing bike here. However an infrequent rider can find satisfaction in this category.

- *Moderate (up to $750)*: Casual riders can find perfectly serviceable and reliable mountain and sports bikes here, as well as reasonable racing bikes. Index shifting is common, and alloy frames are in the picture.
- *Expensive ($750 to $1,000)*: Here you'll find better-quality chrome moly frames in a complete range of sizes, sophisticated components and lighter, more responsive bikes with high-performance potential and good reliability for serious riders.
- *Deluxe (over $1,000)*: This category covers all the bases in the best available bikes. You get maximum performance, the lastest high-tech developments, the prestige of brand names, and the best workmanship available. Most of the really expensive models are racing bikes, custom-built versions of which can cost up to $5,000, like the ones I race.

Used Bikes?

In most of this section I'm assuming you'll be buying a new machine, but a good used bike is another possibility for limited budgets. It's really only a good idea for the more expensive categories because the frame and components are more likely to remain in good condition, plus the fact that owners of expensive bikes tend to take better care of them. Some shops sell reconditioned bikes, and sometimes they have notice boards where private owners can advertise. It's wise to have a reputable mechanic give a privately owned used bike a checkover before you buy. But the most important consideration is whether or not the bike fits you.

Bike Fit

If your bike doesn't fit right it won't work right, and all the high-priced components will be wasted. That's because you, the motive power, won't be in the most efficient and comfortable position to ride properly. Also, improper fit can adversely affect you, the motive power, in the form of injuries and damage to muscles and joints. Once you and your bicycle are broken in, getting in the saddle should be almost as comfortable as settling into your favorite armchair.

Once you've chosen the type of bike you want, the final choice is made according to the size of the frame. Then the saddle, handlebars and pedals are individually adjusted to fit your physique. Better bike shops sometimes have a special fitting apparatus for you to sit on, and it determines all the correct dimensions. Otherwise, there are several methods of arriving at the right size for you.

Frame Size

The correct frame size is essential for proper balance, optimum efficiency and comfort. Frame sizes are based on the measurement from the center of the axle on the bottom bracket to the top of the seat tube and are usually expressed in inches. Most quality bikes come in four sizes: 19, 21, 23 and 25 inches. Standard mountain-bike frame sizes are: 17, 19, 21 and 23 inches.

The starting point for determining your frame size is to straddle the bike without your shoes on. There should be about 2.5 centimeters (1 inch) of clearance between the top tube and your crotch. Mountain bike frames are up to 10 centimeters (4 inches) smaller than road frames, with a desirable straddle clearance of that amount.

The mathematical methods of determining the right frame size are based on typical anatomical proportions. In one method, you choose a frame size equal to two-thirds of the inside length of the leg (from crotch to sole), or one-third the person's height. A more precise method is to measure the distance from the top of your femur (upper thigh bone) to the sole of your foot, then subtract 34 centimeters (13.5 inches).

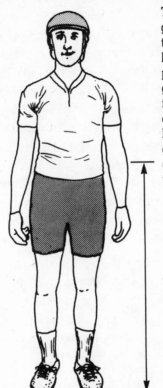

The first step in getting a proper fit is to ascertain your lower body proportions. Probe gently with your fingers to find the top of your hip bone below the rib cage, and measure the distance from there to the sole of your foot.

top of hip bone to sole

Once you've got the right frame size for your height, the rest of the bike is brought into line by adjusting first the saddle, then the handlebars and the pedals to your individual physique.

Saddle Adjustments

The saddle is adjustable for height, distance from the handlebars and tilt. The adjustments are made by loosening bolts in the seat post and saddle. Make sure you tighten them fully after adjustments so that the saddle doesn't move while you're riding.

- *Height*: A saddle that is too low will impair power on the downstroke of the pedals and can cause aching quadricep muscles. Too high, it can cause pelvic rock, where your bottom moves back and forth with each pedal stroke: besides being wasted effort this contributes to a sore seat. When your saddle is at the right height your leg is almost fully extended on the downstroke when your *heel* is placed over the pedal axle; there should be just a slight bend in the knee when the *ball* of your foot is on the pedal axle. To find your saddle height I recommend a simple formula. Devised by scientists in England, it establishes the distance from the pedal axle to the top of the seat as a percentage of the rider's inside leg measurement and accommodates two skill levels. For novice riders: inseam measurement x 1.03. For experienced riders: inseam measurement x 1.09.

- *Distance from the handlebars*: Next, the saddle is adjusted for distance from the handlebars so as to place your legs properly over the pedals for maximum efficiency. The correct distance places your knee joint directly over the front pedal axle when the pedals are in a horizontal position. To find this position, sit in the saddle and grasp the handlebars on top, above the brake levers. To be precise, you can suspend a weighted plumb line from the protuding bone on the outside of your knee (shin anterior bone) and move the seat forward or backward until the line is directly over the front pedal axle.

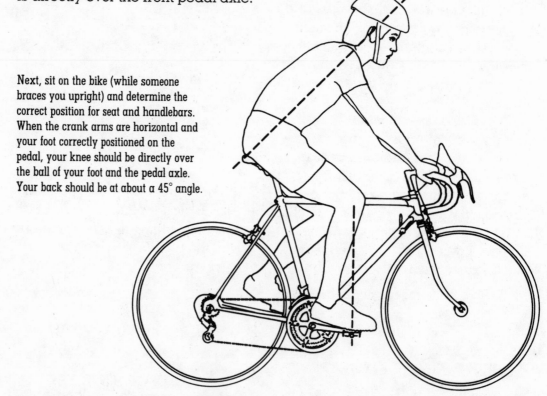

Next, sit on the bike (while someone braces you upright) and determine the correct position for seat and handlebars. When the crank arms are horizontal and your foot correctly positioned on the pedal, your knee should be directly over the ball of your foot and the pedal axle. Your back should be at about a 45° angle.

- *Tilt*: Finally, the saddle is tiltable, so that you can regulate your position over the handlebars, avoid pain and fatigue, as well as optimize steering efficiency. Most people ride best with a level saddle, and some prefer the nose tilted slightly up. Too much downward slope of the saddle either to the front or back, sometimes done to ease soreness, will have you sliding off and having to brace yourself with your arms, which can cause soreness in the arms.

Handlebar Adjustments

The position of the handlebars affects the incline of your upper torso. They are adjustable in height, distance from the saddle and tilt, depending on the way you prefer to ride. Racers prefer a lower profile, with the upper body bent at a more horizontal, aerodynamically efficient angle. Casual riders and tourers usually prefer a less-sharp angle, while older riders may desire an almost upright position. The flat handlebars on mountain bikes are not usually adjustable.

- *Height*: Generally, handlebars should be no higher than the saddle. Fast riders have them set as much as 5 centimeters (2 inches) below the saddle height. Handlebars are raised or lowered by moving the stem, but don't extend it past the safety marker, which is stamped on the stem.

Continue adjusting to the perfect position by comparing these factors: when the pedal is at the bottom of its revolution, your leg, with the foot correctly positioned on the pedal, should be very nearly straight, with just a slight flex at the knee. (With the heel on the pedal, the leg will be fully extended.) The saddle top should be at the same height as, or at most 5 cm.(2 inches) above, the top of the stem.

● *Distance from the saddle*: As a rule of thumb (or forearm and fingers) the distance from the top of the handlebar to the nose of the saddle should be about the length of your arm from the elbow to your outstretched fingertips. This distance, a function of stem height, frame size and horizontal seat adjustment, should result in a riding position with an upper body angle of about 45 degrees and with your elbows slightly bent, which enables them to better absorb road shocks. If this is not achieved it may be necessary to get a different-sized stem for your bike. Everyone is different: I have a relatively long upper body in comparison to my legs, so I have a long bike and a long stem.

Make a final check: the distance between handlebars and saddle should equal the length of your forearm and extended fingers. Remember that everyone's anatomy is marginally different—these are averages—so your final, most efficient cycling position will be obtained by making small adjustments and compromises between these various criteria.

- *Tilt*: Handlebars are adjustable (by loosening a bolt) with respect to their angle to the road. Usually they are positioned so that the drops (the bottom bent part) are parallel to the ground or pointing slightly downward.

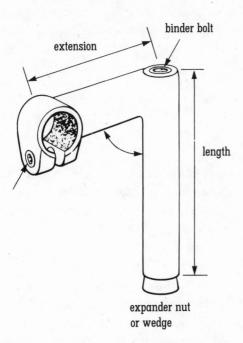

The handlebars can also be rotated by loosening the binder bolt, and moving them up or down. Generally, the bottom drop should be approximately parallel to the ground. Note also the correct positioning of the brakes and brake heads, where you will be resting your hands much of the time.

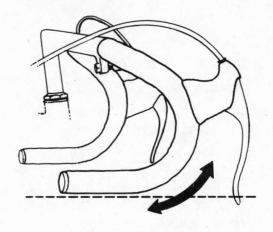

You can fine-tune the bicycle's fit by purchasing the best stem for you. Stems come in different lengths and with various extensions, usually classified in millimeters.

Pedal Adjustments

Properly positioned feet and pedals can improve cycling efficiency by 25 percent or more. Improper positions can result in extra stress on the knee. You should pedal with the ball of your foot directly over the center of the pedal axle. This is best done by using proper cycling shoes with cleats, and pedals with toe clips and straps to hold the shoes in place. The new ski-binding pedal systems are not yet standard equipment on bikes, and clips and straps aren't always available on less-expensive models. If they're on the bike of your choice, the clip-in binding-type pedals are adjustable, as are the cleats on your shoes.

- *Cleats*: They should be mounted on the sole of the shoe so the foot position is parallel with the crank (when the two pedals are at a horizontal plane) for better efficiency and leg alignment. This is the theoretical optimum; however, different people have anatomical differences, and their feet might point in or out slightly. The cleats should also be aligned to match the configuration of the pedals.

- *Toe clips*: There should be a slight clearance of about a quarter of a centimeter (an eighth of an inch) between the toe of your shoe and the clip. This prevents pressure from building up on a longer ride and makes it easier to exit the foot from the pedal.
- *Straps*: Straps should not be cinched up so tightly they cut off circulation or create difficulty in getting the foot off the pedal in a hurry for sudden stops. They should be comfortably snug.

Component Checklist

Before taking the bike you've selected out for a test ride you should "kick the tires," as the car-buying saying goes. Give the bike a check-over to see that everything is in working order and the bolts are all tight. Anything not doing its job should be adjusted by the shop people before you hit the road.

- *Brakes*: Pull the levers hard. The brake pads should grip the rim quickly, well before the cable is fully extended. The levers should stop at least 2.5 centimeters (1 inch) from the handlebars. Lift each wheel, spin it and squeeze the brake levers to check that the brake shoes are contacting the rim properly, with their full surface area.
- *Front Forks*: Lift the front wheel and move the handlebars. They should swing freely. Put the wheel down again and rock the bike back and forth. There should be no play or noises from the headset.
- *Wheels*: Lift each wheel and spin it around. They should both spin freely and silently. Fix your eye on the wheel and a part of the frame or fork to see if there is any wobble, indicating wheels out of alignment. Unaligned wheels will look something like a record with a wow in it as it spins on a turntable. Hold a pencil lightly against the spokes and listen for a steady sound to indicate uniform tightness. Shake the wheels from side to side. Any movement means loose axle bearings.
- *Shift Mechanism*: Suspend the bike from a stand and shift through all the gears to make sure the chain moves smoothly both up and down the gear range.
- *Other Items*: Try twisting the handlebars and saddle to make sure they're firmly fixed in place. Check for play in the bottom bracket by pulling the pedal cranks from side to side. Squeeze the tires to check that they're inflated properly and equally.

The Test Ride

You should run through that checklist again when you take delivery of your bike. But before that, you need to put your prospective bike to the ultimate test: on the road. Begin by giving it a visual once-over, then set off, slowly and carefully at first to accustom yourself to the bike.

- *Visual Inspection*: Examine the bike from all angles to check that the frame is straight and the components line up properly. The finish and paint job should be free of scratches, blisters and blemishes, and there should be no patches of grease or oil.
- *Shifting*: Start riding and shift through all the gears. Vary your speed and seek out a hill to aid in this research. Everything should click into place with precision.
- *Handling*: Check the handling and responsiveness by taking corners at varying speeds. The bike should bend to your will, and corner as if on rails.
- *Steering*: Turn in both directions. The bike should respond swiftly, surely and freely to your directional commands.
- *Acceleration*: Stand up on the pedals and sprint. The bike should give a lively spurt forward, and you should feel it quickly transmitting your energy into speed.
- *Stability*: Relax your grip on the handlebars to check for frame and component alignment. The bike should run true and straight ahead without pulling to either side.
- *Alignment*: To see if the back wheel tracks directly behind the front wheel, ride straight through a wet spot or a patch of dust on the road and check that the tire tracks form a single straight line.
- *Brakes*: Apply them vigorously to check for smooth, sure, easily controllable stops.
- *Silence*: A properly put together bike is rigged for silent running. Any noise indicates a problem somewhere.

Remember that every bike has individual characteristics that are only revealed after you've spent some time on it. The selection process involves a certain amount of gut feeling. So, if the test drive is successful and you like the way your bike feels, buy it. Now you're ready to look at the right stuff to put on it.

The Right Stuff

Walk into a bike shop these days and it seems that more than half the space is devoted to accessories, tools, spares, clothing, and all the assorted gear associated with two-wheeled activity. Few other sports or pastimes have as much paraphernalia associated with them, and the right stuff can greatly enhance the pleasures of cycling. Most bikes come ready for the road or off-road right off the rack, but let's browse through what's available in the way of accessories and add-on equipment, beginning with certain items that belong on any bike ride.

Essential Equipment

Included in the don't-leave-home-without-it category are the necessities for effecting emergency roadside repairs, as well as an item or two for your own maintenance and refreshment. All of this stuff is compact and lightweight and can be carried easily on your bike.

Tool Kit

A bike is made up of close to a thousand different parts, and if you ride it long enough some of those parts will loosen, break or otherwise cease to function properly. When this happens on the road the best defense is a well-equipped tool kit. (The most common problem is a flat tire.) The basics can be packed in a small pouch that fits under the saddle or in the pockets of your cycling jersey. Make sure your kit has tools sized for your bike. Complete prepackaged tool kits are available, or you can buy the items separately. It should be tailored to your own needs, but here's approximately what your tool kit should contain:

- a small, flat-bladed screwdriver, which will also work on cross-shaped Philips screws.
- allen keys to fit hexagonal bolt heads. Three or four of them, sized from 4 to 7 mm, will cover most bolts on a bike.
- a small adjustable wrench to fit other bolts.
- small, needle-nose pliers with a cutter.
- tire levers to pry clinchers off the rim. Two plastic ones will do the job. Tubular tires can be taken off by hand.

- a matchbox-size, tube patching kit for clinchers. They come complete with rubber patches, scraper, talcum powder and cement.
- a spare tube for clinchers in case of serious punctures.
- if your bike is equipped with tubs, a spare tubular tire or two plus cement. No clincher items necessary. (When I'm training on bad roads in Belgium I always carry two spare tires.)
- a cloth to wrap the tools in and clean your hands.
- other useful items: spoke wrench, Swiss army knife, cleaning solvent and/or wrapped moist towelette, and small change—for an emergency phone call should your tool kit not contain what you need to get cycling again!

My personal tool kit consists of two spare tires, and just a spoke wrench, allen keys and a pump. By making sure my bike is well-maintained I can eliminate extra baggage.

Tire Pump

Frame pumps, the kind that mount under the top tube or on the front of the seat tube—the preferred location—don't require clamps. They are longer than the clamp-on type and thus deliver more air per stroke. Make sure your pump fits your tire valves, which are either Presta valves (the kind that have to be unscrewed to let air in or out) or Schraeder valves (like ordinary car-tire valves). The best pumps, made from plastic or aluminum, clamp directly onto the tire valve. The types that must be screwed on are fiddly and waste air pressure, but still do the job.

Water Bottle

Some people might consider a water bottle an optional extra. But in racing and even recreational riding we now know it's a necessity, for it's vital to keep yourself hydrated when cycling, a sport that requires regular replenishment of water. The water bottle is held to the down tube by a cage, usually made from aluminum alloy or plastic. Most quality frames come with brazed-on bosses to accommodate the cage; other bikes have the cages clamped on, usually to the down tube and within easy reaching distance from the handlebars. Cages for mountain bikes are more substantial, and some riders fit two cages and bottles on the down tube to quench heavy thirsts and for longer-distance touring. The best-made bottles are of flexible plastic, with tops that have squirting potential for drinking (water!) and driving. Insulated bottles, or bottle covers, are available for hot drinks or soup in cold weather.

Safety and Security Equipment

Purists like to keep their bikes clean and free of all but the bare essentials, but a strong case can be made for carrying the following items, to help keep you and your bike in one piece, and to help keep your bike period. They are optional items, but if you ride at night and/or park your bike, they become essential.

Lighting

The dangers of cycling after dark are easily understood by anyone who has suddenly encountered an unlighted bike while driving a car. In many places lights for night riding are required by law, and when cycling at night in the country away from street lighting, you need to see where you're going.

There are two main choices of lighting systems—generator or battery operated—which fit to the frame in a variety of ways. Generators are lighter, but have wires running around the frame and depend on your momentum to work (when you stop pedaling, you're in the dark) and sap a certain amount of pedal power. Battery systems are simpler, but heavier, and the charge only works for a limited time. A recent development combines the best of both systems—batteries that are kept charged by a generator. The best lighting systems are compact, lightweight and have high-intensity bulbs, clear for the front and red for the rear. For the real night riders, halogen headlights are great and worth the extra expense.

Other lighting options include leg lights that strap on the arm or lower leg. In the latter position they have the advantage of providing a moving, therefore highly visible, light source, but won't illuminate the road enough for the rider. Also available are flashing beacon lamps that clamp onto the rider's belt or the rear of the bike. The mountain-bike fraternity have popularized the use of miner-style headlamps that clamp onto the helmet.

Reflectors and reflective clothing are effective backups for lighting systems. Reflectors can be attached to the pedals, the rear of the frame and the spokes, though the latter are visible only from the side. Reflective tape strips can be applied to the saddle, rear of the helmet and shoes, and reflective vests are a good idea, as are reflective patches on cycle clothing. Don't forget visibility is a two-way street: make sure cars can see you just as easily as you can see them.

Locks

Urban areas have alarming statistics of bikes stolen per hour. The most effective security system of all is never to leave your bike unattended, or unwatched. If you must park your bike for periods of time there are several types of locks on the market that can be carried in your pocket or on the bike.

The simplest and cheapest locking devices are plastic-covered (to protect the frame) wire cables, locked and unlocked with combinations or keys. Heavier cables are harder to cut through—a favorite trick of bicycle thieves. The best locking devices are the solid U-shaped ones—Kryptonite is a popular brand—which clamp the bike firmly to an immovable object. They're cumbersome to carry but as pilfer-proof as it's possible to be.

Always lock your bike to some substantial stationary object, such as an iron fencepost, but not a parking meter from which the bike can be lifted off. Remember to lock up the quick-release-type front wheel, as well, and remove the tool kit, pump, water bottle—anything not tied down —from your parked bike. I'll cover bike security in more depth later on in the Theft and Security section.

Optional Extras

The following accessories are mainly a matter of personal preference, for they serve specific types of cycling. Before you load your bike up with goodies, keep in mind that anything extra on your bike adds up to more weight you have to haul around and wind resistance you have to overcome. Obviously, mountain and touring bikes are more easily adapted to take heavier loads, but it's unwise to ask even a laden touring bike to carry more than about 20 kilos (44 pounds).

Mirrors

Those who become accustomed to rearview mirrors swear by them. Mirrors can be a real boon in city travel to locate gaps in traffic, or on the open road where you can monitor the progress of overtaking vehicles. But just as you would in a car, it's wise to check what you see in the mirror by looking over your shoulder before you make a move.

There are tiny mirrors that clip onto eyeglasses or helmets, and larger types that fit on the handlebars. Of the latter, the best models clamp directly onto the bar, or into the end of it, or on the brake-lever hood, and are not perched on the end of a stalk, which causes greater vibration. They should be mounted within reach of your line of forward vision so that you can keep one eye on the road ahead as you consult the mirror. Wide-angle lenses are also available, but it's even more difficult to gauge the speed of approaching traffic in such mirrors.

Racks and Carriers

Some touring bikes, road or mountain versions, come with racks already installed; mine have alloy racks mounted over the rear wheel. Bolt-on versions, hardware included, are available for installation over both the front and back wheels. Most of the cargo weight should go on the back carrier. For longer touring trips, saddlebags, or panniers, are designed to be draped over the front and rear carriers. Constructed of weatherproof fabrics, they're available in various configurations, with extra pockets and compartments. They must clear the chain and spokes, and should be as low as possible for stability. I'll go into this in more detail in the Touring section.

Other travel bags, with clear plastic inserts on top for maps, are designed to hang from the handlebars. Straight handlebar models can take traditional carrier baskets.

Child Seats and Trailers

Seats for children are another available carrier item for bikes, and because of their precious cargo they must be well-designed. The best models, made of heavy-duty plastic, fit over the rear wheel, but should not be placed on top of a carrier rack. Seat belts are important, and the seat design should include a guard to protect the child's feet from the spokes. The recommended maximum carrying weight for a child is 18 kilos (40 pounds). Even though there are good products available, I still feel it's a great risk to ride with small children in traffic and I recommend riding in parks or areas without cars. I may be one of the best riders in the world, but I would think twice before carrying my child through busy city streets.

Bike trailers are another way of transporting children or goods. The better-designed models are lightweight but strong, have windscreens and all-weather protective coverings, high-quality wheels and narrow tires, and a sturdy and reliable hitch system.

Fenders

Racing-bike purists tend to consider fenders as something for wimps. They wear their stripes of mud and water thrown up by the wheels like badges of honor. However, commuters in office clothes, or long-distance tourers on vacation who must continually confront the elements, or any rider interested in creature comforts, should consider fenders. The better designs are easily installed and taken off, have plastic mudguards at the bottom of the front fender, and are made of plastic (less durable), stainless steel or aluminum. Without them on a rainy day, road water and grime will soak you thoroughly.

Computing Devices

Computing devices, usually just called computers in bike jargon, are among the most popular bike accessories, and there are models on the market that give you a comprehensive picture of anything you'd care to know about your bike and your riding self. They can keep track of speed, distance, elapsed time, the time of day, cadence, pace, and more. I use one for both training and racing, and they're great for monitoring your performance and motivating yourself.

For races the distances can be preprogrammed so that the computer can give you a preview of the exact location of difficulties, such as an upcoming mountain climb, the feeding zone, or more importantly, the finish line. Triathletes and serious fitness riders combine bike computers with heart monitors to monitor their bodies more closely. The best computers are not much bigger than a watch, weigh only a few grams, and attach to the handlebars at the head tube.

Floor Pump

A good, solid floor pump is a required item for serious cyclists. Bike-tire pressure needs continual topping up, and a frame-mounted pump isn't powerful enough to inflate them to the required 100 psi-plus pressure.

Gas-station air hoses are not a good idea, either, because of inaccurate pressure gauges and the risk of the extra pressure blowing up a bike tire. The solution is a floor pump with an attached tire-pressure gauge, kept wherever you store your bike.

Car Racks

Racks for carrying bikes on cars are needed to transport your bike over long distances you may not wish to ride. The choice is between roof racks and trunk-mounted racks. The latter are second-best because the bikes (trunk models can carry up to three bikes) can easily be scratched, and even a slight tap from the bumper of a car behind can damage them. However, trunk racks are usually more easily installed and cheaper than rooftop models. Roof carriers are more solidly anchored and can carry up to six bikes, as well as other cargo, and are the best bet for really long journeys.

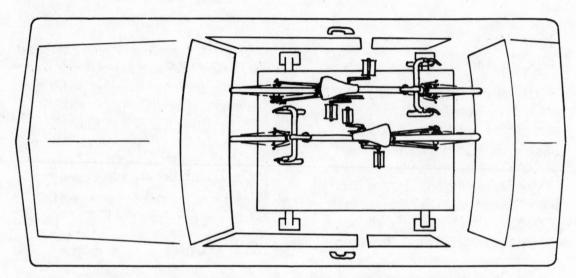

Modern car racks hold up to six bikes on the roof, so the whole family can take their bicycles along for a ride in the country. Some use heavy-duty bungy cords to fasten the bikes down; other use a form of quick-release skewer similar to those on bicycle wheels, to secure the bike. The key to saving space is to alternate the bicycles head to tail on the rack.

Other Accessories

Bells or horns (handlebar-mounted), chainguards (to keep clothing away from the chain) and kickstands (to prop up a parked bike) are traditional accessories seldom used these days, but still available for those who want them.

More exotic add-ons are the wind-cheating clear plastic fairings, like the windscreens on racing motor-bikes, designed to give the cyclist the maximum aerodynamic advantage. They remain at the far end of the popularity totem pole and are only of interest to real speed freaks, as are the disc wheels on the market, modeled after the real thing on time-trail bikes.

New equipment is being developed regularly for the mountain-bike enthusiast, including such items as skid plates, which fit under the bottom bracket (to prevent damage from rocks) and shoulder slings (to carry bikes over unridable terrain). More of that in the Off-Road section.

Wind trainers and other similar devices to convert a bike into an indoor exercise machine are becoming increasingly popular, and are serious rivals to the traditional exercise bike. The rear wheel sits on a roller that whirls fan blades to create wind resistance, thereby increasing pedaling effort. I'll talk more about them in the Fitness section.

That just about covers bikes. Now let's do the same for the cyclist's body.

Bike Wear

Only a few years ago people in proper cycling regalia were the subject of ridicule in some parts of the world. Not anymore. Now everybody wants to look like a bike racer, and that's good news for recreational riders. What we racers have always worn has been updated and adapted for "civilian" use, and with the cycling boom, bike clothing has become high fashion. It's colorful and fun, with an aura of eccentricity that makes it even more desirable for the fashion-conscious. But real cycling clothing is above all functional and practical, the most important item of gear after the bike itself, and absolutely essential for serious cycling. Here's a look at what you need to wear, starting from the top.

Helmets

You should wear a helmet at all times when riding. Treat it like the seat belt in your car and put it on every time you sit in the saddle. Three-quarters of all cycling fatalities are caused by head injuries, and the vast majority of those victims could have been saved by helmets. (In this case I'm afraid you'll have to do as I say, not as I do. The macho world of European bike racing is back where the game of hockey was a few years ago, and we usually race helmetless. The most head protection you see in a race is of the ineffective leather-padded hair-net variety, though hard-shell helmets are mandatory in some types of racing in certain countries. I used to play hockey at a fairly serious level and welcomed the coming of helmets. I look forward to the day when bike racers see the light as the shinny players did and start to protect their heads.)

Bike helmets are becoming more and more sophisticated, and like helmets in other sports, they must meet certain government-set standards of safety. The better helmets will have a sticker saying they've been certified. They usually have hard plastic outer shells with padded inner liners designed to absorb shock.

Helmets should be lightweight and comfortable, with adjustable chin straps and inner headbands for a snug custom fit. Bright colors are a good idea for greater visibility, and streamlined, aerodynamic designs are desirable. Ventilation is also important since cycling heads will sweat, even in cool weather.

All this helmet talk relegates traditional racing caps to a secondary role. Still very much a part of bike style and lore, the little peaked caps with the brand names on them, worn backwards in races for better aerodynamics, can still be worn in après-cycling situations. Under your helmet they can help absorb perspiration and provide extra warmth in cold weather. Woolen versions are available for winter riding, and the peaks of caps can also serve as sun visors or rain shields.

Eyewear

Besides the sun's glare, a cyclist's eyes are subjected to dust and grit, even the occasional stone, raised by traffic or the wind. And when you ride at speed, the wind in your eyes can cause them to burn or water. Riding like the wind also turns insects into dangerous projectiles, and even rain drops can hurt your eyes. For these reasons some kind of eye protection is important.

Ordinary glasses or sunglasses will do the basic job, but there are several brands of specifically designed cycling goggles with plain or tinted lenses (gray or green for sunlight, plain or amber for bad weather) that are distortion-free and shatter-proof. They're highly styled, wraparound models giving better peripheral vision, and constructed so that the frames are located out of your line of forward vision when you're bent over the bars.

Clothing

I'm developing my own line of cycling clothing, and as a designer I'm concerned with two key aspects: form and function, which are critically interrelated. Form includes style and fit. The clothing must look good, and from a practical point of view it has to fit well to do the job. Sloppy, loose-fitting clothing increases wind resistance and slows you down. Seams, stitching and bunching can cause chafing, rashes and misery on a cycling body.

Fabric choice is important, too. Form-fitting fabrics improve the look—assuming your body looks good!—but the material also has to allow for perspiration evaporation, provide warmth when wet, dry quickly, be reasonably weatherproof, lightweight, and so on.

Besides visual appeal and higher visibility, color selection also involves considerations of heat and cold: light colors deflect the sun's rays, darker ones absorb them. Once upon a time wool and cotton were the main fabrics used in cycling clothing. But the trend is to synthetic fabrics like lycra and polypropylene, which hug the body, wick away perspiration, help maintain optimum body temperature, wash easily, dry quickly and are very durable. Another, emergency, function of cycling clothing is to help protect your skin from abrasion in a fall.

That's some of the theory behind the thinking on the drawing board. Here's how it works in the finished products.

Jerseys

Jerseys (the name comes from the knitted woolen fabrics once used for cycling tops) are pullovers shaped and cut to keep your backside covered when you're bent over the handlebars. They usually have a zip at the neck which can be raised or lowered to help regulate body temperature, and pockets on the lower back to carry such items as snacks, spares or extra clothing. Jersey sleeves are short for summer and long for cold weather or winter.

Shorts and Tights

What you wear on your posterior and lower extremities can make or break your cycling day. Proper cycling shorts are not as critical on shorter rides, such as commuting to the office, but in the long run they're the essential buffer between you and the saddle.

The key ingredient of cycling shorts is a piece of leather, or sometimes a synthetic, called a chamois (pronounced "shammy", after the European wild goat from which the material originally came), strategically located inside the crotch area. The chamois provides extra padding, protects the skin against chafing caused by friction and absorbs perspiration.

Any seams or stitches in the delicate area should be well-tailored so as to prevent saddle sores. The tight fit of shorts prevents them from bunching up while you're pedaling. Shorts are cut high to keep the waist covered and reach to mid-thigh so that your legs won't chafe against the saddle or top tube. Though other dark colors are used, black is favored for shorts because it masks sweat and grease stains, as well as absorbing body heat better to warm up the main cycling muscles—the quadriceps in the thighs. However there are new trends toward wild colors, all the better for rider visibility.

Shorts are intended to be worn without underwear and they should be washed frequently to prevent bacteria from perspiration from flourishing, which can cause infections. Most serious cyclists have at least two pairs of shorts; full-length tights are also available for cooler weather. I probably use and abuse two dozen pairs of shorts in a full racing season.

Touring shorts and pants have a

looser fit than racing shorts, and more pockets. Some tourers wear traditional knickers and gaiters, and there are mountain-bike pants with padded knees. Any longer cycling trousers must be snug around the lower leg so as not to interfere with the chain.

Gloves

Cycling gloves are no poseur's affectation, and play a key role in cycling. Their padded palms, usually leather, cushion the hands against road shocks and help prevent the numbing, blisters and chafing that can result over the long haul. They provide protection against scrapes, help cushion the impact of a fall, and can be used to brush away potentially puncturing debris on the tires. The open fingers of cycling gloves leave your digits free to work on the brake and gear levers. The fabric backs can be used to brush away the sweat on your brow. Summer gloves have mesh backs for ventilation, and there are full-fingered, insulated gloves for cold-weather cycling. We racers used to have difficulty finding a good rainy cold-weather glove, but now there are neoprene-type gloves, like those used by scuba divers, in which your body heat warms up the absorbed rainwater, and so your hands are kept warm.

Shoes

In performance terms, shoes are the single most important item of bike wear. Studies have shown that proper cycling shoes can save up to 20 percent of the rider's energy. The key factor is the rigid sole, which prevents the arch from flexing and therefore transmits all the foot power to the pedal on the downstroke. By distributing the weight of the foot evenly, the stiff sole also prevents the pedal from digging into the foot at just one spot and causing discomfort or fatigue.

Racing shoes with cleats, fixed to the pedals with straps, or one of the newer strapless ski-binding-style systems, are the most efficient, because they maintain the power during the upstroke of the pedal movement. The best types have adjustable cleats so that the foot can be custom-fitted to the pedals. But these shoes, which have no heels, are not meant for walking.

Touring shoes are a compromise. They have stiff soles but resemble running or athletic shoes, with rubber tread patterns on the bottoms that grip the pedals better. Mountain-bike shoes or boots are heavier and wider versions of touring shoes. Besides being quite walkable, touring and mountain shoes are useful for city cycling because they aren't fixed to the pedals with a cleat system but grip the pedals with a serrated sole.

The best cycling shoes are lightweight, with inner sole stiffeners of plastic or light metal, and made of leather, suede or synthetics. Some have mesh uppers for better breathability, and those with velcro fasteners are easier to adjust. Like any shoe, a proper fit is important to prevent the foot sliding around, which is uncomfortable, inefficient and can cause blisters.

Socks should be thin, made of wool, cotton or blends of materials that breathe and absorb perspiration. They should have no seams, which might cause blisters, and reach only to ankle height so they don't become laden with water on a wet day. For cold and inclement weather lined cycling boots are available, as are weatherproof shoe covers or "booties," which slip over regular cycling shoes.

Bad-Weather Gear

As a bike racer, particularly in the spring in Europe and in the mountains at any time, I have to wage a constant battle against the elements. I encounter rain, sleet and snow, often on the same day. Couple that with the way a heavily sweating body can become very chilled if a breeze picks up, and with the fact that the act of cycling creates its own wind-chill factor, and the proper bad-weather riding gear becomes critical, particularly for the body extremities. Fortunately there's all kinds of stuff on the market to combat the weatherman's worst.

In very cold weather it's best to dress in layers. You're then insulated

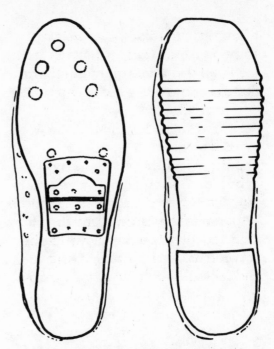

Lightweight cycling shoes have a metal cleat built into the sole. The pedal strap holds the shoe firmly on the pedal so that the cleats are "locked in", allowing you to pull up on the pedal during the back part of the revolution and thus use maximum muscular exertion during the whole cycle, and not just on the downstroke. The latest shoes snap right into the pedal, so that straps are not necessary. Touring shoes have a stiff sole, so that the pressure is distributed away from the ball of the foot, but are minus the cleat, so that you can walk with more ease.

better, because heat is trapped between the layers of clothing and you can peel off outer garments when you get too warm. Suits of underwear made from fabrics like polypropylene wick away the perspiration from the body and are less likely to become sweat-soaked, particularly in stop-and-start situations when you can get a chill. On the coldest days jerseys can be covered by turtlenecks or sweaters, in cotton, wool or fabrics that breathe.

Besides those items already mentioned for the head, hands and feet, the biggest blessing for bikers has been the invention of the windproof, rainproof, breathable fabrics like Gore-Tex (the original). Suits of these high-tech materials allow perspiration to escape while keeping the wind and rain out. Suits specifically designed for cycling have reflective strips for night riding and other important features. Jackets have hoods large enough to cover helmets, adjustable wrist closures and vents to let perspiration escape, and they are long enough to keep the lower back covered as you ride bent over. The tights are cut to accommodate pedaling legs and are narrower at the ankles. We racers use thermal suits, which are rubberized and stretchable for training in the wettest and coldest weather.

For less-foul weather, some specialized jerseys and tights have wind and waterproof panels on the front, and warm knitted fabrics on the back. And there are items like woolen tights, which can be worn with shorts and taken off as things warm up.

PART TWO

Keys to Better Cycling

The Cycling Body

We covered the outside of your body in the last section. Now let's have a look inside. Before I became a full-time bike racer I studied kinesiology, the science of body movement, at the University of Waterloo. This background has been a big help to me in my career, and some knowledge of the cycling body is an important key to better biking for anyone interested in self-improvement.

Your bike is a machine, a combination of mechanical parts that transmits energy into motion. Machines must be powered by a source of energy, which in the case of the bicycle, is your body. In a sense your body, too, is a machine, a combination of physical parts that works to provide the power for your bike. Cycling is about making these two machines work together harmoniously and efficiently.

In automotive terms, you are the engine, and like the internal-combustion engine, you operate on fuel—the food you eat. Your body/engine also needs fine tuning, maintenance and regular care and attention to keep it in good operating condition.

Body Work

The bones, joints, and ligaments of your body, particularly those in the legs, are like a system of levers powered by muscular contractions. The main muscle power in cycling comes from the quadriceps, the large top muscles on the thighs. They contract to straighten the knees, which provide the power for the push on the downstroke of the pedals. (If their thighs are visible, bike racers can be easily picked out in a crowd—they're the ones with the bulging quadriceps.) At the bottom of the pedal stroke the hamstring muscles, on the back of the thighs, contract to pull the pedals back, then the anterior shin muscles and the hip flexors, on the upper part of your thighs, contract to pull the pedals up.

The essential sources of muscle power are oxygen and food. The cardiovascular system (heart and lungs) pump oxygen to the muscles through the bloodstream. The bloodstream is also a pipeline to the muscles for nutrients (mainly glucose, or blood sugar) converted from food (mainly carbohydrates), which are stored in the muscles and the liver. In the muscles the oxygen combines with the nutrients to create chemical compounds, the molecules (mainly glycogen) of which break down to release energy to produce muscular contractions.

Obviously, the fitter you are (that is, the more efficient your cardiovascular system) and the better you eat (the right foods in the right proportions) the better cyclist you'll be. Studies have shown that well conditioned cyclists have up to 80 percent more capacity for pedal power and can cycle that much farther with less fatigue.

Besides being properly conditioned and fed, your body has to be kept as comfortable as possible on the job.

Proper bike fit (discussed in the previous section) and riding position (coming up shortly) go a long way toward this, but there are inevitable stresses and strains involved in the act of cycling. Let's look at how these can be minimized, so that your cycling body works at an optimum level.

Diet and Nutrition

Few other sports require as much energy expenditure and endurance as bike racing, so a racer's success depends to a large extent on eating the right foods to keep the energy level at its highest. The good news for every cyclist—for that matter, everybody—is that the best diet for racing is also the best diet for an all-round healthy lifestyle.

We now know from extensive experiments conducted on athletes—often cyclists—that the ideal everyday intake of food should consist of a well-balanced diet, made up of about 65 percent carbohydrates, about 20 percent fats, about 15 percent protein (though these percentages vary slightly according to the authority being cited), minerals, vitamins and plenty of water.

Carbohydrates

Carbohydrates, which consist of atoms of carbon, oxygen and hydrogen, are the most fuel-efficient food for cycling muscles—and for the brain, by the way, which runs almost entirely on glucose derived from carbos. Carbohydrates come in two main varieties: complex and simple.

Simple carbohydrates are just sugars. They are commonly contained, in too much abundance, in many junk foods and drinks: pop, desserts and candy in particular. Sugar gives you a temporary carbo hit for a burst of energy, but then leaves you more tired than before.

Complex carbohydrates (found in

pasta, rice, vegetables, whole grain foods and fruit) are the best energy source, because your system takes longer to metabolize them, like a slow-burning fuel. Complex carbohydrates also promote muscle growth, and they contain fiber. Fiber is only partly digested, and the residue helps keep the intestinal tract cleaned out, eliminating potentially toxic waste products from the system.

Muscles also burn fat, mostly during steady, less strenuous activity, but when you're pedaling vigorously, carbos become more important, and during real bursts of power you're burning carbos almost exclusively. Unlike fats, which can be stored in huge quantities in the body, carbohydrate energy (glycogen) can't be stored in quantities large enough to fuel the cycling fires for very long—only enough for not much more than two hours of heavy-duty riding. And when you run out of carbo power, you're out of gas. It can happen very suddenly and underlines the importance of carbohydrates to the working body.

Sudden energy depletion is the syndrome that marathon runners refer to as "hitting the wall" and we cyclists call "bonking." Fatigue hits you over the head like a brick, your muscles burn like crazy and may cramp up, and you may feel dizzy, nauseous, and uncoordinated. Bonking is avoided by consuming carbohydrates regularly, in larger quantities before a longer ride and topping up your tank with smaller doses during the ride. Before a race, we consume huge plates of spaghetti, potatoes and rice, along with cereals and bread. We often do this at breakfast on race day, and with over a hundred racers sitting down to this kind of feast we tend to get strange looks from the personnel and patrons in restaurants, but it sure works on the road.

Bonking aside, the more active you are, on or off your bike, the more carbohydrates your body needs. But don't eat more than you can burn off before the next pit stop, because carbos contain calories, too, and the excess will be stored as body fat.

Fats

Fat has a bad name, but it's also an important source of muscle power. Fats take a backseat to carbohydrates because they require much more oxygen to metabolize, and so it's harder to turn them into energy. Fats are a less-efficient fuel, therefore, but they're more concentrated, containing more energy potential than carbos. Because they're slower to metabolize, fats—and proteins to a lesser extent—come into play after glycogen has been used up and so become the main source of energy during longer rides. The fitter you are, the more efficiently you can burn up fat, and that's why bike racers and other serious athletes have a very low percentage of body fat.

Fats are found in nearly everything edible, including the best carbohydrate sources, so that you don't need to seek them out; in fact, it's best to avoid really fatty foods. They take longer to digest, using up energy in the process, and besides being unhealthy and unattractive, excess fat interferes with the body's cooling system and restricts the amount of oxygen the blood can transport to working muscles. Your daily ration of fat, which should be about 20 percent of your food intake, is especially concentrated in dairy products and meats, which also happen to be good sources of protein.

Proteins

Proteins contribute less than 5 percent to cycling energy, but they're important in creating enzymes that act as catalysts used in the metabolic process; also, the cells of the body are composed mainly of protein. Thus, protein is vital to rebuilding cells, and the cycling body, any body, needs a constant supply of protein since it can't be stored like fat. However, protein is not easily digested, and that process uses up extra energy. Protein-rich foods, therefore, should only be consumed well before a bike ride. Eggs, dairy products and meats, as well as all types of beans, contain plenty of protein.

Minerals

Minerals are essential components in the enzymes that metabolize carbohydrates, fats and proteins into energy. Nearly all the minerals found in the ground, including aluminum, copper, iodine and nickel, fit into this category, and our daily requirements are easily obtainable in a well-balanced diet. However, minerals are easily sweated out of the body and care must be taken to replenish supplies after heavy cycling, particularly potassium, iron and sodium.

Potassium helps delay muscle fatigue, iron (along with protein) is a major ingredient in hemoglobin in the blood (important in carrying oxygen to the muscles), and sodium (salt) is vital to controlling the water content of the body. Iron deficiency anemia, often indicated by lethargy, can be a problem for athletes, particularly for women, and it can certainly slow down a cyclist. Potassium, sodium and magnesium are some times called electrolytes because of their role in the transmission of neural impulses. A severe shortage of them in the body can cause muscle cramps and lead to heat problems, including the potentially deadly heat stroke.

Some athletes take electrolyte drinks, containing concentrations of those minerals plus sugar (glucose/glycogen), as well as salt tablets, especially in hot weather. It is generally felt that salt tablets are not a good idea, and there are differences of opinion as to the effectiveness of electrolyte, or mineral replacement, drinks. A better idea might be to eat a banana (particularly good for potassium), green vegetables, raisins and red meat (for iron) and vegetables, fruits and grains (for sodium). In other words, eat a balanced diet rather than artificial concoctions to get your quota of minerals and vitamins.

Vitamins

Vitamins are organic substances that release and control the enzymes during the energy-making process. Vitamin A is found in vegetables, Vitamin B in meat, eggs and milk, Vitamin C in citrus fruits. The key to getting an adequate range and number of vitamins is to eat a wide variety of fresh, better quality, non-processed foods. I like to take a daily multivitamin/mineral pill as insurance. It's at worst harmless, and may be worth the taking.

Water

The water bottle is one of the most important cycling accessories because water is absolutely essential for human life, let alone cycling. Nearly three-quarters of your body weight is made up of water, and when you lose some of that you must replenish it, fast. Besides being used to transport all the substances needed for energy, water flushes out your system (including lactic acid, a waste product in the muscles that slows you down) and is vital for controlling your body temperature.

When your body's internal thermostat gets too hot, you sweat through the pores of your skin, and the evaporating process cools the body. Unfortunately, this uses up more water, and during a long hot ride up to a liter of water an hour may evaporate from your body. Since your body can only absorb about half a liter (about a pint) an hour, you should top up your tank frequently. I've drunk up to a dozen bottles during a single hot stage of the Tour de France, and in a one-day race where I have to ride for seven hours in the heat.

When to Eat and Drink

You can't pig out on food and expect to ride in comfort. Besides the extra weight and the bulk in your stomach, the digestive process uses a lot of blood to break down food and thus interferes with bringing oxygen to the muscles for energy. This process can be quite prolonged; for instance, it can take up to eight hours to digest bacon, which is mainly protein and fat. In contrast, boiled rice, which consists mainly of carbohydrates, takes about one hour to digest.

Thus, the trick is to eat a light-carbohydrate meal not later than about one hour before a major bike ride. Ideally it should be consumed from two to three hours before, to assure that the digestion is complete and the food is metabolized into energy. You should also prepare for your ride by drinking water, even if you're not thirsty, well before you pedal away.

If you're riding for an hour and a half or longer, you should bring something to replenish your energy supply. Bananas are excellent as quickly digestible sources of carbohydrates and potassium, and they come in their own containers that easily stuff in your jersey pocket. Other fresh fruits, such as apples and pears, are also excellent sources of nourishment on the road, as well as good sources of water.

In longer races we latch onto feed-bags, called *musettes*, provided by our crews, and eat on the fly. The fare is often small sandwiches containing honey or jam, ham and cheese for a longer race, dried fruits, apple tarts, and natural fruit. Often, near the very end of the race we drink a *topette*, almost pure glucose syrup, to give a final boost and prevent bonking. A favorite food of touring riders is a mix of nuts, grains and cereals, sometimes called trail mix and known to canoeists as "gorp", which keeps pumping the carbos into the body.

Cycling jerseys have pockets on the back where you can carry snacks, a spare tube, or other necessities, out of the way.

As I've already mentioned, you should take a swig from your water bottle every 15 minutes or so, more frequently in hotter weather and if you're really hammering.

Conditioning

Although cycling itself will get you fit and improve your stamina, you should do some conditioning before you attempt strenuous cycling. You have to be somewhat physically fit to take advantage of cycling's physical benefits, as well as its pleasures. You've got to push yourself on your bike to reap those cardiovascular rewards, even if you're riding just for fun, or to and from work. Cycling will lose much of its appeal if you tire easily. So, regular riding will gradually improve your fitness, but a conditioning program will give you a headstart and keep you out in front.

Even if biking takes over your life, you should complement your riding with exercises that involve those areas (mainly the upper body) that cycling conditions to a lesser degree, and you should also spend some time caring for the muscles used in cycling. As well as the thousands of kilometers I log on training rides, often more than 1000 kilometers a week in preparing for the season, I devote a lot of time to fine-tuning my body in workouts. A regular off-bike conditioning program will improve your performance on the road, lessen the likelihood of injuries, enable you to ride more comfortably and safely, and generally make you a better cyclist.

Exercise Caution

A well-conditioned cycling body has endurance, strength, flexibility and coordination. Achieving the desired condition requires subjecting your body to a certain amount of stress, and this should be approached with caution, particularly if you are older or not currently physically fit. The process takes time, and you should build yourself up gradually, using the following guidelines:

- Get a doctor's advice before you embark on any strenuous conditioning program, particularly if you're older and unfit.
- Begin any exercise activity, including cycling, slowly, to warm up your muscles. When you're finished, gradually slow down again.
- Avoid jerky, bouncing movements that might cause muscle strain. Gently stretching the limbs into position and holding them there is best.
- Be careful not to push yourself too hard. The old "no pain, no gain" theory may be dangerous and in the long run is not as efficient as a workout of painless, but steady intensity. No need to bust a gut. Slow and steady wins this race.
- Consider rest to be part of your conditioning regimen. Your body needs time to recover, and a fit but exhausted body defeats the purpose.

Frequency and Intensity

The prescribed formula for achieving a desirable state of fitness is to gradually build up to a point where you can comfortably do three 45-minute workout sessions a week. Appropriate programs should include warming-up and cooling-down periods, and exercises should involve all parts of the body. About 20 minutes of each session should be devoted to aerobics, which accelerates the heart rate to improve and maintain cardiovascular endurance(heart/lung efficiency).

The intensity of the aerobic component, which you can get while riding your bike or from other types of exercise, can be monitored by measuring your heart rate to ensure that you're working out at a safe and suitable level according to your age. On your bike you can use one of the heart-monitoring devices mentioned in the Right Stuff section, or you can do it yourself by taking your pulse for 10 seconds and multiplying by six to calculate the number of beats per minute.

Measure your heart rate in the middle of your aerobic activity and compare it to the following formula, which shows the desirable upper and lower heart-rate limits according to your age. The idea is to work out within these ranges, below which you're not getting the training effect, and above which you enter a danger zone.

Age (Years)	Heart-Rate Range (Beats per minute)
20–30	140–175
31–40	130–160
41–50	122–150
51–60	115–140
60 plus	100–125

Warming Up

You must warm up before you work out. Throwing yourself abruptly into strenuous activity can cause injuries, and at the very least you will take longer to recover from your workout. A warmup does exactly that: warms up your muscles gradually by increasing the blood flow through the fibres and makes the muscles, tendons, and ligaments more flexible and pliable so they're better able to perform under a greater workload. This includes the most important muscle in the body—the heart.

When you're out on your bike you can supplement your warmup by simply pedaling easily in a lower gear for five to ten minutes to iron out the kinks. But you should still limber up before riding to help prevent stiffness and ward off soreness in the saddle. The best way to do this is to spend ten to fifteen minutes on a thorough stretching routine, with special emphasis on the muscles used in cycling.

Stretching

Ideally your stretching routine should begin with some kind of brief, gentle cardiovascular activity, such as lightly running on the spot, taking a brisk walk or a short bike ride, to get the blood flowing. Another round of stretching should be done after a heavy workout or bike ride.

Ease gently into each stretch, hold each position for up to a minute, then ease out of the stretch. Do not bounce. Stay relaxed. The whole point of stretching is to expand and contract the muscles in a relaxed manner, which also helps to relieve accumulated tension from head to toe.

The following stretches are performed while standing, sitting and reclining. Hold each stretching position for at least 30 seconds.

Standing Stretches

- *Neck rolls (for the neck and shoulder muscles)*: Keeping your shoulders relaxed and your back straight, slowly rotate your head from side to side, then up and down, then in circles.
- *Shoulder rolls (to loosen up the shoulders and upper back)*: Lift your shoulders up, forward, down, back, then repeat the movements, while holding your arms either at your sides or extended horizontally.
- *Side stretches (for the shoulder, arm and side muscles)*: With your feet slightly apart and your heels flat on the floor, reach your arm down one side toward your toe as far as it will comfortably go and hold that position. Do the other side. Reach above your head with the other arm.
- *Toe touches (for the lower back, hamstrings and knees)*: Relax your upper body and bend your knees slightly as you bend forward from the waist and reach toward your toes, touching them if you can—but don't force it, and don't bounce.
- *Knee squats (for the lower back, groin and legs)*: With your feet flat on the floor, your back straight and your arms extended, slowly lower yourself to a sitting position and hold it. You can also do this with your back against a wall.

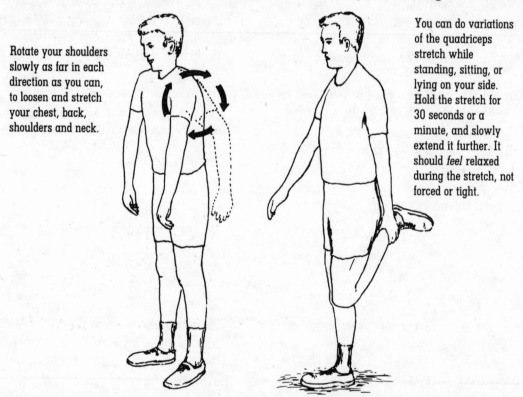

Rotate your shoulders slowly as far in each direction as you can, to loosen and stretch your chest, back, shoulders and neck.

You can do variations of the quadriceps stretch while standing, sitting, or lying on your side. Hold the stretch for 30 seconds or a minute, and slowly extend it further. It should *feel* relaxed during the stretch, not forced or tight.

- *Quadricep stretches (for tops of thighs, cycling's most important muscles)*: Reach behind and grasp one ankle, bending the leg at the knee, and pull it up behind you to the buttocks. If you wish, place your other hand on a wall for support (though a balancing act will also improve coordination), and hold the position. Repeat with the other leg.

- *Lower leg stretches (for the calves and Achilles tendons)*: Lean forward with your hands against a wall and extend one leg backward, keeping the knee locked and the heel down. Hold that position, then bend the stretched knee (for the Achilles tendon) and hold that. Repeat with the other leg.

Sitting Stretches

- *Hamstring stretch (for the lower back and groin)*: Sit on the floor and extend one leg straight out from the body. Tuck the sole of the foot of the other leg against the thigh of the extended leg. Slowly bend forward from the waist and try to reach the toes of the extended leg. Hold that position, then repeat with the other leg.
- *Groin stretch (for the quadriceps and lower back)*: Sit with your knees apart and bring the soles of your feet together and as close to your body as is comfortable. Slowly bend your upper body forward from the waist and hold.

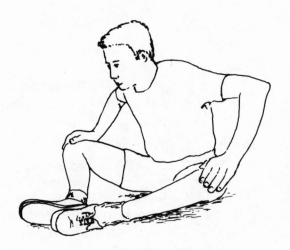

Left: The groin stretch is another standard for loosening the thighs, buttocks and lower back. You can create your own variations to emphasize various parts of the body.

Below: Pull your knee up towards your chin, as shown. You can also straighten your leg, or drop it over left and right, to get the full benefit of the stretches.

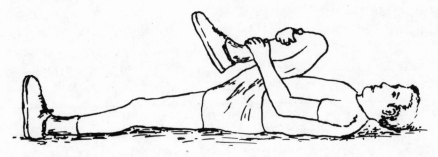

Reclining Stretches

- *Thigh tucks (for the quadriceps and lower back)*: Lie flat on your back and, with one leg bent at the knee, pull up the other thigh toward the upper body and hold. Repeat with the other leg.
- *Body extension (for the whole body)*: Lie with your lower back pressed flat to the floor. Stretch your arms over your head and extend your legs as far forward as you can. Reach with your fingers and point your toes and hold.

Upper-Body Exercises

Cycling is great exercise for the lower body, but the upper body tends to get left out of the action. Thus, many serious cyclists, and all racers, work on improving their upper-body strength. The need for this is particularly important in off-road riding and in all-out sprinting on the roads when your bike will flop around beneath you unless you counteract the pumping action on the pedals by pulling very hard on the bars to keep all your power on the road. A strong upper body will help any cyclist during hard acceleration, climbing hills, battling winds and generally keeping control of the bike in emergencies.

To build up my upper-body strength I've been involved in weight training for many years and highly recommend it. Make sure you get expert advice when you start; have someone develop a routine best suited to your personal needs. Nowadays I do a lot less weights than when I was an amateur rider specializing in track events (I lifted weights up to three times a week then), because we race so often I have very little time for weight workouts. Still, in the winter I like to go to the gym to keep the muscles toned and ready for hard training on the bike when the good weather returns. And there are other ways to give your upper body a workout without having to invest in your own weights or going to the weight room at a gym.

In the off-season it's important for me to get off the bike and do other activities to keep fit. Besides going to the gym, I play hockey and do some cross-country skiing. Swimming, tennis, squash, racquetball and handball are also excellent sports to improve your upper-body strength. The trend among fitness buffs these days is toward cross-training, which involves combining different activities as part of a regular routine. This is how the very popular triathlon began, and those athletes who combine swimming, cycling and running are about as fit as you can get.

Fitness classes are another way of conditioning the cycling body. All properly organized workouts involve a healthy component of upper-body work, and some of them are geared specifically to improving muscular strength and endurance. Most of them will include variations of the following two traditional upper-body strengthening exercises, which you can do anywhere at any time.

- *Situps (for the muscles in the abdomen and lower back)*: Lie with the small of your back pressed to the floor, your knees bent and your feet together and flat on the floor. Clasp your hands behind you head and slowly raise your head and shoulders from the floor (it can be dangerous to raise your upper torso too high, especially if you have back problems), then slowly return to the floor. Repeat the movement, smoothly and rhythmically, as many times as you can comfortably do so.
- *Pushups (for the muscles in the upper back, arms, chest and shoulders)*: Support your body with your palms and your toes and raise your body until

your arms are fully extended, then slowly lower your body almost to the floor, before raising yourself again. Repeat the movements smoothly and rhythmically, concentrating on keeping your back flat throughout. Less demanding, but still excellent, are pushups from your knees instead of your toes. Varying the width of your hands, from directly beneath your shoulders to wider than your shoulders, will spread the effectiveness of the workout over your upper body.

Cooling Down

You should never stop an exercise session cold turkey. You should ease out of it gradually, so that your muscles don't seize up. Cooling down also helps prevent lactic-acid buildup, which causes fatigue and soreness, and it allows you to recover from a workout more quickly.

Cooling down involves gradually reducing exercise intensity before coming to a stop. On a bike ride you can simply reduce your speed and pedal in a lower gear. In a workout you should spend the last 10 to 15 minutes tapering off, ending the session with stretching exercises, concentrating on them even more thoroughly than during your warmup.

Massage

People often ask me why bike racers shave their legs. The main reason—beside making it easier to repair cuts and abrasions after falls, and less painful to remove adhesive bandages—is that a smooth skin surface makes it easier for the masseurs to do their job. Massage is an extremely important part of bike racing, and none of us could ride the way we do without the continued efforts of our team masseurs. I'm also fortunate to be able to get an excellent massage at home—Elayne is a trained masseuse.

Massage promotes blood circulation and stretches and relaxes the muscles so they can perform better. After a strenuous performance, massage relieves muscle swelling, soreness and tension, and reduces fatigue.

If you're a serious cyclist I recommend that you make massage part of your conditioning regimen. Make regular visits to a professional or get a book on the subject so you can learn self-massage or how to perform it with a friend.

A rudimentary self-massage can be performed by lying with a pillow under your head and your legs propped against a wall. Apply massage oil, available from health shops, to your legs and massage each one by kneading the muscles with both hands, using circular motions on troublespots, and stroking towards the heart.

Riding Comfort

Unlike many sports, which subject the body to potentially crippling punishment, cycling is relatively easy on the rider. Most physical problems take the form of minor discomforts, mainly to those parts of the body resting on the bike. But although the aches and pains start out as minor, they can become major if ignored or not treated early on. Here's a troubleshooting guide to potential cycling sore sports and what you can do about them.

Cyclist's Seat

This problem, more pronounced until your seats—your own and your new bike's—are broken in, can really only be cured by riding. As you become accustomed to sitting in the saddle your bottom will toughen up and your saddle will gradually assume the shape of your posterior.

The most comfortable saddles have foam inserts and are leather-covered. (In the old days leather saddles were preferred but required up to 1,000 kilometers before being completely broken in.) Particularly sensitive posteriors can be babied by using padded saddle pads or covers (from bike shops) or investing in wider, padded saddles with springs.

Numbness in the crotch area can be caused by an improperly tilted saddle or a saddle that's too high.

After your original bike fit you should move your saddle only in very small increments to any new position. Temporary numbness on the road can be alleviated by moving around in the saddle and/or standing on the pedals for a while.

Genuine saddle sores are a rarity, which is a good thing because they can be a serious condition; blisters may deteriorate into boils and open wounds. Saddle sores are caused by friction, chafing and allied irritations, aggravated by perspiration, and are best avoided by riding with proper chamois-equipped cycling shorts, which you wash regularly. You can also apply petroleum jelly or skin cream to your crotch area to prevent friction. If a sore begins to develop you might have to stop riding until it goes away.

Sore Hands

The best way to avoid this problem is to keep moving your hands to different positions on the bars. Each new position puts the pressure on a different part of your hands. You can also shake them out periodically—but one at a time!

Wearing padded gloves and using cushioned handlebar coverings are insurance against your hands becoming sore or numb. Continuing problems in this area might be caused by an improper riding position, which pushes too much of your weight over the handlebars. This can be cured by moving the seat and/or handlebars. Refer back to the Bike Fit section and check out the Riding Position and Posture sections, coming up soon.

Sore Upper Body

When your arms become fatigued, your shoulders, neck and back can also be affected. This is another reason for improving your upper-body strength and for thorough stretching as part of your cycling routine. But the problem may be caused by the handlebar-stem position. If it's too long you have to reach forward as you ride, which locks your elbows. Without bent elbows to absorb road shock, your arms become tired and tense. When the stem is too short you have to ride in a hunched position, which is also inefficient and uncomfortable. Check your stem length, according to the Bike Fit section, consult the upcoming Riding Position and Posture sections, and always ride with your shoulders relaxed.

Another way to relieve upper-body troubles is to stretch while you're riding. You can do neck rolls at any time, but don't lose sight of the road. Shrug your shoulders up and down and rotate them forward and backward. With a bit of practice, and keeping one hand on the bars, you can bend an arm over your head to stretch it and windmill it in your shoulder socket for a moment.

Sore Knees

If your knees are sore, it usually means that you're pedaling at an improper angle or that the saddle is wrongly positioned. Don't pedal through knee pain, since the action can lead to serious problems with tendons and ligaments that might force you to stop cycling.

Your knees should be moving only in a vertical plane and not from side to side. If the pain is on the inside or the outside of the knee you might try changing the position of your foot on the pedal. I think the ideal position is with the foot parallel to the crank and the ball of the foot immediately over

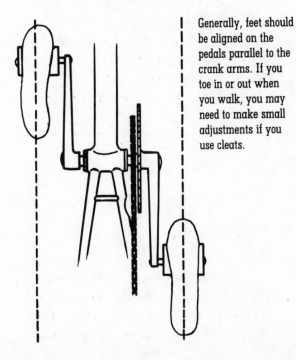

Generally, feet should be aligned on the pedals parallel to the crank arms. If you toe in or out when you walk, you may need to make small adjustments if you use cleats.

the axle of the pedal. But my ideal positioning might not suit your particular anatomy. Experiment a little, and when you find a comfortable solution, reset the cleats on your shoe to align your foot properly.

If the pain is behind the knee, your saddle may be too high. If it's on top of the knee, your saddle may be too low. The saddle may be too far forward or back. Consult the Bike Fit section again, and check that your bike is set up properly for you. But if you have a persistent knee problem discuss it with an expert in your bike shop.

Sore Feet

If your feet become sore or numb it means the blood circulation is not as it should be. This can be caused by too-tight shoes or toe straps, or soles that aren't thick enough and thus transfer pedal pressure to your foot. Your feet swell as you ride, so you may have to loosen the shoes or straps accordingly. For sole problems you might investigate special insoles (from bike shops) that help cushion the feet.

Bike soles that bend under pressure can cause arch problems, for which arch supports are available. If you have particularly tender feet, less-serious touring or mountain-bike shoes may be the solution. But toe clips or system shoes that lock you to the pedals help take the pressure off your foot on each upstroke so that your foot gets brief but continual respite during the act of pedaling.

A large part of being able to ride comfortably depends on mastering some essential skills in the saddle, particularly riding position and posture, and that's what I'll cover in the next section.

Skills and Techniques

Almost any adult can ride a bike by just hopping onto the saddle and pedaling, and that's one of the beauties of cycling. But learning to ride properly, mastering your bike so that you become one with it, is essential to riding safely and exploiting all the sport has to offer.

You should be confident, relaxed and comfortable in the saddle, so that you can cycle with style and efficiency. Your control of the bike should become second-nature, so that you can give the necessary attention and care to riding safely while still being free to enjoy all the satisfactions and rewards of cycling. Let's look at some of the fundamental skills one at a time.

Riding Position

The most basic prerequisite is correct body position. It's not only important for good aerodynamics—overcoming wind resistance—but also for cycling efficiency: maximizing your muscular power with the minimum of effort. And proper alignment lessens strain and discomfort that can numb the body and detract from the pleasure of riding. In short, if you don't sit right, you can't ride right.

In assessing the relative merits of the upright or inclined riding positions, offered by flat or dropped handlebars respectively, drops win hands down. The lower you are over the handlebars, the more evenly your weight is distributed over the bars, saddle and pedals, and the more control and stability you achieve. Taking the weight off your buttocks also frees your legs to transmit power to the pedals more efficiently, with the large muscles running from your back through the buttocks to the legs coming into play. As a bonus, pressure is reduced on the load-bearing portion of your anatomy on the seat—the spot that most easily gets sore. The inclined position also reduces the frontal area that has to be pushed through the wind. Novices sometimes forget that dropped handlebars offer several options of hand positions that can be adopted over the duration of a ride. This helps to lessen the buildup of strain on the arms and, more importantly, enables you to assume a variety of stances better suited for particular circumstances.

However, flat handlebars, especially on mountain bikes, are well suited for the job. They give the greater leverage necessary for hauling your bike over rough country, and the upright position gives you a good view of approaching hazards. And since this branch of cycling usually involves less prolonged time in the saddle, with dismounting more frequent, the comfort factor is less of an issue. Mountain-bike handlebars are still evolving, though, and in some parts of California, droplike handlebars are increasingly seen up in the hills, and some city bikes are also sporting them these days. If you've chosen to go the flat-handlebar route, riding posture is still important.

Posture

When the height and angle of the saddle and handlebars are properly established, your upper body is bent at 45 degrees for the "standard" riding position, and less when you drop lower on the handlebars. The correct posture, though it changes somewhat the lower you go, works like this:

- Concentrate on bending from the waist and keeping your back flat.
- You should be able to lean forward with your arms outstretched and grip the handlebars comfortably, without strain.
- Your shoulders should be square (not hunched, which interferes with proper breathing) and reach about midway between the saddle and the handlebars.
- Your arms should be slightly bent at the elbows, which helps absorb road shock more easily and keeps you more relaxed.
- Keep your arms close in to the body for a better streamlined effect.
- Concentrate on keeping your upper torso relaxed so that your lower body does all the work. This enables you to breathe better and avoids tension buildup, which causes fatigue.

Handlebar Positions

There are four main ways to grip dropped handlebars, each one affording respite for hands and arms, and enabling you to deal with changing conditions as you ride. Generally speaking, the lower you drop, the faster you go, and vice versa. Here's a rundown of the basic positions from top to bottom:

- Grip the bars fully, one hand on each side of the stem. This, the most upright position, is restful and relaxing and helps relieve tension in the upper body and pressure on the hands. This top handlebar position is also efficient for climbing while in a sitting position on the saddle. The grip near the stem is useful for one-handed operation while reaching for water or food. However, your hands are farthest from the brake levers in this position, and the upright posture is the least aerodynamically efficient.

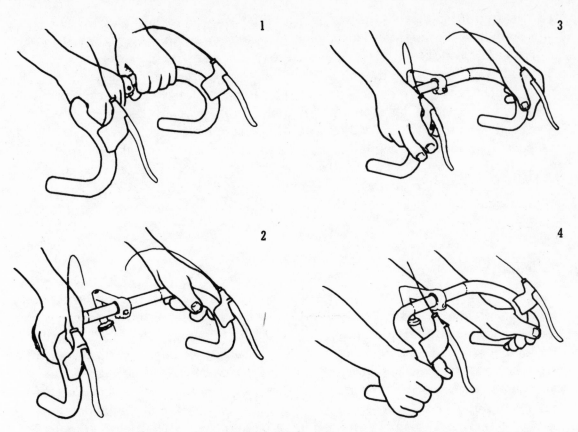

There are four basic positions on the handlebars, though you can move your hands for minor variations. In *position 1*, your hands are on top, next to the stem. This is the most upright position, and is also favored for hill-climbing (though riders typically bend over a little more while climbing). *Position 2*, with hands at the top curve, puts a little more pressure on the heel of the hand, but is a welcome change on a long ride. In *position 3* the hands rest on the brake hoods. This is the standard position for much riding, streamlined for less wind resistance but not all the way down where breathing is sometimes constricted. The down position, *number 4*, is for sprinting and real power riding, and good for gaining speed on downhills, with easy access to brakes.

- Grasp the bars at each extremity of the top part of the handlebar, just at the point where they curve down and forward. This wider hold keeps the bike more stable, but the hands are still some distance from the brake levers should an emergency situation arise.
- Rest the hands on the tops of the brake-lever hoods with the thumbs hooked over the hoods and the fingers on the bars beneath the levers, or with the top two fingers on the brake levers. This is the normal position, favored by most riders most of the time. The lowered body angle affords good forward visibility and is more streamlined, while providing excellent support for the upper body. It's also good for panic braking, especially when you ride with two fingers resting on the brake levers. With your arms straight and your thumbs hooked on the brake hoods your body won't move forward under sudden deceleration, and you're less likely to fly over the handlebars. It's also the preferred position for standing out of the saddle while climbing steep hills.

- The drop position, with the hands gripping the lowest portion of the bars beneath the brake levers, is excellent for panic braking, because you're in a lower, more stable position. It's also the grip where you gut it out on the road. And the grip for no-holds-barred, all-out racing effort while sprinting or riding into a strong headwind, and for recreational riding the only place to be when you're descending a hill fast. It's the most stable and most aerodynamic position, with your hands reasonably close to the brakes and best positioned for maximum leverage on the brakes and better steering control. However, it's the least-comfortable handlebar position and can't be maintained for long without discomfort.

Pedaling

Pedaling is the heart of cycling, and the whole point of the exercise is to keep the pedals turning as efficiently and effortlessly as possible. A good way to understand this is to imagine a revolution of the pedals as consisting of four equal parts, with the top being the 12 o'clock position, and so on. Most of the power comes from the forward and down strokes, between the 12 and 6 o'clock positions. But efficient cycling requires equal effort on the last half of the rotation, with your leg/foot power pulling up. This is where cleated shoes or toe clips and straps, or a ski-binding-type system, are essential. All pedaling should be done in perfect circles with continuous and equal motion throughout each revolution of the crank.

Here's how to put the plan into action:
- The ball of the foot, not the arch or heel, should be positioned directly over the axle of the pedal. Cleats will help.
- Toes should be pointing down slightly throughout each revolution with the heels slightly raised on the downstroke and slightly dropping on the upstroke phase.
- Ankling, pivoting the foot at the ankle with each revolution of the crank (which will make the heel drop slightly from 5 to 7 o'clock and lift from 9 to 12 and through to 5), helps smooth the circle and promote fluidity.
- Think about turning the cranks in a smooth, continuous, rounded motion, not in separate segments, which can lead to pedaling in "squares" as opposed to perfect circles.
- Concentrate on pumping from the thighs, where the muscle power is, while keeping the ankles loose and applying equal pressure on the pedals throughout each revolution.
- Keep your feet working in tandem. As one is pushing forward and down, the other is pulling back and up.
- Knees should pump up and down like well-oiled pistons, with no jerky movements or wasted side-to-side motion.

● The upper body should not move very much, except in rhythm with the pedaling, and the hips should not swivel in the saddle. Legs should be doing all the work while your upper body provides stability.

Cadence

Cadence is the number of times you turn one pedal in one minute, and proper cadence is a vital key to more efficient cycling. It's a function of fitness and terrain, and is closely related to proper bike gearing. Your goal should be to ride in gears that enable you to comfortably maintain a faster cadence over any terrain. A quicker pedal rate is less fatiguing, even going up hills, because your legs tend to tire more quickly from pedaling slowly using greater force— which can also cause knee and leg injuries—than from pedaling quickly with less effort. In the long run, you will be a better cyclist if you learn to cover the ground at a faster cadence in a lower gear, rather than a slower cadence in a higher gear.

Once you have developed more strength and stamina you'll find that you can maintain a faster cadence in higher gears. Most novices begin cycling at a slower cadence of around 50 to 60 revolutions per minute, experienced riders pedal at a rate of from 80 to 100 rpms over flat terrain and seldom less than 50 on hills, while racers can maintain a cadence of 120 or more. Cadence is called spinning at anything over 90 rpm.

Here's how to improve your cadence:
● Determine your cadence by counting the number of pedal revolutions in 10 seconds and multiplying by six. Some cycle computers include a cadence readout function.
● Build up your cadence gradually by dropping to a lower gear so that you are pedaling faster, and concentrate on keeping relaxed and smooth, not bouncing in the saddle.
● Downshift to a lower gear whenever pedal effort becomes greater. Keep your pedaling relaxed.
● When you want to go faster, pick a higher gear and pedal harder, but keep relaxed.
● Concentrate on rhythmic pedaling and applying even power throughout each pedal stroke.
● Stay in lower gears for a period of time, perhaps several weeks until you become accustomed to pedaling in a relaxed and efficient manner.
● Build up your power and endurance by climbing hills in a higher gear.
● Concentrate on maintaining an even cadence and learn to adapt it to the conditions.
● As you become more fit, you will be able to pedal easier in higher gears, even while climbing hills.

Shifting

Obviously, maintaining an efficient cadence depends greatly on using the gears properly. Through experience you get to know when to change gears by feel and you select a higher or lower gear as required to keep your legs pedaling at a comfortable cadence. The key to efficient gear selection is learning where the various gears are and how to engage them smoothly.

Your bike is in its lowest gear when the chain is on the smaller chainring at the front and the largest cog on the freewheel at the back. Looking down from the saddle, this means that the chain is positioned on the far left of both the chainring and freewheel. In the highest gear the situation is reversed: the chain is on the largest chainring and the smallest cog, both of which are on the far right from the perspective of the saddle. All the other gears are between these two extremes.

The lefthand shift lever, which controls the front derailleur, moves the chain on the front chainrings; the righthand lever, which controls the rear derailleur, moves the chain on the rear freewheel cogs. Most shifting is done with the righthand shift lever, the left being used to move between general ranges of gears.

Downshifting, or gearing down, requires moving the chain to larger cogs (on most models, by pulling the righthand shift lever toward you) and to the smaller chainrings (on most models, by pushing the lefthand lever away from you). Gearing up requires the opposite: moving the chain onto smaller cogs—pushing the righthand lever—and to larger chainrings—pulling the lefthand lever. Broadly speaking, you downshift when pedaling becomes too difficult, and you shift up when it becomes too easy.

Mastering shifting requires practice. If you're a beginner, or you're starting out on a new bike, run up and down the gears frequently to see how each one feels. Start off in a low gear on the freewheel and shift up one gear at a time. Switch to another chainwheel and go back down through the gears. Repeat the process if you have a third chainwheel.

Now here are some shifting tips:
- Develop a smooth and fluid shifting technique. It's more efficient and easier on the shifters and derailleurs, the most delicate parts of your bike.
- Always anticipate the need to change gears ahead of time and shift before you find yourself spinning aimlessly or bogging down.
- Use the appropriate hand for shifting, on either the right or left side. Keep the other on the handlebar near the stem to maintain control of your bike.
- When shifting, ease up slightly on the pedal pressure, but you must keep pedaling throughout the maneuver.
- Stepping down one gear at a time when downshifting is best. Higher gears may be jumped one or two at a time but make sure the chain is well engaged before you put pressure on the pedals.

- Avoid a gear that stretches the chain across from the outside cog to the inside chainwheel, and vice versa. These extremities are inefficient gearwise because they're usually duplicated somewhere else in the gear range and cause extra wear on the chain.
- If a gear is noisy, move the shift lever back and forth slightly to properly align the chain.
- Shift to a lower gear when coming to a stop so you'll be ready to start up again in the right gear.

Gear Development

Number of teeth on front chainwheel

	28	29	30	31	32	33	34	35	36	37	38	39	40	41	42	43	44	45	46	47	48	49	50	51	52	53	54	55	56	
12	4.98	5.14	5.34	5.51	5.69	5.87	6.04	6.22	6.40	6.58	6.77	6.94	7.12	7.30	7.47	7.65	7.83	8.01	8.18	8.36	8.54	8.72	8.90	9.07	9.25	9.43	9.61	9.78	9.97	12
13	4.59	4.76	4.92	5.08	5.24	5.41	5.57	5.74	5.90	6.07	6.23	6.40	6.57	6.73	6.90	7.06	7.23	7.39	7.55	7.72	7.88	8.05	8.21	8.38	8.54	8.70	8.87	9.03	9.20	13
14	4.27	4.42	4.58	4.73	4.89	5.04	5.19	5.34	5.49	5.75	5.80	5.94	6.10	6.25	6.40	6.56	6.71	6.86	7.01	7.17	7.32	7.47	7.63	7.78	7.93	8.08	8.23	8.39	8.54	14
15	3.98	4.12	4.27	4.41	4.55	4.69	4.84	4.98	5.12	5.27	5.41	5.55	5.69	5.84	5.98	6.12	6.26	6.40	6.55	6.69	6.83	6.97	7.12	7.26	7.40	7.54	7.69	7.83	7.97	15
16	3.75	3.88	4.01	4.14	4.27	4.40	4.53	4.67	4.80	4.93	5.07	5.21	5.34	5.47	5.60	5.74	5.87	6.00	6.14	6.27	6.40	6.54	6.67	6.81	6.94	7.07	7.20	7.33	7.47	16
17	3.51	3.64	3.77	3.89	4.02	4.14	4.27	4.40	4.53	4.65	4.78	4.90	5.02	5.15	5.27	5.40	5.52	5.65	5.78	5.90	6.03	6.15	6.28	6.40	6.53	6.66	6.78	6.90	7.03	17
18	3.32	3.44	3.56	3.68	3.80	3.92	4.04	4.16	4.27	4.38	4.50	4.62	4.74	4.86	4.98	5.10	5.22	5.34	5.45	5.57	5.69	5.81	5.93	6.05	6.17	6.29	6.40	6.52	6.64	18
19	3.14	3.25	3.36	3.48	3.59	3.71	3.83	3.94	4.05	4.16	4.27	4.38	4.50	4.61	4.72	4.83	4.94	5.05	5.17	5.28	5.39	5.50	5.62	5.73	5.84	5.95	6.07	6.16	6.29	19
20	2.99	3.09	3.20	3.31	3.41	3.52	3.63	3.75	3.85	3.95	4.06	4.16	4.27	4.37	4.48	4.59	4.70	4.80	4.91	5.02	5.12	5.23	5.34	5.44	5.55	5.66	5.76	5.87	5.98	20
21	2.84	2.94	3.05	3.15	3.25	3.35	3.45	3.56	3.66	3.76	3.86	3.96	4.07	4.17	4.27	4.37	4.47	4.57	4.67	4.78	4.88	4.98	5.08	5.18	5.29	5.39	5.49	5.59	5.69	21
22	2.71	2.81	2.91	3.01	3.10	3.20	3.29	3.39	3.49	3.59	3.70	3.79	3.88	3.98	4.07	4.17	4.27	4.37	4.46	4.56	4.66	4.75	4.85	4.95	5.04	5.14	5.24	5.34	5.43	22
23	2.60	2.68	2.76	2.84	2.92	3.00	3.09	3.17	3.15	3.34	3.42	3.62	3.71	3.80	3.90	3.98	4.08	4.18	4.27	4.36	4.45	4.55	4.64	4.73	4.83	4.92	5.01	5.10	5.20	23
24	2.48	2.57	2.68	2.75	2.84	2.93	3.02	3.11	3.20	3.29	3.38	3.47	3.56	3.64	3.75	3.82	3.91	4.00	4.09	4.18	4.27	4.36	4.45	4.54	4.62	4.71	4.80	4.89	4.98	24
25	2.39	2.47	2.55	2.64	2.72	2.81	2.90	2.99	3.08	3.17	3.25	3.33	3.42	3.50	3.58	3.67	3.76	3.84	3.93	4.01	4.10	4.18	4.27	4.35	4.44	4.52	4.61	4.70	4.78	25
26	2.30	2.38	2.46	2.54	2.62	2.71	2.79	2.87	2.95	3.03	3.11	3.20	3.28	3.36	3.45	3.53	3.61	3.69	3.78	3.86	3.94	4.02	4.10	4.19	4.27	4.35	4.43	4.51	4.59	26
27	2.21	2.29	2.36	2.44	2.52	2.60	2.69	2.76	2.84	2.92	3.00	3.08	3.16	3.24	3.32	3.40	3.48	3.56	3.64	3.72	3.80	3.87	3.95	4.03	4.11	4.19	4.27	4.34	4.42	27
28	2.13	2.21	2.29	2.36	2.44	2.52	2.60	2.68	2.75	2.83	2.90	2.97	3.05	3.13	3.20	3.28	3.36	3.43	3.51	3.59	3.66	3.75	3.82	3.89	3.97	4.04	4.12	4.19	4.27	28
29	2.06	2.13	2.20	2.28	2.35	2.42	2.49	2.57	2.64	2.72	2.79	2.86	2.94	3.01	3.08	3.16	3.24	3.31	3.39	3.46	3.53	3.60	3.68	3.75	3.82	3.90	3.97	4.04	4.12	29
30	1.99	2.06	2.13	2.21	2.28	2.35	2.42	2.48	2.56	2.63	2.70	2.77	2.84	2.92	2.99	3.06	3.13	3.20	3.28	3.35	3.42	3.49	3.56	3.63	3.70	3.77	3.85	3.92	3.98	30
	28	29	30	31	32	33	34	35	36	37	38	29	40	41	42	43	44	45	46	47	48	49	50	51	52	53	54	55	56	

Number of teeth on rear sprocket

Development (in meters) for 27-in. and 700-mm Wheels

Gear Selection

An essential key to efficient cycling, particularly over uneven terrain, is having the right gears at your disposal. I've already covered some of this ground, but once you've been riding for a while you may find that the gear combinations that came with your bike aren't entirely suitable for your needs. If so, you can get exactly the gears you want by changing the freewheel, the chainrings (or add a third chainring), or all of the above. You can have this done by an expert, or you can do it yourself, as discussed in the next section. Once you've mastered gear selection you can have various options on hand and substitute cogs, or complete freewheels, as required.

Through riding experience you'll know that using a higher gear gets you going faster, but can be tiring, while a lower gear is more restful, but covers less ground in the same time. That's how they feel in the saddle. To understand why this is so and to optimize the gearing on your bike, you need to take a closer look at development—the distance traveled per crank revolution in a given gear.

Development can be calculated by using the formula outlined earlier under Gears, but in the preceding table all the mathematics have already been done. According to the number of teeth on the rear freewheel cogs and the number of teeth on the front chainrings, the table shows the development in meters for a 700-millimeter (27-inch) wheel.

From the table you can see that the highest gears will carry you 9 meters or more with each turn of the crank. These gears are best suited for level terrain. For hillier country the chart shows that lower gears develop as little as 2 meters per crank revolution. As a rough guide, the most practical usable extremes from high to low gear are 8.5 and 2.0. A high maximum of 8.5 will have you flying along over the flattest terrain, but only if you're very fit, because this requires heavy-duty leg effort. Most recreational riders will be happier using a high gear of from 6 to 7 meters, while

you're unlikely to need anything below 3.0—unless you start tackling mountains.

So, the first step in selecting your range of gears is to choose the maximum and minimum gears, according to your state of fitness and the terrain where you ride. What you choose between these extremes is a matter of preference, which will come with riding experience. To get a headstart, you can examine the various possibilities using the Gear Development Table. For example, let's look at a typical 10-speed arrangement (you can easily extrapolate to 12, 18 or 21 gears):

	13	15	17	21	24
52	8.54	7.40	6.53	5.29	4.62
42	6.90	5.98	5.27	4.27	3.75

This example is biased in favor of higher gears and would be most suitable for fairly level terrain, perhaps some hills that aren't too steep. For very hilly country, or off-road use, it would be useful to have more lower gears. One way of achieving this would be to have a 30-tooth cog on the freewheel which, with the 42 teeth on the chainring, would give a low gear of 2.99. This option would provide a good climbing gear, but would result in a large gap between the combinations of gears. Remember, too, that extreme crossovers of the chain—from the chainring to the freewheel—are to be avoided, and that the ideal gear selection has a minimum of duplication of gears. These considerations bring up another important factor in the gearing department: shift patterns.

Shift Patterns

Some gear changes require two shifts, moving both the front and back derailleur—called double shifting—while some shifting can be done with one derailleur only. This latter maneuver is faster and more efficient, for instance, at the bottom of a steep hill where you don't want to lose momentum shifting into your best climbing gears. Furthermore, big differences between gears—when you abruptly jump from a fast-spinning lower gear to a higher one, or vice versa, when you shift from a very high to a very low one and are spinning madly without getting anywhere—are hard on your legs. This all boils down to the need for a selection of gears that minimizes double shifting by maximizing the useful range of gears available on each chainring (no duplication), and that progresses from low to high in approximately equal steps. In other words, you need to be concerned with shift patterns.

To examine the options here we can assign numbers to the developments used in the previous 10-speed example, applying 1 to the lowest gear and 10 to the highest. This gives the following shift pattern:

	13	15	17	21	24
52	10	9	7	5	3
42	8	6	4	2	1

As you can see, an even progression up through the gears would require shifting both derailleurs for most gear changes. This shift pattern would keep you very busy should you be ascending an increasingly steep hill. In addition, position 5 is wasted, since it is virtually the same as position 4 (5.29 and 5.27, respectively). Of course, you could skip a gear or two, but a more efficient arrangement, in fact the theoretical ideal, would look like this:

	15	16	17	18	19
52	9	8	7	6	5
42	5	4	3	2	1

Here, you have all the higher gears on the larger chainring, which can be selected progressively by moving the rear derailleur only. Then, when you start to climb, you can shift to the smaller chainring and select the lower gears by again moving the rear derailleur only. This pattern still has one duplication, but the fact is, it is virtually impossible to find ten combinations that have no duplication, and it's better to have it as in this pattern, on the "ends" where it is more easily skipped during a series of quick shifts.

Thus this pattern eliminates double shifting, but something else has been sacrificed: the cogs run from 15 to 19 (rather than 13 to 24), so you've lost part of your high and low range. Furthermore, besides minimizing the need for double shifting, one of your goals in setting up a personal shift pattern should include establishing a pattern that minimizes large differences between chainrings (which make shifting harder), so that the steps between gears feel about equal.

One way of arriving at this latter arrangement is to translate the differences between gears (i.e. between developments) into percentages, the ideal being to have the percentages as close to equal as possible. Experts have calculated that racers are comfortable with small steps between gears in increments of 5 percent, riders interested in the training effect might have 7 percent, while recreational cyclists might be best served with spaces between gears of up to 12 percent. For example, the lowest gear in our original 10-speed example was 3.75 meters. Using an equal increase between gears of 10 percent we can calculate the developments necessary to establish an ideal shift pattern by adding .375 (3.75 × 10%) to each gear. Thus the 10 gears would have developments of 3.75, 4.13, 4.50, 4.89, 5.25, 5.63, 6.00, 6.38, 6.76 and

7.13. You would then go to the full table and pick combinations of chainrings and cogs that give you these developments.

However, before you can achieve the ideal shift pattern, there are such practical considerations as derailleur capacity (the gearing range it can handle), compatibility between crankset and rear derailleur, the availability of suitable chainrings and cogs in the range supplied by your component manufacturer, establishing a pattern that is easily remembered (so you don't have to look down to see what gear you're in), and so on. Work out what you'd like to have on paper, then discuss it with an expert to see how feasible it is. You may have to make some compromises.

One place you shouldn't have to compromise, though, is in braking.

Braking

In most cycling situations the brakes are used mainly to regulate speed to maintain control of the bike. Emergencies may require panic stops. In both cases it's important to know what happens to your bike under braking so as to avoid skidding or flying over the handlebars.

Under deceleration your weight is transferred forward, which tends to push the front wheel down and lift the back wheel up. Consequently most of the stopping power—up to 80 percent—is on the front brake, and the front wheel can take more braking than the rear before it starts to skid.

But too much braking at the front can cause rear-wheel liftoff and the risk of somersaulting over the bars. This is counteracted by activating the rear brake, but only to a degree that maintains traction and stops short of causing a skid.

It's a good idea to use both brakes simultaneously, with more pressure on the front one, though many riders use the front brake only some of the time. However, it's essential to use the back in emergency stops, and it's important to practice panic braking frequently so that you know how your bike behaves when you slam on the brakes. Keep seated with your weight balanced on the saddle and the handlebars, a position that places you ready to react to emergencies.

Slippery conditions call for particular attention to braking. Rain, dust, grit or oil on the wheel rims prevent the brake shoes from doing their job efficiently, as well as reducing tire adhesion on the road, which promotes skids and lessens stopping power. In these situations use a gentle pumping action and apply pressure to both brake levers lightly and evenly. This quick on-and-off action cleans the rims and avoids skids.

Descending steep hills requires frequent applications of the brakes, which can lead to heat buildup and thus decrease braking efficiency; a tire on the rim might loosen, or even burst. Excessive heat buildup can be controlled by frequent pumping of the brakes, instead of steady application. On really steep descents, stopping for a while to let things cool off might be necessary.

Here are some tips for better braking:

- Develop the habit of using both brakes, applying about three-quarters of the pressure on the front and one-quarter on the back. (Change this to about 50/50 in slippery conditions.)
- Practice full stops at slower speeds and gradually work up to higher speeds to familiarize yourself with the feel of the brakes and how your bike reacts to braking.
- In heavy braking, slide back in the saddle and push firmly against the pedals to help push your body weight down and lower your center of gravity.
- In situations where you might have to use the brakes suddenly, ride with your fingers on the brake levers.
- Use your body to aid the braking effect. Sit upright in the saddle, which creates more drag, and let your arms and body absorb the decelerating forces evenly, so that you maintain a good riding position throughout the braking action.
- Remember to consider your reaction time in an emergency and be aware of the distance you will travel in the interval before you hit the brakes. This factor, coupled with wet weather, can more than double the stopping distance of a bike.
- Practice heavy braking frequently to keep your reflexes sharp and to get to know your stopping distances in different conditions.
- Don't use your brakes more often than necessary, but be prepared to stop as fast as you possibly can at any time.
- Always be alert during braking in tricky situations: gravel, wet corners, oil, ice, all of which will decrease the braking effect and might cause a slide.

Bike Handling

Once you've learned to ride a bike, you never forget, but you may still be a long way from riding it correctly. For top cycling performance, your own and your bike's, you have to master the techniques necessary to handle every situation you're likely to encounter on two wheels. The skills required begin with developing a proper sense of balance and include riding in a straight line, turning, cornering, climbing and descending hills, finding the aerodynamic advantage, taking bumps properly, and so on.

Balance

All of cycling is a balancing act. Riding a bike involves defying the law of gravity, which contrives to tip it over. If the bike stops moving it falls. Your forward momentum is what keeps you upright, and the faster you go, the easier it is to maintain equilibrium. Slow speeds exaggerate the state of imbalance and it pays to study the phenomenon closely.

When you slow to a crawl you can feel the bike start to lean over to one side. You counteract that by turning the wheel slightly or shifting your body weight to the opposite side, the latter movement being the more subtle. But the counterbalancing effect will last only a moment and you must bring correcting movements into play again, either by moving the wheel or your body weight. Once you are more experienced you can use gravity to your own advantage. For example, you can use a state of imbalance to make slow turns by simply leaning to one side; the bike will follow. You can also learn to stand in the pedals to keep your center of gravity centred and lower when cornering sharply.

Riding a Straight Line

One of the most noticeable differences between pro and amateur riders is that the pros can ride as straight as arrows, keeping the wheels steady on a straight and narrow path with no deviations, all the while pedaling furiously. The best riders can also do it while moving at very slow speeds. Mastering this skill is important for several reasons.

First of all it helps improve your sense of balance. From a practical point of view, riding in a straight line avoids wasted effort from wandering wheels and is crucial in the art of drafting (which I'll cover later). Holding your bike steady is also important to keep you in line in heavy traffic where straying a few centimeters off line can cause accidents.

Practice riding in a straight line these ways.

- Ride beside the painted line on the shoulder of a road and concentrate on keeping your wheels exactly the same distance from it for a period of time.
- Relax your arms and your grip on the handlebars and gently guide your bike with your body. Any steering corrections should be made by slight movements of the hips.
- Concentrate on smooth pedaling, applying the pedal pressure straight down and not from side to side, which causes wobbling.
- Avoid abrupt shifting of gears. Keep a light grip on the handlebar with one hand as you move the lever with the other. Don't look down.
- Keep your eyes focused some distance ahead, about 5 meters (16 feet), when you're moving at a rate of 25 kilometers (15 miles) an hour. The faster you're traveling, the farther ahead you should look.
- Practice keeping the bike in line while glancing back over your shoulder to check traffic.
- Practice your hand signals while maintaining a straight line.
- Vary your speeds until you can keep on track while riding very slowly, an indicator you've mastered the skill.

Turning

At first glance, turning seems the simplest of bike skills. You change direction by steering the front wheel, and the back wheel follows suit. Yet being able to place your front wheel precisely where you want it to go takes some practice, especially if you're under duress.

At slow speeds, as mentioned in the section on balance, you can take advantage of your bike's tendency to topple and simply lean in the direction you want to turn. You only need to move the handlebars to bring the bike back into balance. This turning method is relatively imprecise and not fast enough for emergencies.

Often you have to turn quickly at speed, and there is very little room to maneuver or for error; such is the case when you suddenly encounter a sewer grate, or a child or dog running in front of you. Quicker turns require more input from the handlebars accompanied by a greater shift in weight. It's best to practice turning first at slow speeds away from traffic, then turn more sharply more quickly until you know by instinct how far you can go.

Cornering

Taking a corner at high speed is one of cycling's biggest thrills and one of the most satisfying. It can also be quite frightening if you're unsure of yourself, and inexperienced cyclists often get into trouble when negotiating a bend at speeds beyond their capabilities. Regardless of your skill level, corners must be treated with respect, and the starting point for proper cornering technique is an understanding of the factors involved.

At slower speeds you can steer your bike through a corner using the handlebars. You turn the front wheel in the direction you want to go, and the rear wheel follows. The situation changes dramatically when you're traveling faster because the two wheels become more independently minded. When you turn the front wheel it takes the rear wheel longer to react. It continues traveling straight ahead, and if it's not brought back into line very quickly the bike will jackknife and you risk being thrown off.

To solve the problem you have to lean the whole bike in the direction you're turning and steer with your hips. To prevent the bike from skidding out from beneath you as you lean, particularly on sharper bends, you must lower your body's center of gravity as much as possible.

In criterium events, through city streets, racers depend heavily on their cornering skills, and I spend a lot of training time working on my technique. You shouldn't try to corner at racing speeds until you've completely mastered the necessary skills, but even recreational cycling involves the same procedure: setting up for the corner, choosing the best line through it, and positioning your body properly.

Corner Setup

Preparation for a corner mainly involves adjusting your speed to suit the conditions. All braking should be done before you start to turn since braking in mid-corner can cause a skid. However, an advanced skill is to be able to feather the brakes very lightly to control cornering speeds. I do this sometimes when going through a downhill hairpin, but it should only be attempted by experienced riders.

Your cornering speed depends on such variables as road-surface grip (the slippier, the slower), the sharpness of the bend (the sharper, the slower), visibility (the less you can see, the slower you should go), the type of bike you're riding (racing bikes corner best), traffic conditions (particularly oncoming), and your skill level. Run all this information through your mental computer, decide on the safest speed and brake accordingly—before you enter the corner.

Line Choice

Plan your route through the corner with care. The wider your arc, the better, since it allows you to maintain more speed throughout and you don't have to play catchup when you exit. Think about making the corner as shallow as possible, by cutting across the apex (middle of the corner) and flattening out the bend. For instance, approaching a lefthand bend you would move out to the right side of the road, providing the coast is clear of traffic, and veer left across the apex in as straight a line as possible. The right choice of line should have you emerging at the exit of the corner without having to make any abrupt corrective steering movements.

For smoother technique, focus your gaze about 4 or 5 meters (13 to 16 feet) ahead, and consider the various parts of the corner (entry, apex and exit) as a whole. Be sure to plan an exit line that won't place you in danger of oncoming traffic. Once you're committed to the line don't change it drastically, or you risk encountering the dreaded skid demon. Try to keep your speed regulated so you have a little bit of line change in reserve for such sudden hazards as potholes. Remember, the faster you're going, the less chance you have of changing your line safely.

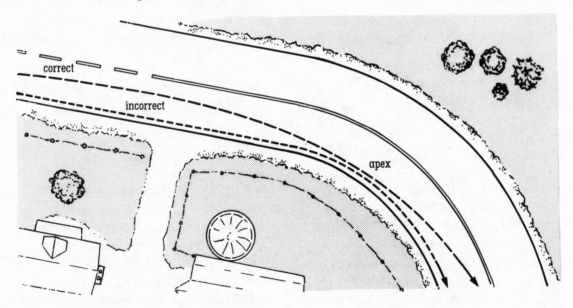

correct

incorrect

apex

Cornering: the shallower the arc, the more speed you can maintain; the sharper the turn, the more you will have to slow down. Proper cornering requires a combination of judgement, balance, planning—and, of course, is premised on having safe access to the room required.

Body Position

In a race my bike and I sometimes lean at an angle of 30 degrees or more. It looks precarious but is really quite stable, and the degree of lean depends on speed, line and traction, and will vary throughout the corner.

The faster the speed, the tighter the line and the better the tire grip, the more lean required. You're more upright on the entry, the greatest lean comes at the apex, and you straighten up again at the exit. Here's how it works in a corner.

- Leave your bike in the gear you plan to use after the exit of the curve.
- Drop low in the saddle with your back flat, your elbows bent and your arms relaxed.
- The best handlebar position is your hands inside the hooks, on the front of the drops beneath the brake levers.
- Start to lean to the inside of the curve. Coast through it. Stop pedaling as you begin the turn, keeping your inside knee up and out for balance.
- Stop the pedals in the vertical position, the inside pedal up (at 12 o'clock) and the outside pedal down (at 6 o'clock), and begin to transfer your weight to the outside pedal.
- Stand on your outside leg and place your weight over it to anchor your center of gravity. Press harder on the outside pedal in the apex, and balance your upper-body weight on the saddle and handlebars.
- Rotate your hips in the direction of the curve and let your outside knee, which should be slightly bent, follow through.
- Bend the inside knee and point it to the inside of the corner. This improves stability and balance by directing your weight into the turn.
- Once past the apex, gradually decrease your lean, even out your weight distribution, bring your body back into line and resume pedaling as soon as you can.
- If you *do* want to pedal through a turn, hold the bike in a more upright position and move your body out over the side of the bike on the inside of the turn.

- Be careful pedaling in the apex of the turn when you're leaning at an acute angle, because you might touch the inside pedal on the ground and cause a fall.

That's how the technique works in theory, but it takes a great deal of practice to put it all together for fast, efficient, confident and safe cornering. Work on it in non-traffic situations and gradually build up your speed before you try hard cornering on the road.

Leaning: Drop the shoulder, turn the knee out, and keep the inside pedal up.

Hills

Once you learn to take hills in your stride you've eliminated one of cycling's few negatives. The problems presented by hills can be ironed out through improved technique so that mountains become molehills.

While the challenge of climbing requires extra effort, what goes up must come down and your descent is your reward for the climb, though no less involving. Let's look at both sides of the hill story.

Uphill

In racing there is the tradition that climbers are born, not made. Physique, large lung capacity and low body weight certainly play major roles, but anybody can help even the score by working on their hill-climbing skills. While I'm not supposed to be a good climber, I've recently improved by leaps and bounds, and you can, too, by employing strategy and making the best use of your body and your bike.

Plan your assault on a hill by selecting your climbing gears so as not to lose momentum, and shifting down as required. Aim for a cadence throughout the climb of between 60 and 80 rpm. Once you've made those preparations you have a choice of climbing while sitting in the saddle or standing on the pedals, each method requiring a different approach. On hills with varying pitches you can switch from one to the other.

Sitting

Climbing while seated is technically the most efficient method and is most effective on gradual inclines and longer climbs because you can better conserve energy. Here are the finer points of climbing from the sitting position.

- An upright posture is best so you can relax and breathe more freely. (Aerodynamics are less of a factor in climbing.)
- Grip the handlebars on either side of the stem for better leverage. Pull back on them as you pedal.
- Shift your weight to the back of the saddle so that most of it is over your legs (for greater leverage) and the rear wheel (for more traction).
- Concentrate on maintaining a steady cadence and even rhythm, applying even pedal pressure throughout the full range of motion.
- Focus only a short distance ahead to avoid being discouraged on a long ascent, and be patient. Slow and steady thinking wins this type of race.
- Avoid too much wobbling or weaving from side to side. If such motion starts, choose a smaller gear.

Standing

Standing up as you pedal brings more of your upper-body strength into play, which supplements the leg effort and involves rhythmically rocking the bike from side to side. Standing enables you to maintain a better power output by using more of your body weight in the force of pedaling, the full force of each leg being accentuated by the side-to-side motion.

Standing also helps you gulp in the maximum oxygen, affords an opportunity to bring more muscles into play, your back and upper body included, and stretch old ones; as a bonus, it provides relief from saddle pressure. Standing is more tiring than sitting, and normally you stand on shorter, steeper hills or, in racing at least, to climb any hill faster. Here's how it's done.

- Grip the handlebars on the brake-lever hoods and pull up on the opposite side of the bars with each downstroke of the pedals.
- Stand on the pedals and place your body weight forward, over the handlebars and pedals, but keep your shoulders behind the front-wheel axle. Too far forward is inefficient.
- Shift your weight alternately over each leg to set up a rhythmic side-to-side motion, so as to get the full power of each leg onto the pedals.
- Step hard on one pedal as you pull up on the other. Put all your weight into each downstroke.
- Bring the bike back to a vertical position for the fraction of a second between each pedal stroke before you transfer your weight.
- Concentrate on keeping your direction despite the rocking motion of the frame.

Once you've reached the top of a hill continue in the same gear for a while to give your legs a rest while you begin to think about how to handle the descent.

Downhill

After all that climbing, there's a tendency to want to relax as you go down the other side. This is impossible in a race—where you always race down, and certain riders are known for being quick downhillers—and very dangerous in recreational riding. You can put your legs on hold to a certain degree going downhill, but the rest of your body, and most certainly your mind, should be on full alert.

Travelling downhill is dangerous because of the pull of gravity and increasing momentum during the descent, resulting in much greater speeds—probably the fastest you'll ever go on a bike—which mean increased braking distances and higher cornering speeds. Steeper hills have corkscrews and switchbacks, an advantage while climbing, but the reverse while descending. Twists and turns hamper vision and prevent long-range planning, and there is a potential nasty surprise around every corner. Road surfaces may be slippery or bumpy, or both, and the rush of wind hitting your eyes and whistling in your ears is distracting for the inexperienced. Those are some of the reasons you need maximum concentration, a built-in anti-panic device, quick reflexes, well-honed cycling skills and a bike that's working properly.

The other side of the coin is that riding downhill can be extremely exhilarating: the faster, the more fun. But you must ride safely and maintain control at all times. Here's how.

- For very long descents of several kilometers, dress for the occasion with more clothing, especially if you're warm and the air (with the speed-induced windchill) is cooler.
- Shift into a higher gear, maybe even your highest, before you start.
- Ride low in the saddle with your hands on the drops and your fingers on or near the brake levers.
- The safest downhill speed is one where you can still easily brake your way out of trouble.
- Descend only as quickly as you feel comfortable. Slow down to regain control of your bike and your faculties.
- To pick up speed, assume a tuck position with the cranks parallel to the road: back flat and torso lower to the top tube, head down but eyes up, knees and elbows in.
- To slow down, open up out of the tuck and sit up in the saddle so that your body creates air resistance.
- Apply the brakes to further control speed, using the rules and recommendations found in the Braking section.
- Use the brakes more frequently and gently. Don't slam them on, which might cause loss of control.
- Use a pumping action on the brakes to avoid skidding and heat buildup in the rims.
- Adjust your speed according to the situation so that you can avoid any sudden steering action, which might cause loss of balance or adhesion to the road.
- Concentrate on prudent cornering, taking care not to swing wide at the exit, where you might encounter oncoming traffic.
- Start pedaling again as the hill flattens out and take advantage of all that gravity-assisted extra speed while you have it.

Wind Resistance

Wind can be a welcome bonus whenever it happens to be a tailwind—nice to sail easily along with the help of Mother Nature. However, even then your velocity is creating a headwind, and a lot of cycling energy—up to 30 percent—goes into battling wind or air resistance, the required effort increasing dramatically with more speed.

The best defense against the wind factor is to maintain a low profile, keep your body bent well down on your bike. You can also take advantage of the shelter afforded by natural windbreaks, such as dips in the road, trees, buildings—and other riders. Whenever a group of cyclists ride together, they can create their own windbreak and take advantage of the slipstreaming effect, where each rider can take a turn at working against the wind for the common good. This is called pacing (or drafting, in North America).

Pacing

A big part of bike racing, pacing can be used by all cyclists traveling in a group. Everyone lines up in single file and the lead rider bears the brunt of the wind resistance, thereby making it much easier for the following riders and in effect almost towing them along. One rider stays ahead for a period of time, then peels off and drops back into the paceline and another rider resumes the frontal attack on the wind. The same principle applies in a crosswind so that riders fan out beside and slightly behind each other, forming an echelon. The riders on the windward side create a barrier affording some protection for

Pacing or drafting is the cyclist's equivalent of "breaking trail", and isn't just for racers. It adds a spirit of team work to even a good hard recreational ride, and fosters precise, consistent riding. It works whether the wind is from the front or the side.

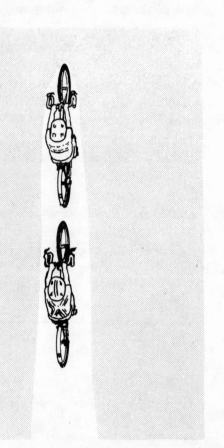

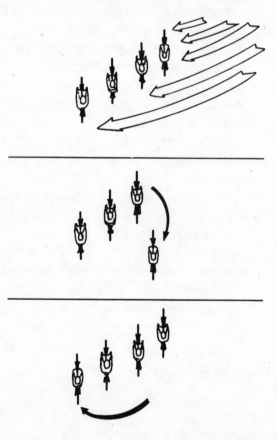

those riding on the sheltered side.

The pacing effect only works when riders are in very close proximity to each other, and so requires cautionary measures by everyone in the paceline or peloton. Even an easy recreational ride by a non-slipstreaming group requires an orderly approach. An unruly bunch of riders is called a pack and is not a desirable state of affairs, from either a safety or efficiency point of view. Casual touring relaxes the requirements somewhat, but since it's always wise to ride in single file, the following rules apply in most group riding situations—though in racing things are sometimes a bit less amicable!

- The slipstreaming effect works best with your front wheel about 30 centimeters (a foot) behind the rear wheel of the rider in front. Racers often come closer, but that entails more risk and requires a relaxed confidence that only comes with experience.
- Wheels should not overlap; otherwise there's a great risk of a spill by the following rider should the front rider have to swerve suddenly. In crosswind situations overlapping can't be avoided and greater caution must be exercised.
- Avoid staring at the rear wheel of the rider in front but use quick glances to watch for such things as unexpected braking in front. Focus farther down the road, using your peripheral vision to take in the scenery.
- Ride defensively and anticipate trouble, but never apply your brakes suddenly without warning those behind.
- Adjust your speed by soft pedaling, spinning the cranks but not applying much pressure.
- Lead changes should take place frequently enough to prevent fatigue at the front. Everyone should get equal time.
- Lead riders should peel off and drop to the back of the pace-line on a predetermined side (right or left) of the pace-line.
- In windy conditions those coming to the front should be given the protected side.
- Leading riders should spot trouble first—potholes, glass, and so on—and pass the information back down the pace-line by means of a quick hand signal.
- Rear riders can pass on warnings of approaching traffic with a shout or a sharp whistle.

Handling Obstacles

In your repertoire of cycling skills, add mastering the ways to handle sudden encounters with potentially threatening obstacles like broken pavement, potholes, curbs, railway tracks, and such assorted debris as glass, stone, sticks, bottles and cans. They can often be handled by avoidance maneuvers, which can be practiced in a vacant parking lot, or some other non-traffic area, by marking out obstacles on the pavement. If you're an off-road rider on a mountain bike this kind of thing will be routine. I'll talk more about it in the Off-Road section.

- Be particularly vigilant when riding along the gutter of an urban street, where most debris collects.
- At slower speeds smaller objects can sometimes be straddled by simply steering to one side for an instant then swinging back on line, so that the object passes between your wheels.
- At lower speeds you can sometimes hop your wheels over obstacles by jumping the bike while pedaling harder, unloading your weight from the front wheel and pulling up on the handlebars. While the front wheel is still in the air, shift your weight off the rear wheel and lift up on the pedals to bring the rear wheel off the ground. This maneuver takes practice. At higher speeds it's possible to jump the whole bike, but this is dangerous for the uninitiated; even pro riders crash trying to do it.
- The force of frontal impacts can be reduced by shifting your weight back to the saddle and lifting up on the handlebars as the front wheel passes over the bump. For rear impacts, shift your weight forward and pull up on the pedals to lift the rear of the bike.
- Bump impacts can be lessened by keeping your body relaxed, your weight evenly distributed, and consciously thinking of your legs as shock absorbers and momentarily lifting your weight off them as you pass over the bump.

PART THREE

A Cyclist's Survival Guide

Riding Safely

Many of the topics I cover in this book are concerned with safer cycling. The reason for dwelling explicitly on the subject of safety is that cycling can be dangerous, and this bad news can be found in accident statistics. The good news is that an analysis of those statistics shows that the likelihood of an accident—the majority of which are the fault of cyclists—can be greatly reduced simply by using precautionary measures.

Safe riding—especially in heavier traffic, where most cycling accidents occur—requires the use of all your faculties and a combination of awareness, alertness, anticipation, concentration, predictable movements, the right attitude, and generous quantities of common sense. The process begins with a thorough knowledge of the law and the rules of the road.

The Law

Safe riding becomes much simpler when you understand that your bike is considered by the laws in most countries to be a vehicle. Thus, you should ride your bike as you would drive a car. If you're unsure about traffic-law details (maybe it's a long time since you studied for your driver's license), get a copy and study them. Regardless of where you live, you'll find references to such illegalities as driving under the influence of alcohol or drugs, driving recklessly without due care and attention, and so on. You're legally bound to behave yourself.

In my home province of Ontario, for instance, the Highway Traffic Act states that a bicycle is a vehicle, and a cyclist, as a vehicle operator, has a right to use the road. With that right comes a responsibility to obey the laws and follow the rules of the road. Thus, cyclists must ride on the right-hand side, look and signal before turning, obey all traffic signals, follow rules of right-of-way and general road conduct, carry proper lighting at night, and so on—just like any motor vehicle. In California and several other American states a cycling misdemeanor is treated like any other traffic violation: it is marked against your driving record and can raise your car-insurance rates.

A major virtue of treating bicycles as vehicles is that everyone knows where they stand; motorists and cyclists are equals and both should behave responsibly, according to the laws and accepted rules of behavior. However, human nature being what it is, the system often breaks down and as a cyclist you have to make allowances for that.

Attitudes

Once you begin to realize that your bike is a vehicle you're well on the road to safer riding. You must also hope that motorists realize this, too. Unfortunately, a great many of them don't. Many motorists seem to resent having to share the road with a mere human-powered, two-wheeled device. Traffic bullies are to be found everywhere, but four wheels against two is unfair, and dangerous. Don't try to fight back if you find yourself being crowded or harassed by a motorist. Ride politely and go out of your way to avoid confrontations. The guy who shook his fist and cursed at you will have to live with his snit for the rest of the day, while you can work off your anger and frustration by pedaling harder.

Your own attitude on the road is vital to safe riding. You should exercise patience, tolerance and understanding (maybe the guy who cut you off was in a rush to get his wife to hospital to have a baby) toward your fellow road users. A show of courtesy on the road is usually rewarded and returned in kind. Riding with goodwill and kindness can generate many happy kilometers—but you don't have to be a wimp.

The meek riders in traffic shall not inherit the earth—or the road. Rather, they're likely to get left behind in the rush. And being too submissive can cause problems, in the same way the dithering, uncertain driver of a car can interrupt traffic flow, cause engines and tempers to overheat and accidents to happen. Ride your bike with caution, yes, but also with confidence and assurance.

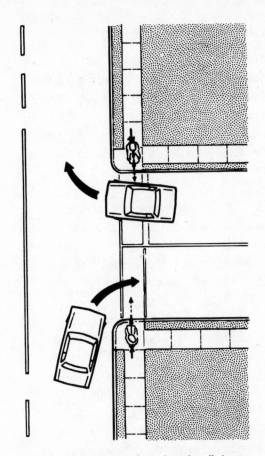

Adult cyclists should not ride on the sidewalk (senior citizens on tricycles are an exception), because motorists don't know whether you will act as a vehicle or as a pedestrian. Riding on sidewalks does not encourage motorists to respect cyclists that *are* on the road, and annoys pedestrians as well. The cyclist coming south (top) is, in effect, riding on "the wrong side of the road", though he's on the sidewalk. The cyclist going north (bottom) is cheating if he expects to have right-of-way as a pedestrian; he should be on the roadway behind the vehicle.

If you consider yourself the equal of anything on the road, you behave more predictably, a vital factor in safe riding. Don't be unpredictable and meander aimlessly, or dart about like a demented doodlebug. Pedal a straight and narrow path, signal your intentions clearly, then act on them decisively.

Alertness

Thou Shalt Remain Alert should be the safe cyclist's first commandment. The heavier the traffic or the worse the road surface and weather conditions, the greater the level of alertness required. It's all right to ride with your head in the clouds on a quiet country road, but doing it in rush-hour traffic brings a risk of a closer encounter with those clouds than you would wish to have.

A high state of alertness, with your antennae quivering and your sensory-input mechanisms geared for action, goes hand-in-hand with acute concentration. The faster you travel, the easier it is to be alert. When all your attention is focused on the uncertainties of what might lie ahead, your degree of alertness is heightened because you're in an advanced state of anticipation—another vital factor in safe riding.

It's similar to driving a car slowly on a wide-open motorway where you have a tendency to be lulled into a state of drowsiness, something that never happens when driving briskly on a twisty road. Racing drivers become much more crash-prone when they slow down. That's one reason for keeping up with urban (not highway) traffic on your bike; the other reason is that when different vehicles all travel at the same speed, traffic flows more smoothly—and safely.

To keep alert on a bike you obviously need lots of feedback from your eyes and, less obviously, from your ears. Keep your eyes peeled (a mirror helps) for any useful information concerning anything that might affect your safe ride. You should become adept at such details as observing reflections in store windows and consulting the shadows on the road beside you.

Keep your ears constantly tuned to the sounds of the road—never wear earphones. Listen to the noises from approaching traffic. Speeding engines, squealing brakes, surges of acceleration, exhaust note variations, gear changes and the like, all have stories to tell a tuned-in cyclist. Learn to separate traffic sounds from the general urban din, and through experience you'll be able to decipher what they mean.

Awareness

If you're new to cycling it won't take long for you to realize the need for constantly scanning the road surface for potential hazards, which might trip you up or cause a flat tire. Anticipating trouble, spotting it, then reacting to avoid it is a fundamental rule of the road. But when you're sharing the road with other traffic you have to broaden your areas of concern far beyond potholes, glass and the like. You must be flexible, able to compensate quickly and adjust your position in response to new circumstances. In this way you'll be able to maintain your hard-earned momentum, as well as avoid trouble. To be successful, you have to plan your moves ahead of time.

During any ride in an urban area you must exercise your powers of observation in all directions, taking note of the road surface, oncoming traffic, following traffic, road signs, pedestrians, animals, weather conditions—everything that's going on and particularly anything that might interfere with your safety. Ride defensively and always expect the unexpected.

Positioning in Traffic

Where you locate yourself in moving traffic depends on your degree of confidence, skill level and fitness, as well as traffic density and speed. Proper positioning gives you, and others, a safety margin to work with in times of emergency, and can shorten the distance from A to B.

The best position is to be fully integrated with the traffic flow, most practical in lighter traffic at speeds of up to 40 kilometers (25 miles) an hour. You can assume a position in the middle of the traffic lane and ride as if you were another vehicle. As such, you shouldn't tailgate; always stay at least two bike lengths behind any vehicle in front of you (no vehicle drafting allowed!), preferably more, and increase that distance when traveling at faster speeds.

The other position involves sticking closer to the edge of the traffic lane, about one meter (just over a yard) from the curb. Here you're somewhat removed from the cut and thrust of the mainstream traffic, but you'll need to exercise extra caution to avoid such hazards as parked cars, road debris and unseeing or unsympathetic motorists who might contrive to invade your space. This position is also the one to use on the open road

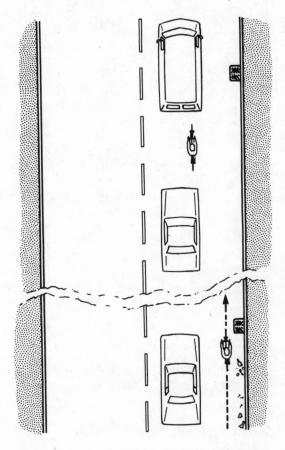

Merge with the traffic flow if you are moving at the same speed as the cars, or if the roadway is too narrow to use your "own" lane at the right. If you are moving significantly slower, or there is room, ride to the right, but still far enough away from the curb so that debris and sewer grates are missed without swerving left.

where the speed limits mean cyclists have to play second fiddle to motor vehicles.

Your riding position on your bicycle is also very important in heavier traffic. Upright is best, particularly at intersections, and your hands should never be far from the brake levers. It's also advisable to keep toe clips loose or ride without them.

You can be on the safe side when you change lanes in moving traffic if you treat each lane-change as if it were *two* changes. (1) Look, signal, and move from the *right* side of the lane to the *left* side of the same lane; (2) then look, signal, and move to the *right* side of the new lane.

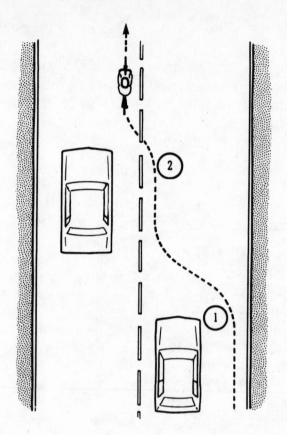

Signaling

Using hand signals is essential to make others aware of your intentions, but you have to first master controlling your bike with one hand, because the signaling hand causes a slight imbalance. You also have to be able to steer straight ahead while you're looking elsewhere: behind to check following traffic, and to either side before you turn.

Before you change direction you must look behind to make sure it's safe to do so. A mirror helps, but you should also practice shoulder checking, looking over your shoulder, or under (if you're in the drop position),

to check that the coast is clear. You have to be able to do this while maintaining control of your bike.

In some situations you might also have to provide an audible signal of your approach—to pedestrians with their back to you, for instance. A bell or horn mounted on your bike can be used, or you can yell or whistle. Do anything you can to make sure others are aware of you and of what you plan to do.

When hand signaling you should make your signals well in advance. Hand signals vary somewhat from region to region and country to country. Here are the recognized signals.

Left Turn: Raise your left arm and extend it horizontally from the shoulder, pointing left.

Right Turn: Either (a) raise your left arm to shoulder height with your elbow bent and your hand held vertically, or (b) raise your right arm and extend it horizontally from the shoulder, pointing right.

Stop or Slow: Either (a) raise your left arm to shoulder height with your elbow bent and your hand held straight down, or (b) raise your right arm halfway, about 45 degrees, to a horizontal position.

Basic Riding Rules

- Ride on the righthand side of the road (or on the left in England, Australia and some other countries) and travel in the direction of the traffic. Riding against traffic is illegal and unsafe—especially on one-way streets. So are U-turns.
- Obey all traffic signs and signals as if you were driving a car. This means proceeding with caution, slowing or stopping when instructed to do so, and yielding to other traffic and/or pedestrians. Watch for crosswalks, passengers getting off public transit vehicles, and so on.
- Ride in a straight line (no weaving), stay in single file (if you're in the company of other cyclists), and keep in your traffic lane (either in the middle of it or closer to the curb).
- Signal your intention to make any directional change. Use hand signals well in advance, and use an audible signal, a yell or a bell, to warn those who might not see you of your approach.
- Pass slower vehicles on the left (or on the right in countries where they drive on the left). This occasion arises mainly when a vehicle ahead of you slows to make a righthand turn. Check behind and signal before making your lane change.

- At stop signs, yield to pedestrians crossing, then yield to other traffic, before entering the roadway.
- On sidewalks, where cycling is permitted, yield to pedestrians, give audible warnings, pass with care and ride slowly. Make sure it's legal before riding on sidewalks. (Regulations vary in municipalities; in Toronto only bicycles with 60-centimeter (24-inch) wheels or smaller may be ridden on sidewalks.)
- On cyclepaths ride in a straight line, keep to the right (or left in countries like England), check behind and signal (visually and audibly) before passing on the left.

Intersection Procedures

Most cycling accidents happen at intersections because traffic-speed differentials are higher, vehicles are moving in opposite directions, traffic tends to back up, the danger of confusion is high, and cyclists are harder to see. Motorists have a tendency to ignore anything not on four wheels themselves. When making a move in an intersection it's a good idea to try to make eye contact with opposition motorists in your path, to make sure they see you. All intersection maneuvers require special attention.

- Watch for vehicles crossing your path—right, left and center, and coming from behind, if you're turning left.
- Stay in front of, or behind, all vehicles turning in an intersection, never to one side (especially the right), since they may not see you.
- At traffic lights, allow yourself enough time to stop and/or turn before the light changes—remember, you have much less acceleration than a car. Don't try to anticipate green lights or beat amber or red lights.
- Making a Right Turn: Check behind, signal, stop if necessary, yield to pedestrians and oncoming traffic, signal, then turn.
- Making a Left Turn, Option A: Become a pedestrian, which may be advisable in heavy traffic. Dismount, walk your bike across the road via the pedestrian crosswalk, and resume riding in the new direction.
- Making a Left Turn, Option B: Perform as a motor vehicle. Stop if necessary, check behind, signal, edge over to the left of your traffic lane well in advance, yield to oncoming traffic in the intersection, then turn left.

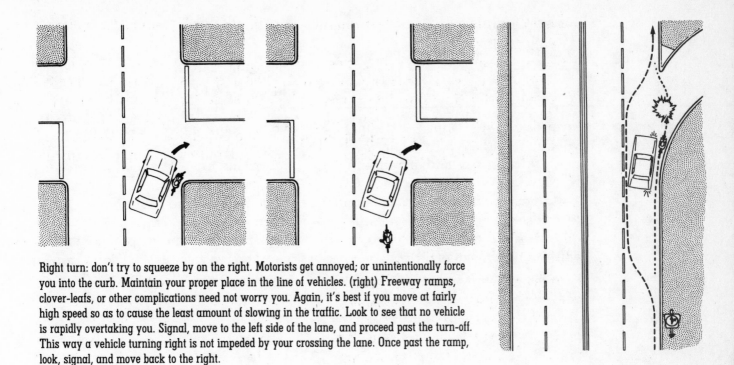

Right turn: don't try to squeeze by on the right. Motorists get annoyed; or unintentionally force you into the curb. Maintain your proper place in the line of vehicles. (right) Freeway ramps, clover-leafs, or other complications need not worry you. Again, it's best if you move at fairly high speed so as to cause the least amount of slowing in the traffic. Look to see that no vehicle is rapidly overtaking you. Signal, move to the left side of the lane, and proceed past the turn-off. This way a vehicle turning right is not impeded by your crossing the lane. Once past the ramp, look, signal, and move back to the right.

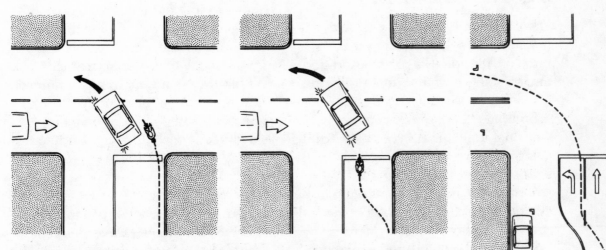

Left turn: don't try to sneak through on the right side of a turning automobile. The driver coming from the left times his approach to enter the intersection immediately after the vehicle turning left has cleared it—and he cannot see the cyclist. Typically, however, the motorized vehicle turning left will accelerate more rapidly than the cyclist, leaving the rider exposed to the now rapidly approaching car. To be safe, stay in line behind the turning car, so you are visible the whole time. (right) The arrow shows the correct path for a left turn through a multi-lane roadway.

Route Choices

Roads and streets with traffic lights at major intersections are your safest bet. Back streets may allow more leisurely riding, but parked cars are hazards and stop signs will destroy your hard-earned momentum, wear down your brakes, and increase the risk of errors.

Many motorways are out of bounds to cyclists and will have signs at entrances to that effect. Highways with paved shoulders are a boon to cyclists, as you can ride further away from the faster vehicles and the ensuing blasts of wind they produce. On all open roads you can ride closer to the shoulder (due to things like the absence of parked cars), and while cycling-touring pleasures increase on less-traveled roads, there, too, you tend to find more road-surface problems, twists, turns and reduced visibility. (See also the Touring and Commuting sections.)

For serious training I prefer wide-open spaces with no stop signs, traffic lights, little traffic and smooth surfaces—surely the cyclist's utopia!

Speed and Momentum

The ideal in city traffic is pedaling nonstop and seldom using your brakes. This helps keep you alert and makes you ride with forethought, and it's also more practical and safe.

Stopping and starting is more wearing—on you and your bike—and less efficient, and slower speeds expose you to more dangers. It's safer to keep up your momentum in city riding and better to ride at the speed of traffic, if possible. This is because speed differentials increase the accident rate and when you keep up with other vehicles you can more easily spot trouble and plan your moves ahead. The reverse is also true in that other vehicles are better able to see you and avoid you when you're traveling at their speed. You should ride briskly to be able to act and react, but keep something in reserve for emergencies, where acceleration might be required. Remember that the point of this exercise is safe riding, and you shouldn't try to race with vehicular traffic.

One way to maintain momentum is to learn traffic-light timing patterns and pace yourself between them, slowing down slightly or speeding up to time your arrival at the green lights. Maintaining your position in moving traffic is a key to avoiding stop-and-go situations. You might also indulge in a certain amount of what is called traffic jamming, which is taking advantage of your bike's comparatively small size to work your way through slowly moving traffic. It should only be done at slow speeds and your overtaking maneuvers should be conducted legally and with a certain amount of discretion, since stalled motorists might get annoyed to see you passing them. Don't abuse the technique.

Safety Tips

- Try to keep pace with traffic and maintain your momentum, but keep your hands on the brake levers.
- Ride defensively. Always assume the worst and that every situation is an accident waiting to happen.
- Stand out in the crowd. Wear colorful clothing. Put a flag on your bike, a bell, a horn—do everything you can to be seen and heard.
- Move your eyes constantly to keep track of ongoing developments. Constantly monitor the sounds of traffic.
- Watch for idiots. Make sure you're not one yourself. Behave predictably. Don't make a move unless the coast is clear.
- Be especially alert for suddenly opened parked-car doors, wide mirrors on larger vehicles, and unexpectedly stopping vehicles.
- Look for escape routes, such as driveways, open gates and gaps between parked cars, for emergency situations.

What I've given you in this section is just an overview of riding safely. I recommend that you join a cycling organization, study pamphlets, books, films and videos on the subject, take lessons (see the Cycle Sources section), and generally proceed with caution on the road. Meanwhile, here's how to safely handle some of the more frequently encountered cycling problems.

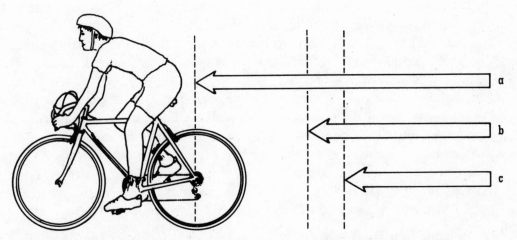

Both brakes must be used for quick, stable braking. The braking distance with rear brake only is *a*; front brake alone, *b*; using both brakes, stopping distance is *c*. You can see that the *front* brake does most of the braking.

Problem Solving

Most of the slings and arrows of outrageous fortune to which you as a cyclist are subjected can be minimized if you're prepared for them. The following list, in alphabetical order, covers the main types of troubles you're likely to encounter and offers some suggestions on how to avoid or survive them.

Accident Avoidance

A study on cycling accidents has shown that traveling 16 kilometers (10 miles) by bicycle is no more dangerous than traveling 48 kilometers (30 miles) in a car or 1,600 kilometers (1,000 miles) in a plane. Accidents will happen, but it's safe to say that cyclists can vastly improve the odds against them by practicing safe, defensive riding. Beyond that, here are some specific measures to be taken against some of the leading factors that contribute to accidents.

- *Inexperience*: If you're new to cycling, proceed with greater caution at all times until you've logged plenty of time on your bike and feel confident you can handle it in emergencies. Stick to easy riding conditions, regarding roads, traffic and weather, until you gain experience.
- *Overconfidence*: As an experienced rider, don't let down your guard for a moment. The more you cycle the more you will be aware of potential problems. Stay alert and be prepared for emergencies. I still consider every vehicle I meet on the road a potential danger.
- *Fatigue*: A tired rider is much more accident-prone. Be especially careful after a hard ride and try to limit longer rides to 100 kilometers (62 miles) to lessen risk. (See Fatigue section.)
- *Bad weather*: Riding in inclement weather and after dark greatly increases the dangers. Slow down in the wet, be well lit after dark or in the fog, and stop when conditions become severe. I simply don't ride in fog.
- *Traffic bullies*: Your bike is no match in a close encounter with a four-wheeled vehicle (or motorcycle) driven by a belligerent driver. Be particularly alert at the times and places (such as the closeness of drinking establishments) when and where the most idiots are on the road.

Despite your best efforts, you may be confronted with the likelihood of an accident, in which case you've got three main last-minute options. For the most part these avoidance maneuvers depend on how much time you've got to react, and you should try to maintain what I call quick calm. Don't freeze up or panic, but try to behave logically. Here are your options:

- *Brake hard*: If you're far enough away from the problem you can hit the brakes and come to a safe halt. Be careful of skidding, particularly on wet surfaces, and of locking the front wheel, which might send you over the handlebars.
- *Turn abruptly*: This is often an instinctive reaction and can be employed to avoid potholes, suddenly opened car doors and such, but care must be taken not to lose control of your bike in a front-wheel skid.
- *Speed up*: You may be able to accelerate away from potential trouble—wayward children, dogs and the like—providing you're in a low-enough gear and have the energy and power to effect a quick burst of speed.

In some situations, a surprise dog attack, for instance, you may be able to employ all three methods of avoiding trouble: braking first, then steering to one side of the animal, then making a run for it. (More of this under Dogs.)

Accident Survival

To update an old saying, a gram of prevention is worth a kilo of cure, and the few grams of a cycling helmet are essential weight in a wise cyclist's survival kit. Even when an accident is inevitable, there are some desperation steps an alert cyclist can take to lessen its severity and aftermath. Should you be the victim of an accident, or be present at one where another cyclist is involved, here are some precautions:

- Even if you and the bike are still mobile, don't try to ride away immediately, but check over both. Retire to a safe position if you're in traffic. Give yourself time to recover from any shock. Make sure you're not suffering from a hidden injury and examine your bike to make sure it's still roadworthy.
- If you're able to ride away, proceed with more caution than usual since you may be dazed or experience delayed shock. If you've had a heavy jolt it may be wiser to walk your bike for a distance to recover and clear your head.
- If you have any injuries that prevent riding but aren't crippling, seek the necessary first aid, or apply it yourself. When touring it's a good idea to have a first-aid kit with you and know how to use it.
- With more serious injuries lie still and wait for help. Don't try to move if you suspect broken bones or head injuries. Get professional medical attention and X rays as soon as possible.
- In personal injury or property-damage incidents, summon the police so that an officer can file the accident report you may require for insurance purposes. Get names and addresses. Take photos or make a sketch of the circumstances.

Animals

Part of the touring or country-riding experience is confrontation with animals, often in the form of flocks of sheep or herds of cows. The appropriate action here is to stop well short of the herding operation and let the farmer and the dogs get on with their job. Fortunately, these working dogs are usually too busy to pay any attention to cyclists. Riding into the pack can startle the animals and cause mass confusion or a stampede. Resume your journey when the road is clear.

Horses and riders, particularly thick in English country lanes, call for special precautions. When you come up behind a horse and rider unseen, you risk frightening the horse. Try to announce your arrival, by ringing your bell or speaking softly. Once the rider is aware of you and has a firm grip on the reins, overtake with caution and give the horse as much room as possible. Riders will usually thank you for this—though the riders on a fox hunt in England once berated my co-author for running his

bike across the scent of their quarry and causing confusion among the hounds. The fox escaped.

All-terrain adventurers may have to contend with more dangerous critters. Avoid any overly friendly animal—especially foxes—in areas prone to rabies outbreaks. Covered legs, heavy-duty riding boots or shoes and snake-bite kits are advisable for riders who frequent rattlesnake country. Haste should be made in the opposite direction from any female bear with cubs, and all brown bears should be given a wide berth.

Small creatures, such as squirrels, mice, pheasants and partridges, that suddenly dart across the road are other hazards that can distract a cyclist. Be very watchful, especially in wooded areas, along hedgerows or where there is long grass beside the road. My co-author reports several close encounters and near misses with pheasants, particularly during fast, corkscrewing descents down hills when the birds had no warning of his impending arrival.

Dogs

I love dogs and have two of them at home. But dogs and cyclists tend to mix like oil and water. And, just as oil and water present precarious surfaces for riding, dogs have to be treated with caution on the road. Just

the other day, as I was working on this part of the book, a Great Dane nearly ran me down! Not all dogs chase bikes, but enough do to qualify dogs as one of cycling's worst hazards.

Besides frightening cyclists, which can cause them to crash or swerve into traffic, dogs that love to chase vehicles can cause injuries by hitting the bike or falling under its wheels, not to mention biting the rider. Most dogs announce their intentions by growling and barking, but silent surprise attacks, where the dog sneaks up behind and snaps, are worse, giving the rider little time to react. Here's how to defend yourself when man's best friend becomes the cyclist's worst enemy.

- You can outrun most chasing dogs, since they are mainly intent on defending their own territory. Once you've ridden beyond the property they call home, they'll usually give up the chase.
- If you're unable to beat a hasty retreat you might try discussing the situation in a friendly manner, speaking in soothing tones to the dog. But it's usually more effective to adopt an authoritative pose and speak sternly. If the chase persists, most dogs will respond to short, sharp commands like "Stop!" or "Stay!"
- During the period of time the dog is alongside your bike, you might consider lifting your foot on that side to avoid any snapping jaws, and keep pedaling with the other foot.
- Resist the temptation to kick out at the running dog, as you may lose control of your bike. If you use dog-repellent spray or your water bottle—see below—keep a good grip on the handlebars.
- If the dog attacks on a hill, or if you're otherwise unable to leave it behind, stop and dismount on the side opposite the dog. Keep your bike between yourself and the offended canine and try reasoning with it. Feign friendliness, speaking in a soft voice using "nice doggie" terms of endearment. Often the dog will respond favorably—the thrill of the chase is gone when the chasee stops—and you can walk away before riding off again.
- If the dog is still intent on extracting its pound of flesh—evidenced by continued snarling and growling and bared teeth—you may have to establish your authority by brandishing your tire pump and speaking in a very firm voice. After a short period of standoff the dog will usually give in and slink away.
- To be fully equipped to handle attacking dogs, some cyclists carry discouragement in the form of spray cans of repellent chemicals of the type carried by postmen (some bike shops carry them, instructions for use included). Others resort to squirting dogs from their water bottle, but that may only infuriate the dog more.
- If bitten, get medical treatment as quickly as possible. Report the dog so that it's checked for rabies, especially if the disease is in the area.

Falls

It's a fact of biking life that sooner or later a cyclist will take a tumble, and you should know how to fall properly. Admittedly, falling is difficult to practice beforehand, but I speak to you as one who has had plenty of experience in this regard. Here are some of the ways to minimize the dangers when you suffer a loss of equilibrium on your bike.

- Wear a helmet, padded gloves, and substantial bike clothing. Covered limbs can help prevent skin abrasions.
- If you find yourself airborne, as in flying over the handlebars, try to assume a tuck. The object of this exercise is to protect your head and to return to earth on another part of your anatomy. Put your head down between your shoulders, pull your knees up, land on your feet if you can, and roll forward to help absorb the energy.
- When you reach the point of no return in a skid, slide back in the saddle as far as possible and straighten your arms. Avoid the temptation to abandon ship. Go down with your bike and try to make it a buffer between yourself and any immovable object.
- Instinctively you will try to break a fall with your arms extended. Relax them quickly so as to better absorb the shock and avoid broken bones.

Fatigue

Everyone knows the dangers of falling asleep at the wheel of a car. You're unlikely to doze off while pedaling, but fatigue on a bike is common and can lead to potentially dangerous inattention and slower reaction times. The later stages in a bike race are always the most crash-filled, because the riders are mentally and physically exhausted.

Besides sudden energy depletion, fatigue can be caused by carbon-monoxide fumes (see Fumes), food, alcohol or drugs, cold weather, over-training, or simply boredom from being too long in the saddle. As soon as you feel tired you should do something about it (see below). Before that, you can take some anti-fatigue measures:

- Limit longer journeys and hard rides to your state of fitness. About 100 kilometers (62 miles) a day is a safe distance for the average rider.
- Chronic fatigue can be caused by overtraining. (See Overtraining.) Don't ride hard or far when suffering from this condition. Ease up on your training until you recover. Personally, I welcome this excuse, but too seldom find it.
- Change your riding position frequently. Choose easier pedaling gears. Stop and walk around if you get too tired, perhaps at a variety store where you can find energy food and drink. Stretch your muscles and breathe deeply.

- Don't eat a big meal just before cycling. Carry emergency rations as suggested in the Diet section and nibble frequently to keep your carbohydrate level up. Drink plenty of water.
- Don't pedal and drink. Alcohol first impairs your judgment, then makes you drowsy.
- Drugs and cycling don't mix, either, for the same reasons as alcohol, and alcohol and drugs (medicine included) mixed can be deadly. I am totally opposed to any performance-enhancing drugs.
- Put on more clothing if you feel cold in the saddle. When your body temperature drops, your level of alertness falls right along with it.
- In heavy traffic, drowsiness can be caused by carbon-monoxide fumes. Stop, move off the road and take a minute to breathe deeply and clear out your lungs. Choose cycling routes away from offensive vehicles.
- If fatigue persists during a ride, stop riding. Continue when you're alert again.

Fumes

The combination of oxygen-dependent cyclists, toxic exhaust emissions and polluted air is an unhealthy situation. Bike commuters and urban riders are exposed to a steady diet of noxious fumes. Even a country ride through pleasant landscape can be rudely interrupted when you find yourself puffing up a hill in the wake of a huge truck belching black smoke.

Carbon monoxide, a colorless, odorless gas, is hard to detect in the air, but too much of it is more easily recognized in your body. The symptoms include headache, nausea, dizziness and drowsiness. Fortunately, well-exercised lungs help decrease the negative effects of polluted air by flushing out the impurities, and a healthy diet helps neutralize the toxic effect. Tests have shown that cyclists have less toxic wastes in their systems than motorists, who sit in enclosed cars.

Anti-pollutant measures you can take include riding out in the country whenever possible and not sitting behind heavy vehicles on the open road. In urban areas, make a point of avoiding rush hours and traffic jams, and seek out less-heavily traveled routes. And pester your politicians for more clean-air regulations!

Injuries

Cyclists are prone to certain injuries and health problems beyond the problems of soreness I discussed earlier. If not treated, some of those sore parts of the body can become injuries. Stretching is the best preventive medicine for muscles, and for acute pain rest from cycling is advisable.

Knees are particularly vulnerable to injury, caused mainly by pushing too hard in higher gears, an improperly positioned saddle, or improperly aligned feet on the pedals. The cure is to adjust your cleats on the pedals, your seating position or reduce the forces acting against the knee by pedaling in lower gears. Knee pain can mean the inflammation and swelling caused by bursitis or tendinitis, which can be treated by applying ice to reduce the swelling, then applying heat and massage. Most knee conditions are aggravated by cold weather, so covering up delicate knees and limbs is a good idea.

Tendinitis is a very familiar injury to racers, since it can also be caused simply by pedaling too much. I find I can usually ride through minor cases, but with any severe or persistent knee pain I visit my doctor, who may prescribe an anti-inflammatory. With more acute cases I take a holiday from cycling, and so should you, to avoid developing chondromalacia, an inflammation of the sac of "lubricant" behind the knee cap. Also called runner's knee, this condition can become chronic and requires professional treatment, which may include a prescription for orthotics (shoe inserts).

During the spring racing season in Europe I often suffer from a heavy cold, which doesn't help my performance. The main contributing factors are hard training, which reduces my resistance to disease, and riding in bad weather, which I have to do. I'm looking for a permanent cure, but you can help avoid colds, sinus and bronchial problems by not overtraining, dressing properly to avoid chills and not riding, if you can help it, in cold, wet weather.

Another condition I have to treat from time to time is road rash, the lighthearted name for often very painful abrasions caused by skin sliding over pavement. The prevention, of course, is not to fall, but failing this, shaved legs are easier to treat. The wounds should be washed to remove grit, and antibiotic salve applied to prevent infection. Road rash under clothing should be covered with a dressing, otherwise left exposed to the air.

Insects

We are told that insects are a good source of protein and some people actually advocate eating them. But when biking, a sudden altercation with a winged creature, especially in your mouth or eyes, is disconcerting, particularly when you're traveling fast. It can distract you and result in loss of control. And if the insect happens to be of the stinging variety, it can hurt.

Solutions to these problems include wearing glasses or goggles and being particularly alert for swarms of insects after a rain, in the morning and at dusk, and especially in the spring and fall.

Overtraining

One of the hazards of my profession, as you've doubtless guessed, is overtraining, a condition fitness riders can also find themselves in, especially when they're starting out. It's caused by pushing your body too far and not allowing sufficient time for recovery. The various symptoms are easily recognizable:

- Tendinitis, inflammation and soreness of the knee.
- Lethargy, lack of motivation, irritability and drowsiness.
- Insomnia, chronic fatigue and persistent muscle soreness.
- Headaches, nausea, persistent colds, appetite and weight loss.
- Increased resting pulse rate.

The solution to overtraining is simple: take it easier. Pull in your competitive horns and rediscover the pleasures of recreational cycling for a while. Eat properly, get plenty of rest and give your body time to recover between strenuous workouts.

Road Hazards

A wise cyclist must be prepared to handle a variety of road surfaces and the frequent hazards found on them. Rough roads can shake up you and your bike and cause loss of control, as can the sudden appearance of obstacles in your path.

I covered the subject of handling obstacles earlier on, and you should practice and master the necessary techniques. Here are a few further pointers.

- Develop the habit of continually scanning the road with your eyes focused far enough ahead to provide advance warning of any difficulties.
- Use your peripheral vision to study the road surface, while watching traffic. Be especially careful in heavy traffic, where your forward vision is limited.
- In urban areas ride about half a meter (20 inches) from the curb to avoid the places where debris tends to collect (next to the curb) and give yourself some room to maneuver.
- Be constantly alert for sudden surface changes: potholes left by work crews, curbs, bumps, expansion joints, tracks, oil slicks, painted road markings, and so on.
- Manhole covers are a major threat. They provide less adhesion, especially when wet, and are often raised or lowered in the pavement.
- Sewer grates must be treated with caution. Those with slots parallel to your line of travel can swallow your wheels.
- Steel tracks, train or streetcar, must be treated with respect. Cross them at right angles—checking that traffic is clear first—and when parallel to them don't ride too close.

- Be careful riding on dirt roads and in loose gravel. Avoid sudden turns and panic-braking situations.
- Avoid molten tar on really hot days. It can act like quicksand on your tires, and it's hard to clean off your bike.
- Slippery surfaces call for maximum caution. Besides water, watch for oil, mud, fallen leaves, ice and snow. Metal and painted surfaces—roadmarkings such as crosswalk slashes—are much more slippery when wet.
- Suddenly opened car doors are one of the worst hazards for urban bike riders. Always be on the lookout while passing parked cars. Look ahead through their rear windows for someone sitting next to a door, which they may decide to open. Check the traffic behind you in order to avoid being struck should you have to swerve suddenly to avoid an open door.

Ride at a distance far enough away from parked cars that a suddenly opening door does not force you to swerve left into the path of a following vehicle.

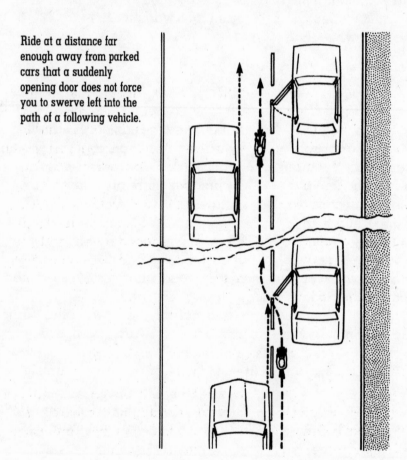

Theft and Security

I mentioned earlier that a sturdy lock is an essential accessory for your bike, and you should buy the best you can afford. The ultimate security system is never to leave your bike unattended. Otherwise, take the following precautions.

- Tether your bike to an immovable object (bike stand, pole, fence), including the front wheel if it has quick-release levers.
- Choose a public location where would-be thieves are more likely to be spotted, and near a light source for overnight parking.
- Remove the water bottle, pump and anything else not bolted to your bike.
- Write down the serial number of your frame and memorize any distinctive features of your bike, to help the police with their inquiries in the event your bike is stolen.

Vegetation

Trees, hedges and shrubs are usually welcome pleasures to a cyclist, but they can also be the source of problems on the road. It's wonderful to take time to smell the flowers on a country ride, but thick vegetation can interfere with visibility around corners—yours and that of oncoming traffic—and canopies of foliage overhead often shut out the sunlight or cause alternating light and shadow, which can impair your judgment. Low, overhanging branches are a danger, as are fallen twigs and branches. Besides being obstacles in your path, sharp twigs and thorns can cause punctures.

Riding through sections of thick vegetation calls for increased vigilance and reduced speed, and you should inspect and clean your tires often.

Visibility

Visibility has two parts: your ability to see and the ability of others to see you. Obviously, visibility is more of a problem after dark, and I'll deal with that first.

Night riding, especially in unlit areas, is potentially very dangerous and should be done with extreme caution. And you should not ride at night on roads you're unfamiliar with. Besides the difficulty in spotting hazards, headlights of oncoming vehicles can be blinding, undipped headlights even worse.

The headlight problems can be alleviated to a degree by wearing a peaked cap under your helmet to shield your eyes from the glare. Don't look straight at the oncoming vehicle, but just ahead of your front wheel, until the vehicle passes. Slow down and be prepared to pull over and stop if headlights are too dazzling.

You must ride more slowly at night and concentrate harder on the road ahead. Use road markings, white lines on the edges and center line, to gauge your position. Your front headlamp beam should be aimed so that you can see the edge of the road, and it should be powerful enough to ill-uminate the road at least five meters (16 feet) ahead, preferably twice that.

Night riders are required by law to have a bright white light on the front and a red one on the rear of their bicycles. (See Lighting.) Reflecting tape on yourself and your bike, garments with fluorescent stripes, reflectors on your bike and lights that clamp on your arms and legs all help make you more visible to motorists. Moving illumination, on your arms, legs and pedals is easier to spot.

Bright sunlight can also present visibility problems. It can dazzle your eyes and those of motorists. When the sun is low in the sky and the shadows are longer you can momentarily disappear from the view of approaching traffic. Be aware of this and be prepared to pull over to the side of the road. Wear tinted goggles or sunglasses, a peaked cap under your helmet and bright clothing.

Fog, mist and fine rain impair your vision, as well as that of the opposition—other traffic—and you should ride more slowly in any bad weather. Tinted lenses help; turn on your bike lights if you have them. Heavier rain, sleet and snow can sting the eyes and obscure the road. In those conditions, slow down even more and stop riding long before you can't see your hand in front of your face, as the old saying goes.

Reflectors, reflective tape, and lights can be included in your equipment in many variations.

Weather

In fine weather, being exposed to the elements is one of cycling's main pleasures, but you must also be prepared to weather the storms of inclement conditions, even gloriously sunny days.

Bright sunlight requires the precautions of tinted lenses for your eyes—visors are also a good idea—and sunscreens to protect your skin from ultraviolet rays. Wind and high altitude increase sunburn. The more sensitive your skin, the higher the number of sunscreen you should use, and lip balm with sunscreen ingredients is also advisable. Cover your limbs on longer rides, and unveil yourself gradually to the sun until you become acclimatized—that is, tanned.

Hot-weather riding calls for preventive measures against dehydration, which can lead to cramps, heat exhaustion and stroke. These problems can sneak up on the unsuspecting cyclist who is being cooled by a breeze and doesn't take notice of the heat. Watch for cramps—painful muscle contractions in the limbs and trunk—and exhaustion—disorientation, nausea, increased heart rate, heavy sweating, fainting. If you ignore these symptoms and suffer stroke—severe thirst, dizziness, profuse sweating, collapse—which is potentially fatal, you should seek immediate medical aid. If a companion appears to be suffering from heat stroke, get him or her immediately into the shade and keep the victim as cool as possible until a doctor comes.

All these conditions can be avoided by drinking plenty of water to keep hydrated, replenishing your system with essential nutrients (potassium, sodium, magnesium—see Diet), avoiding alcohol while riding, keeping your body, particularly your head, well ventilated and well covered from the sun, pedaling easier in hot weather, and not at all in extreme heat.

Guard against cold-weather problems by dressing for the part (in layers, and by extra covering on the extremities—see Bike Wear) and perhaps carrying soup or a hot drink in a thermos, instead of your water bottle. Be aware of the windchill factor, which can drastically multiply the severity of cold temperatures, as does riding in a cold rain. Watch out for hypothermia (drastic drop in body temperature), a very dangerous condition that results in uncontrollable shivering and disorientation, and ultimately death. A victim should be kept warm and a doctor summoned immediately.

Watch out for gusts of wind, which can throw you off balance. On roads frequented by large vehicles like heavy trucks and buses, which generate their own wind storms, brace yourself for a gust as they pass you. Between tall buildings in cities, sudden strong gusts are another potential hazard. Watch for them and brace yourself accordingly.

Precipitation calls for special riding care. Take it easier on wet surfaces, watch out for road spray thrown up by other traffic, and when rain turns to ice, slush or snow, slow right down as you would when driving a car. Easy does it, no abrupt movements, very gentle braking and never in cornering, light grip on the handlebars, light pedaling in a higher gear, no sharp directional changes, and keen anticipation for a skid.

In really rotten weather, head for home, put your bike away, lie in a hot bath—and study the gearing charts.

Maintenance, Adjustments and Repairs

Your bike must be in top form if you want to ride safely, efficiently and comfortably. Adjusting or repairing your bike, besides maintaining it, helps you to better understand and appreciate your equipment which, in the long run, makes you a better and safer cyclist.

Working on your own bike is rewarding and satisfying and gives you a feeling of accomplishment, and it can save you money in two ways: you don't have to pay a bike shop for the tune-ups you do yourself, and better-cared-for components will last longer. Also, you'll ride with more confidence knowing that your bike is roadworthy, and should a problem arise on a ride, a basic knowledge of bike repair can save you from the inconvenience—and humiliation!—of having to walk home or phone someone for a ride.

My racing team includes several professional mechanics who keep my bikes in top shape, so that all I have to do is hop on and pedal away. Our own service vehicles follow us during a race, and if I have a flat or an equipment problem, the mechanics spring into action and conduct pit stops on the fly, so that the minimum amount of time is lost. But I enjoy working on the bikes I keep at home.

Most cyclists, even those who aren't mechanically inclined, find that keeping their equipment in good working order is not really a chore. The feeling is similar to the way people who ride horses look forward to grooming and caring for their faithful mounts. Some people spend hours tinkering with their bikes, even taking them apart completely and rebuilding them, and if that interests you there are several excellent publications that show you how to strip a bike down to its last ball bearing, or how to build your own wheels, spoke by spoke. But even if the idea of getting your hands dirty doesn't appeal in the slightest and you'd rather pay the bike shop to do it, you should still have some knowledge of the fundamentals of preventive maintenance, the necessary adjustments to those components most likely to require them, as well as some basic bike repair. That's what I'll talk about here.

Maintenance Tools

Working on your bike is much easier if you have some workshop space for the purpose; I've set aside a corner of the garage for bikes I keep at home. A raised working surface, a table or bench, in a well-lighted area is the starting point. A really useful tool of the trade is a bicycle workstand, which bolts to the table and clamps the bike in a raised position so that the wheels can spin freely. Some wind trainers will do the trick, and I once used ropes and hooks to suspend the bike by the saddle and handlebars from the ceiling of my basement.

Next, you need some tools in addition to those you carry on your bike. Most households have a number of tools that can be used: assorted screwdrivers, open or box-end wrenches and pliers. Special tools designed specifically for bikes—make sure they fit your particular brand of bike—include such items as a freewheel remover, a third-hand tool, a set of cone wrenches for hub adjustments, a chain-rivet extractor and crank-arm extractor; there are more, and your need depends on how deeply you intend to go into bike repair. If you maintain the hubs and axles you should have a supply of extra ball bearings on hand.

A stockpile of the necessary lubricants and some cleaning solvent is useful, as is a roll of handlebar tape to repair any frayed spots. Most serious cyclists also have a floor pump to supplement the pump carried on the bike, as well as a tire-pressure gauge, which better floor pumps have built in.

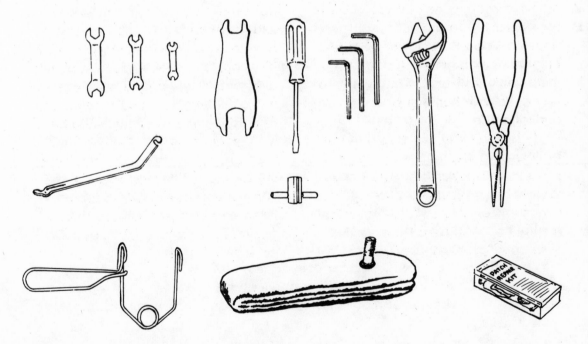

Depending on the type of riding you are doing, and how much work you want to do yourself, you might purchase the tools shown below, and in the following diagrams: wrenches, cone wrenches, screw driver, allen keys, adjustable wrench, miniature needle-nose pliers, tire irons, spoke wrench, third-hand tool, spare tube, tire repair kit.

One of the best investments you can make is a detailed instruction manual, with exploded drawings or photographs, useful for even the simplest maintenance tasks. Some manufacturers supply them with new bikes, and a list of the better books of this type is included in the Bike Book section.

Bike Cleaning

Even if pride of ownership doesn't motivate you to keep your bike clean, there are several practical reasons for removing the dirt, grit, grease and grime that accumulate very quickly on even a carefully ridden bike. Dirty components don't function as well, go out of alignment more quickly and wear out faster. Bike filth, which also has an annoying tendency to rub off on the rider's body, can mask malfunctioning equipment. It's much more pleasant to ride, and work, on a clean bike.

Ideally, you should clean your bike after every ride, rather than letting the dirt build up. This is especially important for those lubricated components, the chain and related items, where dirt and grime gather most. These are the places to begin your bike cleanup, otherwise the grease and oil will smear during the overall washing-up.

- Using a soft cloth or paper towel dipped in cleaning solvent—you can buy ones that spray on and wipe off—wipe the chain, chainrings, freewheel cogs and derailleurs. Stubborn smudges in tight spots can be tackled with a soft bristled brush—a toothbrush works well. Be sure to lubricate the cleaned parts again before using the bike.
- Using another soft cloth, wipe away greasy patches around the brakes, headset, wheel hubs, pedals and bottom bracket. Take care not to scratch painted surfaces.
- If your bike is just dusty you can go over it with a feather duster or soft cloth.
- For heavier dirt, dampen a cloth and wipe down the bike thoroughly, wheels and spokes included, using a noncorrosive household cleaner, dishwashing liquid, or plain soap and water.
- Take another damp cloth and wipe off the bike completely.
- Use still another cloth or soft towel to dry the bike.
- Major cleanups can be followed by applications of car wax to the painted parts of the frame. Metal polishes can be used on aluminum or chromed surfaces.
- For really heavy-duty dirt you can take a hose to your bike (avoid spraying jets of water on sensitive parts) and finish up with a bucket of soapy water, then wipe it dry.

Inspection Checklist

Now that your bike is clean, you can check it over to see that everything is working properly. Most of the items on the inspection checklist are within view, and so you can see how things work and how they can be adjusted. Should your scrutiny turn up any major problems beyond the scope of your mechanical ability or interest, take your bike into a shop and have it professionally attended to. On a new bike you can take advantage of the free tune-up—usually within thirty days of purchase—offered by better bike shops.

A brief inspection after any long ride is a good idea, but once a month you should give your equipment a thorough onceover. Examine your bike visually, bounce it lightly on the front and rear tires to determine if anything is loose that shouldn't be, then take it for a short ride specifically to detect wobbles, squeaks and rattles, paying particular attention to the following points:

- *Brakes*: Check that the shoes are centered properly over the rims and that the pads are not worn too thin. Pull the brake levers forcefully to see that they're up to panic stops, something I always do before the start of a race. Check that the cables have the correct tension, and that the quick-release levers respond on cue. (More to come on brake adjustments.)
- *Wheels*: Spin them and check that the hubs are running freely and the rims are "true," that is, on a level plane. (If a wheel is out of true I recommend taking it to an expert, since trueing them is a delicate job.) If there is any "play" in the axle, the cones may need to be tightened. If there is a grinding sound as the wheel spins, either the cones are too tight, or there is grit in the axle, which should be cleaned out. Pluck the spokes individually to see that the tension is uniformly strong. Make sure the wheels are properly centered and secured in the dropouts, either by the quick-release levers or nuts.
- *Derailleurs and chain*: Shift through the gears to make sure the chain moves properly into position as each gear is selected. Specific derailleur adjustments and chain care are discussed later.
- *Cables*: Check for any looseness. New cables in particular will stretch after the first few days of riding. Cable slackness can be taken up somewhat by screwing the barrel adjusters. If the cable is very loose, pull it through until it's snug, then tighten it up.
- *Nuts and bolts*: Check the nuts, bolts and all fasteners (particularly on moving parts) by hand to make sure they're tight and secure. Tighten as required, being careful not to apply too much force, which might strip the threads.
- *Handlebars and saddle*: Check that they aren't loose and are still properly adjusted for your bike fit.
- *Headset and bottom bracket*: Check for excessive play and looseness. Tighten the lock nut on the headset and the lock ring on the bottom bracket if necessary.

- *Tires*: Inspect the treads and sidewalls for wear, cuts and any foreign objects (glass, thorns and the like), which might work in and cause a puncture. Check that the tires are inflated to the correct pressure as indicated by the manufacturer on the sidewalls. Tire care is discussed in more detail further on.

Lubrication

Most bike squeaks are quickly cured with a drop of oil. Major lube jobs can be done by your bike shop, but it's a good idea to have your own bicycle grease (resistant to water and heat), chain lubricant and medium-weight machine oil (bike shops sell oil in containers with nozzles to reach nooks and crannies), and know where to use it. After you wash and clean your bike, and if you do a lot of wet-weather riding, lubrication is even more important, since water can wash away the lubricants and rust or corrosion occurs.

On many better bikes the ball bearings in the bottom bracket, hubs, headsets and pedals are sealed and prepacked with grease intended to last for the life of the component, but even those can benefit from an occasional greasing. If your bike doesn't have sealed components, the bearings need to be repacked periodically (about once a year) with high-quality grease; some older bikes have grease or oil nipples where the lubricant can be squirted in. A thin coating of grease on the seat post, handlebar stem, cables—especially where they're exposed—and bolt threads helps them perform better and also prevents rust.

Apply oil sparingly to the moving parts where friction occurs. Take special care with the chain, making sure that the lubricant penetrates to the inside of each link, then wipe away excess oil from the outside to prevent dirt buildup. The chain should be oiled most frequently, while other components need only a drop or two occasionally, or when they start to squeak. Every time you clean your bike check to see if lubrication is needed on the derailleurs (the rollers and inner spring on the rear in particular), freewheel (the seams), and the brakes (on the pivot points of the calipers and where the levers and cables meet).

Chain Maintenance

The frequent lubrication necessary on the chain causes a buildup of grime that can interfere with its movement, as well as dirty anything that comes into contact with it. Riding in dusty conditions attracts extra dirt, while wet weather tends to wash away the oil and cause rust. Regular cleaning and relubrication will help control the problem, but every so often you should completely remove all the accumulated guck. This can be done on the bike using a special chain cleaner which is available from bike shops, consisting of a reservoir filled with solvent through which you run the chain. But sometimes the only solution is to remove the chain and soak it in a cleaning solvent.

To remove the chain, first put it on the smaller chainwheel and smallest freewheel cog to lessen the tension. Then, place a chain removal tool (inexpensive at bike shops) on one of the rivets connecting two links and turn the handle to push out the rivet, only as far as necessary to remove the link; don't drive it all the way out, because it's hard to put together again. (Some chains have a master link designed for easier removal.) Once the chain is apart, remove it and immerse it for several hours in a pan of solvent such as paint thinner or mineral spirits.

Let the chain dry before applying fresh lubricant (oil, not grease), then reinstall it, taking care to wind it properly through the derailleur

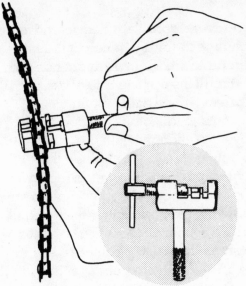

A rivet remover (or extractor) allows you to remove the chain for cleaning, or to add or remove links. Settle the chain into the tool which is notched to fit the links, and screw in the pin until a rivet is pushed almost all the way out. To reinstall the rivet, just put the tool on the other side of the chain and push the rivet back in.

wheels and using the chain tool to push the rivet back in place from the other side. Some people keep a spare chain to use while the other one soaks in lubricant for a few days.

The same method is used to remove a link or two from a chain that has become stretched through wear, though chains are cheap enough that replacing a worn one is advisable. Normally a chain's effective lifetime is about 3,000 kilometers (about 1,800 miles).

Derailleur and Shift-Cable Adjustments

When working on your chain you can also make any necessary adjustments on the derailleurs and their cables. Derailleurs have high and low adjusting screws (sometimes called set-stop screws, and usually marked H and L), which control their range of travel to either side to make the chain line up directly over each cog and prevent it from being dumped (thrown off). With your bike

up on the workstand, run through the gears while turning the pedals. If the chain moves too far to either side (you can see it as you shift gears and you may hear a clicking sound from the chain), use a screwdriver on either of the two adjusting or limit screws, turning them—usually half a turn is enough—to bring the front or rear derailleur back into proper alignment.

If you find the opposite problem,

where the derailleur doesn't move far enough to engage a cog at the far end of the range, you might have to back off the appropriate adjusting screw. Or, the cable might be too loose and fail to pull the derailleur over far enough when the shift lever is fully extended. To tighten the cable, put the shift lever in the lowest position, loosen the screw holding the cable in the derailleur, pull the cable through until all slack is gone, then tighten the screw again.

Precise and noiseless shifting is your goal, except for the "click" in the newer indexed systems. Check once more for the correct cable tension by running through the gears after you've adjusted the limit screws. You can fine-tune cable tension by tightening or loosening the tension screws on the shift levers as required. Indexed shifting systems have a barrel-type adjuster on the rear derailleur, which can be turned by hand to loosen or tighten the cable.

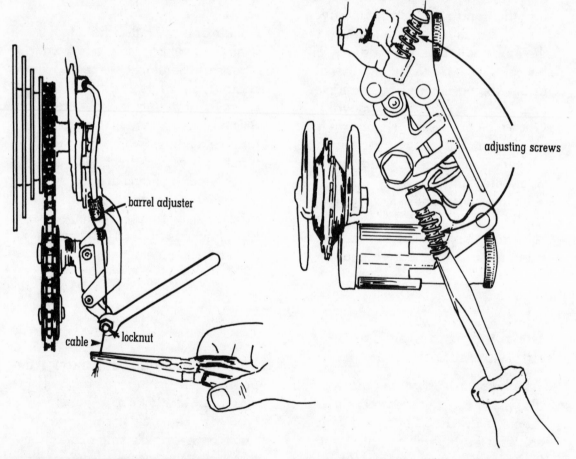

barrel adjuster

cable   locknut

adjusting screws

To tighten the shift cable, first shift the chain to the highest gear (the smallest cog). Loosen the locknut and pull out any slack in the cable, starting near the shift lever, and moving along towards the derailleur. Use pliers to pull the cable firmly through the locknut which you can then retighten. Make a final adjustment if necessary by screwing the barrel adjuster up to tighten the cable or down to loosen it.

The high- and low-gear adjustment screws help control the limits of derailleur movement. The inside end of the screw butts up against a stop, which prevents the derailleur from moving farther. By retracting the screw you allow a further movement; by turning it further in, you restrict the derailleur's movement. Different models have the adjustment screws in different positions, but they are easily identifiable.

Brake and Brake-Cable Adjustments

Brakes need to be adjusted not just for performance but for safety, so check them often. Decreasing performance is indicated when the brake levers move too close to the handlebars before the shoes come into contact with the rims; this is caused by the cable stretching and by brake-shoe wear. The cure is to keep the brake cables taut so there is a minimum clearance of 2.5 centimeters (one inch) between the levers and handlebars when the brakes are applied.

Cables can be tightened by loosening the lock nut and turning the barrel adjusters, then tightening the lock nut again. If more tightening is required you can loosen the screw where the cable attaches to the brake arm or the yoke calipers, and pull the cable with a pair of pliers before retightening the screw. This adjust-

ment is made easier with the help of a friend, or a device aptly known as a "third hand." It clips over the brake arms and counteracts the springs in the brakes, holding them close to the rim while you tighten the cable. If you don't have a third hand, two or three heavy-duty elastic bands will do the trick.

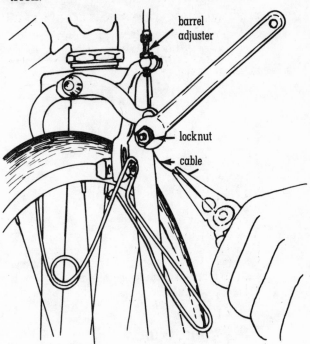

For major brake-cable adjustments, first pinch the brake pads to the rim with a third-hand tool (to offset the opening action of the spring inside the calipers). Then loosen the lock nut that holds the cable to the calipers, pull all slack out of the cable from the brake levers on towards the brake, and retighten the lock nut. The barrel adjustment is for finer adjustments *after* the cable has been tightened. Have the barrel in a *middle* position when tightening the cable, so that you can screw it either up (to tighten) or down (to loosen).

Brakes should be set up so that the brake shoes contact the rim after very little movement of the levers: about 2½ cm. (1 inch).

Brake blocks, the parts that hold the shoes, should be positioned so that the shoes in them come into full contact with the rim when the levers are pulled. They can be adjusted by loosening the bolt on the back and moving the block as required.

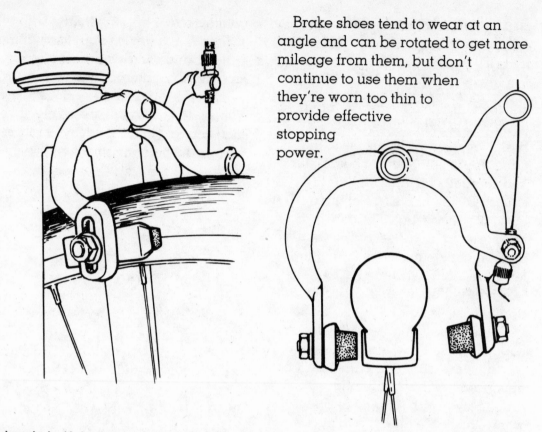

Brake shoes tend to wear at an angle and can be rotated to get more mileage from them, but don't continue to use them when they're worn too thin to provide effective stopping power.

Brake pads should align horizontally and vertically, and be equidistant from the rim, for maximum braking efficiency. When the cables are properly tightened as well, the pads will be only about 30 mm. (⅛″) from the rim. (The examples here show *poorly* adjusted brakes!)

Tire Maintenance

Tire problems are the most common bike ailments, and some preventive maintenance at home can greatly extend their life on the road. You should carefully examine them before every ride, as outlined in the Inspection Checklist.

Basic tire care begins with keeping them properly inflated. Underinflated tires, which tend to pinch the tubes, increase the likelihood of flats or blowouts and rim damage, and are more likely to pick up debris that can cause punctures. Even when your bike is stationary, a certain amount of air escapes each day, and the hand-operated frame pump on your bike

isn't up to the task of inflating them with enough pressure. Service-station compressed-air pumps intended for car tires are too powerful, and you risk a blowout using them on bike tires. So you should use a floor pump, and don't be afraid to exceed the pressures indicated on the sidewalls. Heavily laden bikes, especially on rougher roads, require more pressure, and the rear tire, which bears more weight, should have up to 20 percent more pressure than the front.

At home and on the road you should regularly wipe the tires with a cloth or your gloves to remove any sharp objects. This is especially important if you've ridden over suspect debris. Apply a light pressure to the tread as the tire spins—watch the spokes if you do it as you ride—so you can brush off the offending objects and not work them in.

Presta valves, the ones you have to unscrew before inflating, are most often used on better tires because they hold pressure better than the ordinary Schraeder types. Some of my bikes are equipped with Kevlar reinforced rubber, which prolongs tire life and helps prevent flats. Tubes are stronger than ever these days, and most rims have plastic liners to protect the tubes from the rims. Nonetheless, flat tires are a fact of cycling life and you should know how to deal with them, particularly when they happen on the road far away from your workshop, as is nearly always the case.

Flat Tires

If you've got just a slow leak you may be able to ride on it for a while, stopping periodically to pump it up again. Before you start to work on a suspected flat make sure that the valve isn't leaking, or that someone hasn't let the air out of your tires as a joke. Pump up the tire first and listen for escaping air.

An experienced tire repairer can fix a flat in 15 or 20 minutes, giving the glue time to dry before pumping the tire up again. But if you're in a hurry the best idea is always to carry a spare tube with you—I usually carry two on training rides—and leave the repair work until you get home. With practice you can replace a punctured tube in about five minutes. Here's how to go about it.

Wheel Removal

Before you start, make an effort to find out the cause of the flat and remove the nail, glass, thorn, or what-ever from the tire, marking the spot so you can locate the puncture on the tube inside.

- To remove the front wheel release the levers or loosen the nuts and pull the wheel out of the dropouts.
- The rear wheel is best removed by standing the bike on its nose so that the front wheel lies flat on the ground for support and the rear wheel is in the air where you can work on it. Lying the bike on its side might damage the derailleurs, and turning it upside down can damage the brake cables and scratch the seat.
- Put the bike in the lowest gear, which places the chain on the smaller chainwheel and smallest freewheel cog, to release tension on the chain.
- Open the quick-release lever on the rear brake so that the wheel can easily clear the break shoes.

- Release the wheel levers or loosen the nuts on the dropouts.
- Pull the chain and derailleur back with one hand and pull the wheel out of the dropouts with the other, looping the chain over the end of the axle as you pull the tire away. Sometimes it's easier if you take the chain completely off the front chainring first to gain more slack on the chain.
- Stand the bike upright or lay it down, on the opposite side of the derailleur to prevent damaging it.

Clincher Tire Removal

To expose the tube on clincher tires you have to remove the tire from one side of the rim, which involves maneuvering the bead (on the outer edge of the tire sidewall) off its grip on the rim. This requires the use of the two or three tire levers in your bike tool kit. Care must be taken to prevent pinching the tube and causing another leak; plastic levers are better than metal for this reason.

- Force out any remaining air from the tire and loosen the valve stem.
- Stand the wheel vertically—against your legs for support, if you can—so that the valve stem is at the bottom.
- Insert one tire lever under the tire bead at the top of the wheel, taking care to avoid pinching the tube, and pry the bead up and over the rim.

Insert tire irons one at a time until enough of the tire is over the edge of the rim that you can pry it off with your fingers.

- Leave that lever in place, hooking one end over a spoke if it has the necessary notch for that purpose.
- Insert another lever two or three spokes further on and repeat the prying process, leaving that lever in place, too.
- Insert a third lever, or use your fingers, on the opposite side of the first and pry once more to pull away the tire.
- Now enough of the tire sidewall is released so that you can pull it off by hand, all the way around the rim.
- The tube can be removed after releasing one side of the tire only, but to completely remove the tire you can just repeat the prying procedure on the other side.
- Remove the tube by pulling it out of the tire on each side of the valve stem, which must then be pushed through the rim opening.
- Run your hand around the inside of the tire to see if whatever caused the flat is imbedded in the tire, but be careful of cutting yourself should the offending object be a shard of glass.
- Visually inspect the tire, as well. Sometimes the gash is so large the tire can no longer hold a tube at high pressure.

Tubular Tire Removal

Tubs, which don't have beads like clincher tires, can be rolled off the rims by hand. Stand the wheel upright and brace it between your feet. Grasp it at the top in both hands as if it were a steering wheel, pinching the tire between your thumbs and forefingers. Using a pushing motion, roll a section off the rim—a tight-fitting tire may require some heavy-duty pushing—and continue around the wheel to finish up at the valve stem. Push the stem out of the rim and remove the complete tire.

Tube Repair

If you carry a spare tube you can leave the repair until later. Similarly, most people with tubulars carry a spare tire at all times, because getting at the tube is a longer process that requires undoing the stitching and removing the tube for patching, then sewing it up again. Also, regardless of your type of tires, if you've had a major blowout it's best to throw away the tube.

If the leak is only caused by a pinprick you may have to search for its precise location, beyond the general area you may have noted on the tire tread. Start by reinflating the tube beyond its specified pressure. Pass the tube near your face so that you can feel the escaping air and listen for the hiss. Smaller leaks may require placing the tube in water (applying saliva to the tube is also effective, if perhaps unsavory to some) and looking for bubbles. Dry the tube off, if necessary, and bring your tube-repair kit into play.

- Roughen the area around the hole in the tube (wider than the patch you will use) with the sandpaper, or metal scraper, in the tool kit.
- Clean off the tube and apply a thin layer of glue, slightly wider than the patch, around the hole, then let it dry for two or three minutes.
- Select a suitably sized patch, or cut one to fit, and peel the protective backing from the adhesive side. You might dab a bit of glue around the edges of the patch, too.
- Centering it over the hole, press the patch firmly onto the tube, applying extra pressure around the edges of the patch.
- Sprinkle talcum powder—it should be included in your repair kit—over the patched area to prevent the tube from sticking to the tire, and wait a few minutes before inflating the tire slightly to check that the patch has taken hold properly.

Clincher Tire Mounting

- Do not use tire levers to remount the tire and take great care to avoid pinching the tube in any way.
- Make sure that the inside of the rim is covered with rim tape or a liner to protect the tube from any sharp metal on the rim or spokes.
- Place the valve stem in the rim opening and carefully stuff the tube evenly into the tire around its circumference, using your hands and taking care to avoid twisting or bunching the tube.
- Knead the tire around its circumference to seat the tube properly and work out any kinks.
- Support the wheel and begin to pull the tire onto the rim, starting at the valve stem and working down both sides of the tire away from it.
- More pressure will be required to pull the last part of the tire onto the rim. Work your way slowly, inch by inch. Push hard with your hands and resist the temptation to use a tire lever.
- Center the valve stem and tighten it into place on the rim.
- Partially inflate the tire (about one-third pressure) and knead it, making sure the bead is seated evenly all the way around the rim.
- Inflate the tire fully, close the valve and install the wheel, reversing the wheel-removal process.
- Before riding again, check that the brakes, chain and derailleur are adjusted as they were originally.

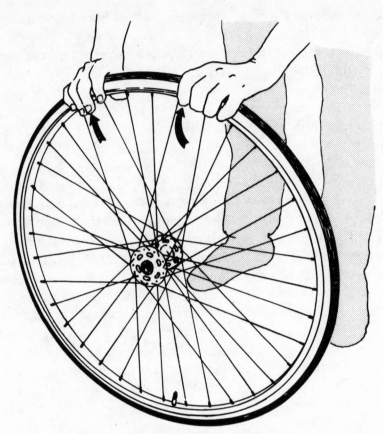

To remount a tire on the rim, reverse the process, starting to pull the tire on with your fingers. You may have to use tire irons for the last few inches, sort of shoe-horning it over the lip of the rim—but be careful not to pinch the tube.

Tubular Tire Mounting

Tubular tires should be reglued to the rims, though you can leave the gluing until later if you're effecting makeshift roadside repairs. Don't corner vigorously without glue, or you risk having the tire roll off the rim. Follow these steps to properly remount a tubular tire.

- Apply a thin coat of glue to the rim and the inside of the tire.
- While waiting for the glue to become somewhat tacky—five minutes at most—you can stretch the tube slightly, especially if it's a new one, to make it easier to slip over the rim.
- Partly inflate the tire to give it some shape, place the valve stem in the rim opening, and begin to pull the tire onto the rim, working from the stem and up each side.
- When the halfway point is reached turn the wheel over and finish positioning the tire on the rim.
- The last bit of tire will require extra effort, and you may have to resort to tire levers, taking care not to pinch the tube.
- Once the tire is seated evenly on the rim, inflate it further and knead out any kinks, making sure the tire is perfectly rounded into position.

- Fully inflate the tire, wipe any excess glue from the tire and rim—and, most likely, your hands.
- Put the wheel back on the bike—reversing the wheel-removal procedure—and check that all adjustments are in order.

Bearing Maintenance

So far I've covered the basics of bike care, dealing with those parts needing the most regular attention. To complete the picture you should have a working knowledge of how to service the bearings in the major moving parts: the front and rear hubs, the bottom bracket and the headset.

Bearings do all the real work in a bicycle, literally bearing the load as the various parts turn. They need tightening, cleaning and lubrication—ideally about every six months, and at least once a year—and replacement when they become worn. Most "sealed" bearings are sealed only to prevent water and grime from getting at them, and they require the same care and attention, though less frequently. Some fully sealed and cassette-type bearings cannot be lubricated and are intended to be discarded and replaced when worn.

Essentially, all the bearings move around axles (the headset can be conceived as just an axle sitting vertically), so if you can handle the bearings in the simplest axle—in the front wheel hub—you can easily move on to the others.

The front hub consists of a quick-release skewer (if your bike has them), a lock nut, washer and a dust cap on each side of the outer casing, or flange (the part the spokes are attached to). The skewers, nuts and washers, and dust caps are on each end of an axle that runs through the center of the hub casing, around which the casing spins on two sets of ball bearings, one at either end of the hub. Each set of bearings revolves on a cone, contained in a cup, or race, located inside the flange of the hub casing. Sometimes the ball bearings are contained in a clip, and in cassette-types the cone-and-cup arrangements are sealed in a one-piece unit. (Some new bikes come with sealed cassette bearings, which require special tools. Check with your bike shop for instructions).

To unveil these inner workings you need two cone wrenches (flat and open-ended, and sized in millimeters—make sure they fit your bike) and a screwdriver. A pair of tweezers to handle the ball bearings is useful, and you should also have a supply of new grease on hand, as well as ball bearings should the old ones need replacing. You begin the operation by removing the front wheel from your bike and placing it over a sheet of newspaper or large cloth to catch any ball bearings that might drop out.

- If your bike has quick-release skewers, remove it by releasing the lever and turning the skewer counterclockwise, while holding the lock nut on the other end of the axle steady with a wrench.
- Put one cone wrench onto the lock nut and the other one on the cone next to it. Turn the nut counterclockwise while turning the cone clockwise and remove them and the washer.

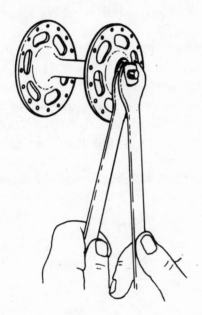

These steps assume the wheel has been removed from the bike. Loosen one lock nut by holding the nut on the other side of the axle with a wrench, or by holding the cone beside the locknut with a cone wrench. Once the lock nut is eased back, you can adjust the cones, or disassemble the axle completely.

- Pull the axle out of the other side of the hub casing and leave the lock nut, washer and cone in place on that side of the axle to simplify reassembling the unit.
- Remove the dust caps by gently (they're quite thin) prying them off with a screwdriver, check to see how the ball bearings are positioned and count them, so that you'll remember how to reassemble them. Carefully remove each set of ball bearings, using tweezers or a screwdriver.

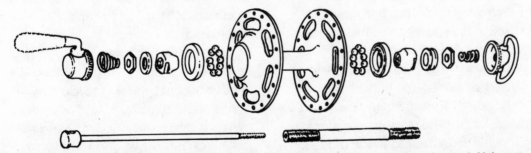

Most axle assemblies are essentially the same—the axle itself with threaded ends where the nuts hold the entire package together, ball bearings which roll between the cones and the specially machined cups of the hub, plus dust caps, washers and lock nuts. With the axle disassembled, you can clean it, inspect the bearings and hub for wear and replace if necessary, or simply repack with grease, for a more efficient ride.

- Clean all parts in solvent and inspect the ball bearings, cones and hub races for wear and tear. Anything pitted or worn should be replaced.
- Pack a small amount of grease into the hub races and set the ball bearings back in place. The grease will help hold them there as you reassemble the unit.
- Press the dust caps back in place, taking care that the bearings remain in position.
- Push the axle back into the hub casing, and on one end of it rethread the cone you removed, winding it up snugly to the hub casing so that the bearings are trapped in place.
- Put the washer and thread on the lock nut to hand tightness, so that the hub is now fully reassembled.
- Adjust the cones by turning them counterclockwise simultaneously so that they are tight against each washer and lock nut. Spin the wheel on the axle to see that there is no excess play from side to side. If there is, loosen one of the lock nuts, tighten the cones a little, and retighten the lock nut. It may take several attempts.
- Finally, tighten the lock nuts firmly with a wrench, replace the quick-release skewers and remount the wheel.

The procedure for the rear wheel is very similar, except you have to remove the freewheel first. And from there, it's easy to move on to the bottom bracket and headset. A good bicycle-repair manual with exploded drawings will help guide you through any tricky parts.

Freewheel Removal

Here we step beyond the bounds of routine home maintenance, but being freewheel-wise opens the door to further cycling freedom. Besides enabling you to maintain it yourself, knowing how to remove the freewheel frees you to change the gearing on your bike as you please.

The freewheel consists of two sections: one that fits onto the hub and the other that the various cogs are threaded onto. Inside it has a complicated arrangement of tiny ball bearings, springs and various bits that are probably best left alone, unless you become expert at bike repair. Note, also, that some freewheels are cassette-types, which require special tools supplied by the component manufacturers. The following instructions are for threaded-type freewheels.

To remove the freewheel you need a freewheel extractor (there are several different types), a large wrench that fits the extractor, and another wrench or a vise. For removing the cogs you need two cog removers or one cog remover and a vise. Once you've taken off the rear wheel, here's what to do.

- On the freewheel side of the hub, remove the quick-release skewer, if you have it, and the lock nut and washer.
- Fit the freewheel extractor into the splines in the freewheel and replace the lock nut to hold the extractor in place.

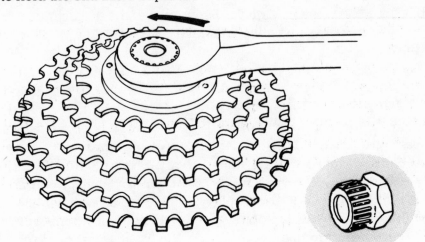

With the wheel removed from the bike, insert the special nut for your type of freewheel into the slots in the freewheel body. Use a wrench to turn it *counterclockwise* off the hub. You'll need a friend to hold the wheel tight when you first loosen the freewheel. Alternatively, put the nut in a table-mounted vise, turn the wheel upside down and settle it over the nut, and then turn the wheel yourself to loosen the freewheel.

- Holding the lock nut on the opposite side of the axle with a wrench (you can also mount that side in a bench-mounted vise), turn the extractor counterclockwise with another wrench.
- When the freewheel is loose, remove the lock nut and turn the extractor by hand to remove the freewheel from the hub.
- To remove the cogs, hold the largest cog with a cog remover while turning the smallest cog counterclockwise with another remover. Usually only the smallest cog is threaded on and the others will simply slide off. But some are all threaded, and inner cogs may be bolted together, so proceed accordingly.

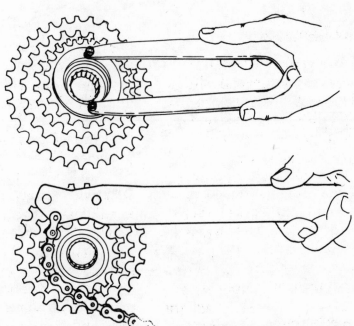

To remove individual cogs from the central freewheel body, first loosen the lockring (this usually requires a special wrench). Mount the gear cluster in a vise, or have someone hold the largest cog with a cog remover, while you turn in a counterclockwise direction with another cog remover, to remove the smallest cog.

- Take note of any spacers between the cogs and make sure you replace them in the same order. When purchasing any new cogs make sure they fit your freewheel. Reassemble cogs by reversing the procedure.
- To remount the freewheel, thread it back onto the hub by hand, taking care not to strip the threads. Tighten it snugly with the extracting tool, but not too tightly. Final tightening will take place as you ride.

Chainring Removal

Mastering chainring removal, which is necessary to get at the bottom bracket bearings for servicing, will enable you to further change your gearing options. The necessary tools vary with component makers, but you will probably need: an allen key or screwdriver, to remove dust caps; a special wrench, to fit the crank bolts; a crank extractor (make sure it fits your type of cranks); and a wrench or allen key, to fit chainring bolts.

Begin by removing the cranks, which can be done with the pedals on or off, to get at the chainrings.

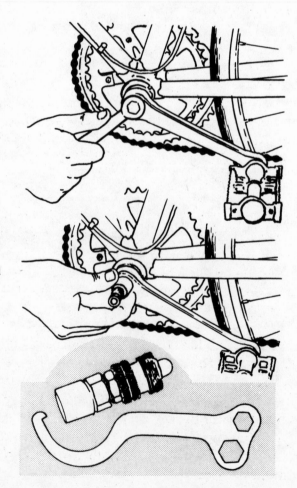

More specialized tools: Use the wrench end to remove the lock nut holding the crank arm on the axle. Then screw the threaded end into the crank arm, and turn the inner sleeve inwards so that its interior end butts against the axle. As it pushes against the axle, it forces the crank arm in the opposite direction until it slides off the axle. Remove the lock ring on the bottom bracket with the hook wrench. Then unscrew the cup, and you have access to the axle and bearings.

- Remove the dust cap on the crank with an allen key, or screwdriver if the cap has a slot.
- Remove the crank bolt and washer with an allen key or wrench.
- To remove the crank from the axle, first screw the threaded end of the extractor into the threaded hole in the crank as far as it will go.

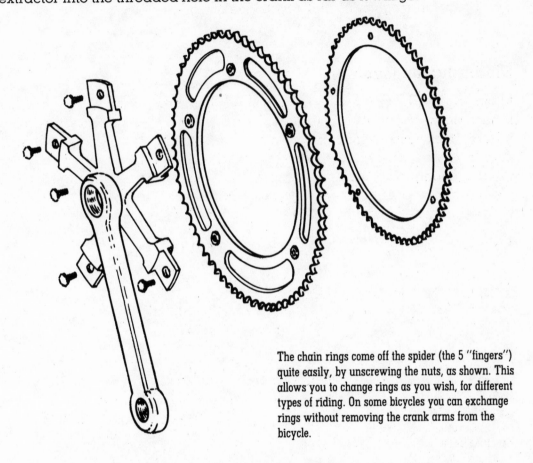

The chain rings come off the spider (the 5 "fingers") quite easily, by unscrewing the nuts, as shown. This allows you to change rings as you wish, for different types of riding. On some bicycles you can exchange rings without removing the crank arms from the bicycle.

- Turn the other end of the extractor clockwise with a wrench, which forces the inside bolt against the tip of the axle, until the crank is pulled off the bottom bracket axle.
- Repeat the process on the other crank.
- Remove the chainring bolts—usually five on a double chainring set, ten on a triple—with a wrench or allen key, whichever fits.

At this point you can change the chainrings, making sure they're compatible with your bottom bracket and drive train components, to effect a different gearing setup for your bike, replace worn or bent chainrings, service the bottom-bracket innards (similar to hub maintenance), and generally clean and inspect everything exposed.

To restore the various items to their rightful places, simply reverse the procedure. After you've performed this operation it's a good idea to tighten everything up again following your first ride.

PART FOUR

Specialty Cycling

Touring

After you've explored all the possibilities closer to home, one of the best ways to broaden your horizons is to explore the world of bicycle touring. If you do it right, there are few more satisfying cycling pleasures than a stimulating ride through new countryside, or a new country. And the whole point of the exercise is experiencing the enjoyment en route, so that the journey, not the arrival, is what matters.

In touring, you travel through scenic countryside at a leisurely pace by a means that enables you to savor and appreciate it most, not insulated in a steel cocoon. It can be a complete sensory experience with the wind in your face and all the sights, sounds and smells under the sun (and rain!) as the terrain unfolds beneath your wheels.

The feeling of well-being on a tour can be one of cycling's greatest highs. The fact that you're working for your pleasure by pedaling only enhances it, such is the feeling of accomplishment at having transported yourself over distances by your own motive power. The sense of freedom and independence, stopping to smell the flowers or to marvel at the view whenever you like, are added attractions.

A tour can be structured and tightly planned, or vague and meandering; you can travel alone, with another, or as part of a group. New friendships can be made, existing relationships more fully realized, and your own self-awareness greatly increased, when you take the time to travel on two wheels. Because the bicycle is a conversation-starter par excellence, a bicycle trip is a splendid way to find out about people and the things they care about.

Since you can tour by bicycle nearly anywhere in the world, you can sample new countries and cultures, or simply get a new, more intimate perspective of familiar ones. And you can do it deluxe (staying in hotels, eating in restaurants) or by roughing it (camping out, doing your own cooking) according to your preferences and budget. The sense of adventure begins the moment you sit down to begin planning your trip.

Planning

Some people feel that meticulous planning detracts from the potential for unexpected adventure in touring, while others regard planning as one of the best parts of the trip. Still others leave most of the arrangements up to someone else by traveling with experienced tourists or signing on with a bike tour. But somebody always has to do some prior thinking, particularly when inexperienced riders are involved.

Useful touring information can be obtained from brochures and pamphlets from tour operators, tourist bureaus, travel agents, bike shops and clubs, and books—several of these are mentioned in the Cycling Sources section. It's even better to hear about touring from people who've actually done it. In larger cities you can often attend slide presentations during the winter by people who've "been there."

Overnight accommodation can take the form of camping (see Camping Gear), bed-and-breakfast homes, hostels, pensions and varying categories of hotels. It can be booked ahead of time if you're sure of your schedule, or you can chance it, which is risky during peak tourist seasons. Food arrangements are similarly variable, whether you do it yourself or stop at eating establishments on the road.

Then, unless you're riding from your home, joining a tour that supplies bikes, or renting a bike on site, you have optional methods of getting your bike to and from the embarkation point of your tour. You can also interrupt the tour with other methods of transportation.

A bike can be carried in the trunk of a car (easier by removing the front wheel and loosening the handlebars in smaller vehicles) or on bike racks. Most airlines will carry bikes as baggage and some of them supply cartons for the purpose and provide packing instructions—you may have to loosen the handlebars and/or pedals to decrease bike width. Most railways will carry bicycles nearly everywhere they go, and many have bike-rental schemes at stations; this method of extending or augmenting road travel is a useful feature of cycling life in many countries, particularly in Europe.

In short, the available options mean you can tailor a cycle tour to exactly suit your requirements. Let's look at some ways to tackle a tour, beginning with the easiest.

Organized Tours

Organized tours are an excellent way to get your feet wet, figuratively speaking, in cycle touring. The most elaborate ones look after every single detail so that you have nothing to do but pedal. You can use the experience on future do-it-yourself tours, or you may succumb to the pampering and decide this is the only way to go. Tours can extend from weekend rides to month-long excursions.

Your fate is in the hands of people who know what they're doing, and very little is left to chance. They choose destinations carefully and with the emphasis on the rewards of novel experiences. They provide support, including such services as looking after all travel arrangements, the supply and maintenance of bikes, overnight accommodation and meals, and often include a following vehicle—sometimes called a sag wagon—to rescue weary tourists and carry luggage so that you can ride unencumbered. They offer a variety of tours to suit degrees of fitness and special interests. Some organizations are now offering fully supported tours on mountain bikes, either as completely off-road adventures, or a combination of road touring and off-road excursions. Study the travel section of your newspaper, or talk to a travel agent, or the people in a good bike shop, for leads.

The only drawback to this type of tour, besides the cost if you're on a tight budget, is that you don't necessarily get to choose your traveling companions. But riding a bike over distances while discovering new sights tends to iron out troublesome personality clashes, and most veterans of organized tours come away with many new friends.

Planning Tips

Whether you go on an organized tour or travel on your own there are some basic considerations.

- Compatibility is important to maintaining harmony under conditions of close contact for lengthy periods of time. Try to work out advance agreements with your fellow riders to establish expectations of each other during the tour.
- Don't bite off more than you can chew on a tour. Work out comfortable daily and total distances beforehand. Approximate reasonable daily distances are: up to 50 kilometers (31 miles) for beginners; up to 100 (62) for experienced riders; up to 150 (93) for very fit and keen tourers.
- Get advance travel and touring information for unfamiliar areas. Bone up on language, culture, customs, currency and the like. Be especially concerned with road conditions, terrain changes (mainly hills), prevailing winds and seasonal weather. Familiarize yourself with local traffic conditions—so that you don't ride through Paris in rush hour!—and the rules of the road. Get large-scale maps well ahead of time and study them thoroughly.
- The most desirable touring roads have fewer hills, are sheltered from strong winds, travel through scenic areas, avoid major urban blight, are relatively traffic-free, and have smooth surfaces. Ideally they will have charming hotels, or full-facility campgrounds, with great food sources, conveniently located at overnight stops.

- Pay attention to overnight accommodation, because proper rest is vitally important on an extended tour. On longer trips it's advisable to book in advance, as you may be too tired at the end of the day to ride around looking for somewhere to stay. If you plan on camping try to do it with someone experienced.
- Consider also the food situation. You may not be on a gastronomic tour, but proper diet and nutrition must be maintained. Investigate the availability of carbo-loading in local restaurants, buying fresh fruit and snacks en route, and so on.
- Make sure your equipment is up to the task. Choose a new touring bike with care. Tune up or overhaul an older bike if necessary, but don't overload it. Carry only what you'll use. I'll talk more about this later on in this section.

Destinations

A cycle tour is much more rewarding on a winding road through a frequently changing landscape. For those with open and inquiring minds, cultural differences add to the pleasures, as do new cuisines and foreign languages. There are certain countries that neatly fulfill all of those requirements and they tend to be smaller, where cyclists can feel intimately involved. And within larger countries there are smaller regions that enhance the touring experience. These are the places where most knowledgeable cycling tourists prefer to wander.

One of the hurdles to overcome is that the best scenery tends to be in mountainous, or at least undulating, terrain, and to explore it you've got to climb. However, vertical landscapes take on a much more manageable perspective when you can lose yourself in spectacular scenery—and when your bike gears are low enough. Another major attraction is riding in areas where cycling travelers are specifically catered to by tourist facilities and respected on the roads by motorists.

You can tour the world on a bike, and a surprisingly large number of people have. It seems that few corners of the planet remain to be explored by bicycle, with Kashmir, Tibet and even Mongolia having recently become the "in" places to tour. Pioneering mountain-bike tourists are also probing such geographic extremities as the Amazon jungle, the Sahara desert, the Arctic, the Alps, Andes and Himalayas. These adventures, or sometimes misadventures, can make for great reading (see Bike Books) but very difficult cycling.

For the purposes of this book I'll confine myself to more practical destinations and concentrate in particular on those I know best. See Cycle Sources to investigate other destinations (the island of Bali is now being featured by several tour operators) and for deeper insights into the following geographical selections.

North America

The Rockies in the west and the Laurentians, Adirondacks and Appalachians in the east are major meccas for cycle touring in North America. The western alpine scenery is unrivaled, but roads are few and far between in the higher mountains, though those through national parks usually have wide shoulders tailor-made for bikes. Accommodation tends to be limited among the high peaks, where there are usually more camping opportunities than hotel rooms. The Quebec Laurentians also lack many paved road options but are wonderfully scenic, particularly in the fall when the leaves change colors. The state of Vermont is renowned as one of the best areas in the U.S. for cyclists, with an attractive Adirondack landscape, lots of charming secondary roads and a wide choice of accommodations.

Both the Pacific and Atlantic coasts are favorite cycle-touring destinations, too. On the west coast, California is the pot of gold at the end of the cycling rainbow, especially north of San Francisco, where mountain bikes first boomed; and in some parts of the state, bikes seem to rule the roads over the cars, which also proliferate there. Canada's east coast has more than its share of scenic landscapes, with the more easily tackled proportions of Prince Edward Island a major attraction.

Touring inland North America, cyclists often have to contend with great distances over boring landscapes that seem to go on forever, from the perspective of a bike saddle. Most tourists seek out the exceptions, such as the Okanagan Valley in British Columbia, the great national park areas in the western American states, and parts of southern Ontario, such as the fruit-growing area of the Niagara Peninsula. (If you ride through Fenwick tell them I sent you.)

Island Countries (Japan, New Zealand, British Isles)

Since endless vistas can be dispiriting and roads stretching as far as the eye can see tend to be intimidating, island countries particularly lend themselves to bike travel. The confined areas are easier to grasp in the mind's eye and distances seem less overpowering. Japan, New Zealand and the British Isles are ideally suited to cycling, being small enough to get a grip on, yet wonderfully varied in landscapes well connected by cycle-compatible roads.

Japan, despite its extreme population density and large urban centers, is very popular with organized tour groups from the West, who confine themselves to more charming, less-peopled areas of the islands. New Zealand, too, is one of the most scenic countries in the world, its splendid vistas inhabited more by sheep than by people. The pace of life is unhurried, and bikes seem to travel at exactly the right speed to appreciate it most. It may seem a long way to travel just to go on a bike trip, but you'll come back from a cycle tour through Japan or New Zealand with a lifetime of memories.

Closer to home for North Americans, the United Kingdom is a touring paradise and wonderfully well organized from a cycling point of view. After all, it was the English who popularized touring by bicycle, and their Cyclists' Touring Club sees to every imaginable requirement, including the provision of the best tour itineraries and listings of literally thousands of accommodations (see Cycle Sources) that cater specifically to cyclists. British Rail is accustomed to handling bicycles, and though certain express trains won't take them in peak periods, bicycles are usually carried in baggage cars free of charge.

But the real beauty of England, Wales, Scotland and both parts of Ireland is just that: the beauty. Many travelers contend that the British Isles contain the most beautiful scenery anywhere. And the diversity of landscape within such a confined area is remarkable. This is where you really get the feeling of exploring on your bike, with something new around every corner of the tiny, perfect roads that will take you into even the most remote corner of "the green and pleasant land."

Any problems with the weather (the creative force behind all that greenery is the frequent rain), or with having to ride on the "wrong" side of the road (it's a cinch once you learn to think left, instead of right) and urban ugliness are easily avoided and more than offset by the charming villages, quaint pubs, historical points of interest and the warm and friendly people.

High overhead, beneath fluffy white clouds floating in a sea of blue, a soaring skylark sings continuously, as if in joyous celebration of such a fine day. Beneath the majestic skyscape, the softly undulating hills are a patchwork quilt of green, bordered by honey-colored stone walls and dotted with placidly grazing sheep. In the valley below, a tiny paved road meanders aimlessly, following the course of a babbling stream where rainbow trout rise from sun-dappled pools. In the grassy verges beside the walls that border the road, butterflies—Small Coppers, Meadowbrowns and Chalkhill Blues—flit to and fro among the flowers: Yellow Wart, Birdsfoot Treefoil and Rock Rose.

Over a humpback bridge and around another corner, beyond a strutting cock pheasant that shows little fear of cyclists, is a crossroads with signs offering a choice of Stowon-the-Wold, Bourton-on-the-Hill, Upper or Lower Swell, Oddington, or Evenlode. Time to dismount, lean the bikes against a wall of Cotswold stone and consult the Ordnance Survey map. Or perhaps to linger a while, to adjust that squeaking brake, give the tires a squirt of air, or to just lie back in the grass and doze.

Put away your cycling computer for a tour through the Cotswold Hills, one of the prettiest of British upland landscapes and a place of timeless beauty best-suited for wanderers without watches. The north and south extremities of the hills, lying about an hour by train from central London, are served by branches of British Rail from whose several stations cycle tours begin.

From the medieval wool market town of Chipping Camden in north Gloucestershire the Cotswold escarpment runs southwest to the ancient Roman spa of Bath in the county of Avon. It's only about 100 kilometers (62 miles) as the rook flies but nearly twice that by the straightest roads on the map, and there aren't many of them. Just over 300 meters (327 yards) at their highest point, Cleeve Hill (which overlooks Cheltenham, another Roman spa site now a showplace of elegant Georgian architecture), the Cotswolds offer idyllic touring options.

Once you're up on the heights it's possible to stay there, cycling along in high gear, following the spine of the escarpment, making use of a network of roads originally built by the Romans and kept up through the centuries. But chances are the perspective from here will distract you, for nestled in the wooded valleys are glimpses of church spires poking above the trees. They signal the presence of many secret villages with enticing names like Guiting Power, Duntisborne Leer, and Hawkesbury Upton. Their muddled streets are choc-a-block with rustic houses, leaning at odd angles after four and five hundred years, and all built of mellow Cotswold stone.

You're guaranteed to find a pub in every second or third village, many of them serving the hearty local brew, Donnington Ale, which is made in the hamlet of that name in a venerable brewery where majestic white swans glide around the mill pond. Any touring day is easily arranged so that lunchtime coincides with your pedaling up to a colorful sign inviting travelers to tarry at the Farmers Arms, the Black Horse, or The Hare and Hounds. Inside, where a cat is likely dozing on a chair beside the open fire in the inglenook hearth, a restorative pint of Donnington Best Bitter, accompanied by a Ploughman's Lunch (bread, cheese and pickled onions), is splendid reward for cycling energy expended. And should you find yourself partaking of victuals in certain establishments such as the Plough Inn at Ford, you will be lunching with the ghost of a certain Will Shakespeare, who frequented the Cotswolds and is said to have penned sonnets over pints in several of these pubs.

A chat with the always friendly publican, perhaps himself a cyclist, can direct you to the churchyard where you can wander among the moss-covered tombstones or sit beneath the 1000-year-old yew tree. He can also tell you about other establishments farther down the road where bed and breakfast accommodation can be found. And so you push off again and pedal to...who knows where? Sudely Castle (where three queens of England have lived and which is now a museum full of treasures), Winchcombe (originally the capital of the ancient kingdom of Mercia), Hailes Abbey (founded in 1243 and now a mysterious ruin), Belas Knap (an eerie Druid burial ground), the charming town of Painswick (nestled on a hillside and calling itself Queen of the Cotswolds) ...wherever your fancy takes you.

Continental Europe

Most of my cycling is done in continental Europe, and though I tend to travel faster than touring speeds, the pleasures of the landscape help distract me from the discomforts of extreme racing effort, and I look forward to more leisurely training rides when I can be more of a tourist. I envy those who can take the time to really savor the sights.

Cycling was born in Europe, and a tour on the spiritual home turf of the bike should be the goal of every serious cyclist. Not just for sentimental reasons, but for the fact that bicycles and touring on them are part of the local way of life in most western European countries. And again, the smaller landscapes, the diversity of scenery, culture, cuisine and history are big attractions for cyclists.

Tourists from North America can fly to a major airport and cycle from there, or they can make use of the excellent rail systems to ferry them to a starting point out in the countryside. It's entirely possible to take in several countries on a bike tour, either by cycling all the way, or hopping on a train to cover more ground faster. Though the distances are smaller in North American terms, with the possible exception of France, that's a cycling plus, and most countries have enough variety and local interest to keep a cyclist fully occupied for the length of a tour. Some people return again and again to the same destination.

In alphabetical order, here's an overview of some of the best cycling countries in continental Europe, and what you can expect.

Austria

This is one country where the postcards don't stretch the truth, and you can easily picture yourself cycling through rustic villages hidden in remote valleys or following the winding path of the storied Danube. The mountains aren't as high as in neighboring Switzerland and the gently rolling Alpine terrain is full of charming vistas. There are plenty of sights on the heights, too, for those who want to climb above it all. The country is divided into half-a-dozen main touring areas, each offering a variety of attractions.

The Austrians are noted for their courtesy, warmth and hospitality, accommodations are spotless, and the hearty cuisine keeps a cycling body well fed. The beautiful medieval cities of Innsbruck, Salzburg, Graz and Vienna are small enough to manage by bike. Austrian trains will take your bike free, as hand baggage, during certain times on weekdays and weekends. Major stations offer a bike-rental service—half price for those with rail tickets.

Belgium

Now here's a country I know as well as my home in Canada, for I live in Belgium during the racing season. I choose to do so, because of the warmth and friendliness of the people, because the countryside is wonderfully suited to bikes, and the fact that bike racing is the national sport. Tourists, too, are well looked after, and you can rent bikes in every one of the over 50 rail stations. There are about 500 campgrounds, plenty of hostels, pensions and hotels, often found in even the smallest villages.

You can cross Belgium by bike in a couple of days, but that wouldn't do justice to what the country has to offer. Though it's densely populated, there are plenty of open spaces surrounding the main urban centers, and you can get lost in places like the Ardennes forest in the southeast, where some of the best scenery is. Little Switzerland, near the German border, comes as a surprise to those who think Belgium is relatively flat. Anywhere you go in the country you'll find charming little villages and lots of history, including numerous battle sites of the two World Wars.

The country is divided culturally and linguistically: the Flemish (who speak Flemish) living in the north and the Walloons (French) in the south. I live in the Flanders area, just inland from the North Sea, and do the bulk of my training over the gently rolling landscape there. I also work at my climbing on the several steep hills in this area, which hosts such famous races as the Tour of Flanders, Het Volk and Ghent-Wevelgem.

France

Cycling aside, France is the favorite tourist destination in Europe, because of its great diversity of scenery, the special ambience of its many regions and of course its splendid cuisine. Almost every visitor quickly feels at home in France, even more so out in the countryside, and while the citizens are sometimes accused of being unfriendly, there are few complaints from those who travel on two wheels.

The French are passionate cyclists. Nowhere else do you see such big crowds watching bike races (literally millions on the Tour de France), and racers like my former teammate Bernard Hinault are heroes of the highest order. All the advantages of such a bike-oriented society filter down to cycle tourists—including free bike transport on all but the express trains—and touring France by bike really puts you in touch with the host of pleasures the country has to offer.

Though it's the largest country in Europe, *la belle* France is relatively sparsely populated, and there are remote regions where you can cycle for many hours without seeing a soul, let alone suffering through traffic problems. The wonderfully varied landscape is interlaced with a network of delightful back roads where you're tempted to just park your bike and feast on the charm, including the local wine, bread and cheese on offer in the *charcuteries* and *boulangeries* found in even the smallest hamlet.

The scenery covers the full geographic gamut, from the high country in the Alps to the east and the Pyrenees in the southwest, the magnificent Mediterranean coast in the south, the charms of Brittany, Normandy, the Loire Valley, the Massif Central, the famous wine and food regions everywhere, the storied cities, and on it goes. There's far too much to take in on one tour, and it's best to take on one region at a time. No matter where you tour you'll find plenty of accommodation, and you'll have many encounters with fellow bike enthusiasts.

Excursions into the renowned French wine country are popular destinations of up-market tour operators, with rides through the adjacent Burgundy and Beaujolais regions particular favorites. Wherever possible, tours stick to the maze of smaller, quieter "D" roads, which run along the Soane river from Dijon in the north to Mâcon in the south. En route cyclists pass by illustrious vineyards and most tours here feature wine tasting as part of the package. Overnight accommodation tends to be luxurious, though the hotels are smaller and older than in North America, and full advantage is taken of the dining possibilities offered by the several Michelin star-studded restaurants in the area. The landscape is gentle, the required cycling effort modest, and daily distances easy. Included in the price of most tours is luggage transportation, morning and evening meals (lunches are bought on the road), with airfare and ground transfers an optional extra. Bikes are supplied by the tour operator who is represented by a tour leader (with full French language capabilities and local knowledge) who guides each group.

Here's how a typical week-long tour might work, starting with a rendezvous point in Dijon (just two hours from Paris via the very fast TGV train) and covering a total of about 150 kilometers (93 miles).

Monday: South for about 30 kilometers (20 miles), along the Grand Crus route on the west bank of the Soane, past the Romanée-Conti vineyard, traditional home of one of the world's most expensive wines. Overnight in a charming inn in the town which is a wine snob's utopia: Nuits-St. Georges.

Tuesday: A leisurely morning's ride (not much more than 20 kilometers, or 12 miles) down to another wine-label town: Beaune, with optional tours to nearby vineyards (Pommard, Meursault, among others), or shopping expeditions in Beaune's fashionable boutiques.

Wednesday: A full day to savor the attractions of Beaune, center of the Burgundian wine culture, with more countryside cycling, perhaps a hot-air balloon ride (very popular in the region), more shopping, and the like.

Thursday: Southward again for about 50 kilometers (30 miles), through several small wine villages with cobblestoned streets, to the cathedral town of Tournus, which also boasts a two-star Michelin hotel/restaurant.

Friday: Visits to such areas as Pouilly-Fuissée near the town of Ige where overnight accommodation can be had in a full-fledged château.

Saturday: Riding now out of Burgundy and into Beaujolais country, destination Mâcon, reached after a leisurely cycle punctuated by wine-tasting stops.

Sunday: Optional rides into the vinous environs of Mâcon, a farewell lunch, and back to Paris by train.

Italy

It's a toss-up between France and Italy as to which society knows how to live best, and the Italians rival the French when it comes to enthusiasm for bike racing. Events like the Tour of Lombardy, Milan-San Remo and the Giro d'Italia are highlights on the European racing calendar, and many of my peers in the sport are Italian.

However, touring in the historic and diverse Italian landscape is not as popular or as highly developed as in France. For one thing, the mountainous spine running down the center of the country and the Alps to the north are where the best touring opportunities are, and the fewer roads there tend to be precipitous and heavily traveled.

The Italian lakes, north of Milan, and the region of Tuscany around Florence—one of the world's most beautiful cities, I think—are favorite tour destinations. Wherever you ride in Italy you're guaranteed to find terrific food—lots of wonderful variations of carbohydrate-rich pasta—plenty of sun, and the friendliest people in Europe.

The Netherlands

Flat terrain, over 10,000 kilometers (6,200 miles) of bike paths, short distances between sights, friendly people—two-thirds of whom ride bikes—and a country where everything works like a charm, are some of the reasons for a bike tour in the Netherlands, probably the most bike-oriented nation in the world.

The whole country, including delightful Amsterdam, is geared for cycling as a way of life, and a tour here has only two negative factors: seemingly incessant wind, because of the flatness of the land and the proximity of the North Sea, and a dense population, which makes those cycle paths all the more important. But you'll seldom find a cycling tourist who doesn't enjoy The Netherlands.

Scandinavia

Scandinavian winters tend to restrict touring to the warmer months when heading north to Denmark, Finland, Norway or Sweden—all highly efficient and affluent countries that welcome cycle tourists—can be well worth the effort. Though they're lumped together as Scandinavia, the countries are quite different from each other in landscape, language, culture and customs.

Denmark makes for very comfortable touring, with mainly flat terrain, excellent roads, plenty of local interest, gregarious people and lots of delicious Danish cuisine. Cycling is nearly as well developed here as in the Netherlands.

Finland's hills are not intimidating, but it's quite a big country where the landscape of forests and lakes tends to go on and on, like parts of North America. There are considerable distances between points of interest, but the uniqueness of the Finns—their language is like no other on earth—and their culture are worthy rewards for persevering tourists.

Norway has the most spectacular scenery in Scandinavia, and some of the best riding/viewing anywhere, especially along the coast around the mighty glacier-bordered fjords. The Norwegians love the great outdoors, which is just as well, since they have plenty of it—the distances between population centers is vast.

Sweden's landscape is less rugged, and cycling is more popular here than in Finland or Norway. There are barren regions and expanses of rock and water, but also plenty of charming rural locales with good roads.

Switzerland

My coach, Paul Koechli, is Swiss, and since I'm now racing with a Swiss team—Helvetia-La Suisse-SMM Uster, with headquarters in Basel—Switzerland is like a third home to me (after Canada and Belgium). It is here that I often take time off for vacations, as well as to train on the roads. It's really my favorite country to ride in because the roads are so well made and maintained, and of course the beauty of the countryside is breathtaking.

The predominance of the Alps makes Switzerland a challenging country for bike touring and the mostly vertical landscape requires a higher degree of fitness. While there are straight stretches in the valleys most roads tend to go up. But the scenic rewards for hill climbers are well worth the pedal.

From a practical touring point of view everything here works with the precision of a Swiss watch—including the bike-carrying trains, which depart precisely on the minute—accommodations are second to none, and the whole country specializes in looking after the needs of tourists.

Those are just a few highlights of some of the touring destinations. You can rent bicycles in nearly every country where cycling is established, but if you're serious about touring you need to know something about touring bikes.

Touring Bicycles

Shorter trips can be made on any bike, but over the long haul you need to ride something more specialized, otherwise the effort you have to put into traveling begins to outweigh the pleasures.

You can get by quite easily for a day or two with an ordinary sports-oriented mountain or road bike. As mountain bikes become more developed, they are beginning to appear in special touring versions, which give you the option of really getting off the beaten track. And certainly, full-fledged racing bikes are capable of as many kilometers as you care to put on them; after all, I tour France for three weeks every July on a racing bike.

While the Tour de France is not a leisurely holiday and pleasure is not the goal—though it feels great when you do well—my long-distance experiences have been put to very good practical use in designing my own touring bikes. For holiday purposes, close-ratio, competition-type gearing is for the birds; you need granny gears and cliff climbers in the lower ranges, and a full spectrum of long-legged gearing options at your disposal. (Remember, what's mid-range for you might be low gear for your companion.) Tubular tires are a greater risk on longer trips, the ride afforded on most non-touring bikes is not the smoothest in the world, and as you sit in the saddle for greater lengths of time you begin to realize all the limitations of bikes not specifically designed for touring.

For extended travel you need to consider a bike that's built specifically for touring, one that can carry heavier loads over varying topography and road surfaces. It should be sure-footed and well-mannered on the road, giving you a smooth ride, stability and safe, sure steering, so that you can relax and take time to admire the passing scenery. You also need quality and reliability so that you don't find yourself spending time stranded in that scenery instead of moving happily through it.

Bicycles made especially for touring are essentially road/racing machines modified and equipped for traveling longer distances. In designing touring bikes, my strategy has been to create state-of-the-art models that are practical, dependable and trouble-free, while maintaining all the qualities and spirit of classic touring machines.

The frames are reinforced for durability and greater load-bearing capacity, and feature touring geometry—less acute angles, more fork rake, for instance—for a smoother ride, with a rear-mounted alloy carrier rack, extra reflectors, and provision on the frame for compatible mounting of extra carriers and touring accessories (two water-bottle mounts, tube-pump-peg mount, front carrier mounts, spare-spoke holder, and so on).

My touring bikes have 18 speeds of full-range gearing, with the emphasis on lower gears for easier pedaling of heavier weights up higher hills, as well as long-legged gears for effortless cruising over flat terrain with the wind at your back—the tourist's dream!

They feature powerful cantilever

brakes for bringing a heavily laden bike to a safe, sure stop, and more robust wheels and tires. The wheels are reinforced and have heavy-duty 14-gauge spokes (36 on the front, 40 on the back), and the tires are reinforced puncture-proof cushion types. The handlebars are special touring *randonneurs* for long-distance comfort, as is the anatomically sympathetic touring seat.

Those are the essentials you need in a touring bike. Next you have to decide what extras you're going to carry.

Accessories

Your bike shop has all kinds of stuff to put on your touring bike. What you choose is a function of what you intend to carry, and this in turn depends on the type of touring you're going to do, and how long you're going to do it.

More on what you need is coming up soon. Meanwhile, here are the main touring-bike accessories available. Some of these items are discussed in more detail in the earlier Right Stuff section, and I'm assuming you'll always carry tire-repair items, a pump, a lock, a small tool kit, and at least one water bottle.

- *Lights*: Essential for night riding and advisable for any journey likely to include riding time close to dawn or dusk. Generator lights tend to be brighter, but cost you pedal power. Battery lights wear out, but stay lighted when you stop pedaling and can be useful around a campsite—the choice is yours.
- *Safety flags*: Some people add to their daytime visibility by adding a fluorescent flag to their bicycles.
- *Fenders*: Probably a good idea for longer trips in wetter climates. The longer you stay on the road, especially in countries like England, the more likely you'll get rained on, and fenders can help make you less miserable by keeping the flying wet-road crud out of your face and off your back.
- *Racks*: Strength (for loads) and rigidity (so they won't buckle under weight or wobble and hit the spokes) are the main requirements here, lightness of weight being taken for granted. Rear racks—standard equipment on my tourers—carry the most weight and should be well supported with struts firmly attached to the frame, and for better stability should allow loads to be carried as far forward as possible. The best front racks place loads down near the wheel hub for a lower center of gravity. Their attachment should in no way interfere with the steering.
- *Panniers and bags*: Panniers are the saddlebags that fix to the racks and are used to carry your gear. The front ones are about half the size of the rears, and both types should be sturdily constructed from waterproof fabrics and have reflective materials on them. Single compartments are standard

(Left) Panniers come in a range of quality, prices and extra features. Front panniers are a necessity for tour-camping. They should go low on the wheel to keep the center of gravity down, and be easily detachable for those quick pit stops. (Right) The handlebar bag attaches to a frame that fits over the handlebars. One of its valuable features is a plastic sleeve on top which holds a map so you can navigate and ride at the same time.

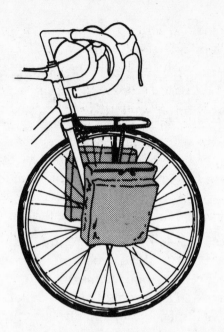

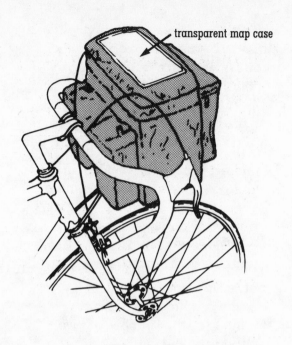

transparent map case

issue, but separate interior sections and zippered outside pockets are useful for more extensive touring. Saddlebags, which fit to the rear of the saddle like tool kits, are another option, as are the more useful handlebar bags. Handlebar bags, which become easily detached tote bags, should have a built-in rigid frame for anti-sway reasons, and their mounting should not interfere with the brake levers or steering in any way. They should have lots of pockets—for snacks, sunglasses, gloves, tissues, and so on—and a transparent, waterproof flap on top to carry a map.

What to Carry

On an all-inclusive package tour with a following vehicle transporting your luggage, prearranged overnight accommodation and catered meals en route, you needn't worry about anything other than filling the water bottle. Other types of touring require more self-sufficiency, the ultimate being a lengthy bicycle camping trip where the tendency is to want to bring everything, including the kitchen sink. Don't.

Remember, everything you carry on your bike is going to cost you in terms of extra pedaling effort, and any bike overloaded like a beast of burden is going to object like a contrary mule—unpredictable handling, instability, or total collapse.

The trick to deciding what to take on a bike trip is to pare everything you think you need down to the barest essentials, put it in a pile, then cut the pile by half again. Even then, you'll likely find some of the stuff you bring is never used during your tour. You might also find that something useful was not included, and you can make up for that oversight on your next trip. Make lists, take pleasure in cutting them down, and keep them for future reference. Here's what you need to consider bringing.

Tools

The better-prepared cycling tourist should carry more items than those in the standard tool kit for everyday biking. What you carry depends on the state of repair of your bike, the extent of your travels and your ability and interest in fixing your bike. In group touring it's possible to assemble a major kit and distribute the tools by weight among the riders.

Besides a tire-repair kit, tire levers, and at least one spare tire and tube (two might be wiser for longer dis-

tances), a screwdriver, needlenose pliers, adjustable wrench and allen keys, useful tool-kit items include: a chain-rivet extractor and spare links, spoke key and spare spokes, a length of cable, lubricants, cleaning solvent, a few extra nuts and bolts, spare light bulbs (and batteries, if you have that kind of system). Much of this stuff can be purchased in all-inclusive kits; otherwise, bundle it in a cloth that can serve double duty as a post-repair hand cleaner.

Clothing

You'll be riding in cycling garb but you'll be riding longer, likely exposing yourself to more weather conditions, as well as appearing in non-cycling situations where cycling apparel might be out of place. Elsewhere I've given you advice on choosing and wearing clothing for all kinds of weather. But on a tour you need more of it, a realistic minimum being an extra change of clothes for riding (while the other is being washed) and a civilian outfit to be worn in après-cycling situations.

Beyond that it depends on how fashion-conscious and fastidious you are.

Some cycle clothing can be dual purpose, like the better-quality weatherproof jackets and trousers, for instance, which help handle nasty weather while you're on your bike and are stylish and practical while you're on foot. To cover your feet, the most functional footwear is of the dual purpose riding/walking variety, though the ideal situation is to wear riding shoes in the saddle and carry alternatives.

Camping Gear

Camping affords the ultimate touring freedom, but it also curbs that freedom, because carrying your own overnight accommodations and cooking facilities can bring you dangerously close to the kitchen-sink syndrome. You might consider bor-

rowing or renting camping gear for your first venture into this aspect of touring, then invest in your own later—after you're quite sure you want to repeat the experience.

Talk to experienced campers before you embark on your voyage into the great unknown. When making purchases, deal with knowledge-able people in bike shops, sports stores or outdoor/outfitting special-ists. The key factor here is keeping the weight and bulk to a minimum. Note that traveling with others means you can distribute the load.

Remember, you need a good night's sleep on a cycle tour to recover from one day's effort and prepare yourself for the next. Sleep-ing bags are the key to overnight comfort on cool nights, and the more expensive ones are better insulated, as well as lighter. You can pamper yourself further with a padded mat to go between your bag and the ground, and the best ones fold up into next to nothing. More hardy tourists can get by with an ordinary ground-sheet or cycling poncho, but the well-cycled body deserves and needs something to insulate it from the ground.

For shelter, the ideal is a compact, lightweight, waterproof, easily erected tent. Some people are happy to sleep under the stars, bringing a poncho or plastic sheet into play for inclement weather. The better touring tents are the types designed for hiking and backpacking, most often sized to accommodate one or two people.

Portable cooking facilities include compact stoves burning different types of fuels, and assorted stacking utensils. Choose the stove according to size, ease of operation, safety (some fuels are more volatile than others) and smell (certain fuels are less odorous). A wide assortment of compact, self-stacking utensil pack-ages are available.

You'll also need food to cook, and it's best to do your shopping late on each riding day so you don't have to carry extra weight and bulk. All you need to pack is snack food (plus basic survival rations if you're extra cau-tious) as long as breakfasts, lunches and dinners can be bought en route. Concentrate on carbos (refer to the Diet section), and take a swig from your water bottle every few kilo-meters.

Maps

Maps are your passports to cycle-touring adventures. Besides prevent-ing you from getting lost—though that can be an entertaining adventure in itself—they'll help prepare you for what to expect on the road. The more adven-turous like to navigate by compass.

Specific country and geographical maps are needed to plan your route before you leave home. Once on the road you should have more detailed topographical maps and perhaps city maps. The best ones will show con-tours and elevations—so you can spot the hills, and brace yourself or take avoidance action—indicate road sur-

face conditions, point out sight-seeing opportunities, and so on.

Carry your large-scale touring
map in the plastic sleeve on your
handlebar bag so that you can keep
track of where you are and where
you're going as you ride—keep one
eye on the road as you consult your
map.

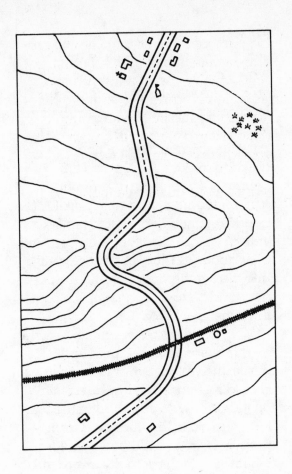

Topographical maps are
useful for planning tours.
The thin wavy lines show
contour and elevation
(check the map for scale),
so that where the lines are
very close together the
land slopes steeply; where
they are farther apart, the
incline is more gradual.

Miscellaneous Items

You'll need a kit of personal toiletries,
plus sunglasses, sunscreens, docu-
ments, a wallet with identification,
and a passport if you're touring in
foreign lands. Keep those items up
front in the handlebar bag. Optional
extras include a first-aid kit (a good
idea), flashlight, compass, Swiss
army knife, camera and film, toilet
tissue—more or less according to
your idea of essentials. Seasoned
tourers swear by a supply of plastic
bags for multi-purpose use—dirty
clothes, weatherproofing, and so on—
on a cycle trip.

Packing

Proper weight distribution and the
location of the cargo is critical on
your touring bike. Get it right and
your bike's stability can even be
improved; get it wrong and you'll
upset your bike's balance, causing it
to behave unpredictably, the worst
scenario being a severe shimmy at
high speeds, particularly likely to
happen on downhill descents.

Before packing your gear you need
to determine how much weight you're
carrying. This can easily be done by

putting your stuff on a bathroom scale. Give or take a kilo or two (you'll need more clothing for cooler weather, for instance), a comfortable load containing everything you need for a tour of several days, without camping gear, can be accommodated in about 10 kilograms (22 pounds). If you're carrying your accommodation, add about 5 kilos (11 pounds). A heavy-duty touring bike will take more than that, but anything over about 20 kilos (44 pounds) puts it into the heavily-laden-vehicle category and beyond a reasonable comfort zone. Less is best.

Most of the cargo weight should be over the rear wheel—about two-thirds; the weight over the front wheel should be carried as low as possible on the bike. With one-third of the total load carried in low-mounted front panniers, tests have shown that front wheel stability is actually improved over that of an unladen bike. But a heavy handlebar bag has the opposite effect, serving to upset the balance of the front wheel and cause unstable steering.

Handlebar bags should only be used to carry lightweight items. And individual bags should be packed with heavier items at the bottom to lower the center of gravity. You must also consider arrangement of your cargo in their containers, burying anything you won't need on the road and making sure items you'll use during your ride are the most accessible.

While your goal is to travel as light as possible, fully packed panniers and bags are best, since they're less likely to flop around and interfere with the spokes. Some panniers have built-in stiffeners, otherwise you may need to use a packed item or a piece of thin plywood to do the job. Finally, all baggage-carrying facilities should be firmly closed and tightly secured to your bike during your daily rides, though you may wish to detach them and use the panniers and bags as suitcases at night.

You'll find your loaded bike is quite a different beast from the one you rode away from the bike shop. Handling characteristics will have changed, and the extra width and bulk of the panniers must be accounted for in tight squeezes, crosswinds and the like. You should take your loaded bike on a trial run to familiarize yourself with what to expect on your tour.

Touring Fitness

It's a good idea to do a little extra preparation in the area of personal fitness, too, before embarking on an extended journey, or else that idyllic picture you have of pedaling serenely and leisurely through pastoral wonders can have a threatening cloud on the horizon—your exhausted body. Even when you're quite fit for regular riding around home, you may not be up to comfortably logging longer distances day in and day out on a tour.

Before embarking on a tour of several days duration you should condition yourself for the rigors of the road, both to get your muscles in shape and to toughen up your posterior. To avoid turning a tour into an endurance test, keep the daily distance easily manageable, somewhere on either side of about 100 kilometers (62 miles). Though most organized tours involve less distance than that, even then you need to be prepared for several hours in the saddle over several days. And don't forget you'll be sleeping in unfamiliar beds or on the ground, which might interfere with your rest and recovery from sore muscles and fatigue. Remember to include a few minutes of stretching and warmups at the beginning of the riding day, and a cooldown at the end.

Before you depart, I recommend that you gradually build yourself up to be able to ride farther than your planned daily touring distance, then work at maintaining that distance for several consecutive days until you're confident about managing the total tour distance. Do it first on your unloaded bike, then with all your gear (or load your bike with a similar weight). Work at conditioning yourself as discussed in The Cycling Body and Fitness sections, and remember to eat properly and stretch regularly, then test yourself by taking a weekend trip, including an overnight stop.

Off-Road

Mountain, or all-terrain bikes (ATBs), are mentioned throughout the book, but in this section I'll talk about the branch of cycling they were invented for, or in fact created: off-road riding.

Mountain bikes are one of the most exciting developments in the history of cycling. And the phenomenon is growing and changing so that their short history is regularly being rewritten. Their versatility means that cyclists have a viable alternative to traditional bikes in nearly every branch of the sport. But they began as all-terrain bikes, and that's where they literally took cycling to new heights and broke new ground.

Mountain bikes are descended from the heavy-duty balloon-tire coasters that served cycling Americans for many years before the English racers came on the scene. As with many trends, this one began in California and was pioneered by a few eccentrics who wanted to break from tradition. Their main purpose was to develop new ways to have fun, improve fitness and seek challenges—in locations away from traffic-laden thoroughfares and polluted urban centers.

There's a rise of land in the rolling countryside of Marin County, just north of San Francisco called Mount Tamalpais—known locally as Mount Tam—and it was here that mountain bikes first took shape. Many local running enthusiasts regularly trotted up and down Mount Tam's fire roads, rough trails intended for use in times

of forest fires. In the mid-1970s a handful of hardy souls began to tackle the trails on battered old coaster bikes. They called their sport "clunking," and the bikes became known as "clunkers." It wasn't long before courses were laid out, stopwatches came into play and competitions for clunkers began.

One fire road in particular became popular—a rugged and precipitous trail of about 3 kilometers (1.86 miles) with grades and slopes as much as 20 percent, and terrain of dirt, grass, gravel, rocks, boulders, shrubs and fallen trees. In their quest for more speed the clunker fraternity tended to destroy their machines, and by the time they reached the bottom the coaster-type brakes were red hot and smoking. The hubs had to be taken apart and repacked with grease, and the trail became known as Repack Road.

News of the Repack races and the concept of clunking spread quickly, and riders began to modify their bikes, borrowing ideas and components from BMX (smaller runabout bikes developed for kids), cyclo-cross and road racing, not to mention motorcycling. The earliest hybrid clunkers featured such modifications as flat and wide motocross racing-type handlebars and brake levers from motorcycles, drum brakes on the front and rear wheels, big, fat knobby-treaded motocross-type tires, and 5- or 10-speed derailleur gearing systems from road bikes, all mounted on a rugged coaster frame (mostly from venerable Schwinn bicycles).

By 1976 the supply of suitable frames dwindled, mainly because they were destroyed by rough riding, and several Californians began making frames from thicker but lighter tubing intended specifically for off-road use. Responding to the needs discovered in endless field-testing by enthusiastic clunker devotees, the bike builders (off-road riders themselves) incorporated such features as higher bottom brackets (the better to clear obstacles) and quick-release seat posts for instant adjustments to changing conditions on hills.

By 1980 full-fledged mountain bikes were being manufactured in great quantities, and since then their popularity has spread by leaps and bounds, taking them far and away from Mount Tam's Repack Road. Nowadays, most serious manufacturers include a range of ATB bikes. My own line features models designed especially for competition, sports and city or touring use—a reflection of the versatility of these bikes.

The majority of mountain bikes sold these days never get anywhere near a mountain, and many of them never venture off the beaten tracks frequented by traditional road bikes. But they're still built to handle the worst that's thrown their way, and that includes potholed city streets and the rough and jagged pavement surfaces often found on the open road. However, they were not originally intended for use on pavement, and there are some tradeoffs in that area, as I mentioned back in the All About Bikes section.

Though the fatter tires on mountain bikes cause more rolling resistance and are slower, they give a more comfortable ride than narrower tires on road bikes. While the upright riding style creates extra wind resistance, many people find this position more comfortable on a short ride, and for city riding it gives an easier view of traffic.

Speaking as a designer and manufacturer, I can tell you that the whole field of mountain bikes is still in a state of flux with new developments occurring all the time. While the differences between mountain bikes and road bikes have shrunk in the past few years—for instance, some mountain bikes now sport drop handlebars—the two types remain quite distinctive. Certainly there's plenty of room for both in the sport, and I think every cycling enthusiast, confirmed road-bike types included, should also have a mountain bike.

Riding a mountain bike in its natural habitat—off-road—can contribute to an overall improvement of cycling ability on pavement. Once you've mastered balancing and controlling a bike in rough country and become accustomed to losing and regaining traction, you're better able to handle difficult situations on the road. Your cycling body will also be given a strenuous workout, particularly your upper body, from wrestling your machine out there in the boondocks and over dirt and gravel roads. There, too, you won't have to face as much traffic, and the feelings of freedom, exploration and adventure are some of off-road riding's feature attractions.

Bikes

Mountain bikes have evolved more or less into the three categories that I have in my own line: racing (for more serious off-road use), sports (for general riding on and off road) and city/touring, with lots of potential for crossover/multi-purpose use among them.

Besides the general pointers for bicycle shopping that I mentioned earlier in the book, there are some specific things to look for when choosing a mountain bike with serious off-road capabilities.

- *Frame geometry*: As with road bikes, the shorter the wheelbase and the steeper the tube angles, the stiffer the frame. This means more agility and responsiveness (but a harsher ride), better-suited for stump-jumping, rock-hurdling and the like.
- *Frame sizes*: Because bottom brackets are higher, frame sizes (based on the length of the seat tube) are shorter. Because you also need extra crotch clearance (to be able to use your legs as outriggers in rough stuff) you should choose a smaller frame size than on a road bike.

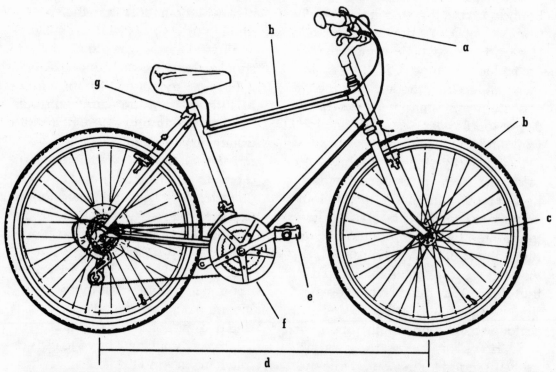

Off-road bikes show a family resemblance, but have a number of unique features. Overall, both the frame and the components are built more strongly to take rugged terrain in stride. Here are things to look for: a. flat handlebars; b. wide, sturdy rims and knobby tires for traction; c. thicker spokes; d. longer wheel base; e. beartrap pedals; f. high clearance for bottom bracket; g. quick-release seat; h. modified diamond-shape (to save the crotch if you become unseated).

- *Seat posts*: A spring-loaded quick-release lever enables the seat post to be adjusted in length as you're riding, raising or lowering your center of gravity: higher for more traction while climbing and lower for more control while descending.
- *Handlebars and brakes*: The flat handlebars have quick-access thumb-shifts for the gears and hair-trigger brakes, usually cantilevers, for stopping on a dime—or on the edge of an unexpected cliff!
- *Gearing*: Triple chainrings, and 15, 18 and 21 speeds are the norm, with wide-range gearing featuring lower gears (than most road bikes) for climbing walls. Cranks tend to be longer for a slower cadence and increased leverage in stand-up-and-pump situations.
- *Tires*: Fat tires with pronounced knobby tread patterns work best in the dirt, but are noisy and rough riding on pavement. There are middle-of-the-road tires with smoother treads, which grip well on or off the road. Another tradeoff option is a tire with a smooth central tread surrounded by knobby sections. Some people keep two sets of tires mounted on rims and change them according to where they ride.
- *Pedals*: Most mountain bikes have "bear trap" pedals, with serrated edges for a better grip. Toe clips are optional, useful for applying the power but sometimes a hindrance when a foot on the ground is needed quickly for balance.
- *Fenders*: Optional, they're useful for protection against mud slinging, though purists like to keep their bikes unadorned and eat the mud. This is why some serious bikes have no mounting points for fenders, (though they can still be attached).
- *Chainguard*: Also called a skid plate, a chainguard is another option, and a good idea in really rough country to protect the bottom of the chainring from being bashed around on rocks, stumps and so on.
- *Shoulder pad*: This optional extra is a pad that fits under the top tube and protects your shoulder when you carry your bike over unridable terrain. A shoulder sling is another variation—some with a pouch for a tool kit and such—the idea in either case being to save your shoulder as you walk or run (in competition) with your bike. Another type of pad fits on top of the top tube, and I sometimes use one of these (originally intended for BMX bikes) to provide cushioning should I suddenly find myself sitting down hard on the top tube!
- *Other accessories*: Heavy-duty water-bottle cages; small, lightweight pumps (some models are stowed against the seat tube); tool kits, with variable mounting possibilities; bike/hike bags that can do double duty; carrier bags, designed to fit out of the way on the frame; and assorted other usual bike items modified especially for mountain bikes.

Clothing

All-terrain clothing, adapted from regular bike wear for more rugged use, is a rapidly developing field. The more intimate contact with the terrain—trees, shrubs, thorns—coupled with the greater likelihood of taking a tumble, has led to the use of stronger, more snag-proof fabrics with padding in vulnerable spots, such as shoulders, elbows and arms, and pockets that close to keep their contents from bouncing out. Besides reinforced jerseys and shirts, many mountaineers wear knickers or trousers with padded hips, thighs and knees, and thick socks. I recently was given a pair of motocross gloves as a gift and find them well suited for rugged off-road work, their extra padding working well to fend off branches and the like.

Helmets for the hills are still the same as those for the roads, but off-road gloves have more padding and there are extra pads available for the elbows, knees and shins, descended from those worn by players in contact sports like hockey. There are several types of elaborately styled boots intended for walking/running/riding, with treaded soles for traction and high-top reinforced uppers for more protection and support.

When riding through elevation changes you need to dress for more temperature variations, using the layering technique and peeling off or putting on clothing as required. You're also more likely to encounter rough weather on the heights, so a stowaway all-weather top is useful.

Thus outfitted, you're ready to tackle off-road riding. And circumstances there require many techniques quite unlike—even opposite to—those used in road riding.

Techniques

Off-road riding is in several ways a whole new ball game compared to normal road riding. New techniques have to be mastered and they have to be brought into play more frequently, sometimes very quickly, as conditions under your wheels change. But everything you need to know begins with basic bike-handling skills, and the essential techniques are relatively easy to acquire through practice. Most of them are concerned with going up and coming down hills, handling obstacles and dealing with uncertain traction. Here's an overview of some of the special off-road techniques.

Climbing

In off-road hill climbing the major concern is keeping the front wheel in contact with terra firma while maintaining traction with the rear. Obstacles should be anticipated and met with increased acceleration, all movements—body and bike—should be smooth and fluid, and cadence should be steady, keeping balanced being all important. The object of the whole exercise is to maintain momentum.

- Preparation for the hill begins with a downshift into the required low gear by pedaling hard for a moment, easing up just as you select the gear. A slightly higher gear prevents wheelspin in loose gravel.
- Keep your weight over the rear axle by sitting well back in the saddle, but lean forward with enough weight over the front to prevent doing a wheelie (liftoff).
- Try to stay seated as long as possible, keeping the power on the rear wheel. (Toe clips help.)
- If you run out of gears and/or steam stand on the pedals with your hips back to keep your weight over the rear wheel, your arms bent and your upper body forward to keep your center of gravity as low as possible.
- During the climb you should help to steer by shifting your body weight, mainly your shoulders and hips, in the direction of the turn so that the front wheel follows their lead. This helps maintain control by making the front wheel more stable over rough terrain.

Descending

Priorities are reversed coming downhill—you need to keep the back wheel down and momentum under control. This is accomplished by proper weight distribution and judicious braking.

- Start by selecting the higher gear, on the big chainring, you'll use at the bottom, which also helps keep the chain tight and in place on bumps. On really steep descents you might lower the saddle to lower your center of gravity.
- Keep your weight toward the rear—more so on steeper hills—keep the pedal cranks horizontal, and your knees flexed to absorb the shock of bumps.
- Your arms should be slightly bent, and most of the braking should be done on the rear wheel as excessive front-wheel braking puts more weight to the front and can cause the bike to flip forward.
- Faster is better than slower to make washboard surfaces feel smoother, but take care to control your speed by braking, because things can get out of hand very quickly. Avoid abrupt steering changes.

Obstacles

Small rocks, fallen trees, hummocks and the like can be negotiated by hopping over them using an "unweighting" technique similar to that employed by downhill skiers (this is described in more detail under Training Tips, coming up). It involves briefly removing your weight from each wheel in turn and pulling them up to clear the obstacle. You have to ride around or climb over major hindrances, in which case a sling or shoulder pad on the top tube helps.

When riding through water you should, in theory, keep moving throughout, best accomplished by using a low gear and pedaling hard. Water deeper than 30 centimeters (one foot) tends to inhibit pedal action—and lets water into the bottom-bracket bearings. If you risk bogging down you should dismount and walk.

Sudden obstacles to be avoided or abrupt turns in a trail may require the use of a skid turn, the elements of which are discussed in Training Tips. Generally speaking, you should try to pick your way over obstacles at slower speeds until you become more skilled.

Experienced off-road riders employ more complicated maneuvers and tricks in really rough terrain, and it seems nowhere is off-limits to these enthusiasts. But this branch of cycling can be dangerous if you don't know what you're doing, and I recommend a cautious approach.

To pursue more advanced techniques you can begin by reading some of the specialist publications listed at the back of this book. Another useful method of learning is to attend courses offered by off-road clubs (see Cycle Sources), and you can also benefit from riding with safety-conscious experts. Meanwhile, here are some training tips to perfect your off-road skills.

Training Tips

The different riding skills for off-road situations can be practiced and perfected on flat terrain and smaller inclines, pavement, curbs and sidewalks included, so that they become second nature when you're performing under the gun and have to be able to respond quickly as conditions change. Work at very slow speeds until you become proficient at these maneuvers.

- Practice using the thumb-shifts on the handlebars (quite a different proposition from the down-tube position on road bikes), accustoming yourself to the longer jumps between cogs on the freewheel and more frequent shifting between the three chainwheels.
- Get used to moving your weight around on your bike, and practice raising and lowering your seat, using the spring-loaded quick-release lever, and lifting the front and back wheels as you ride. Try it on curbs.

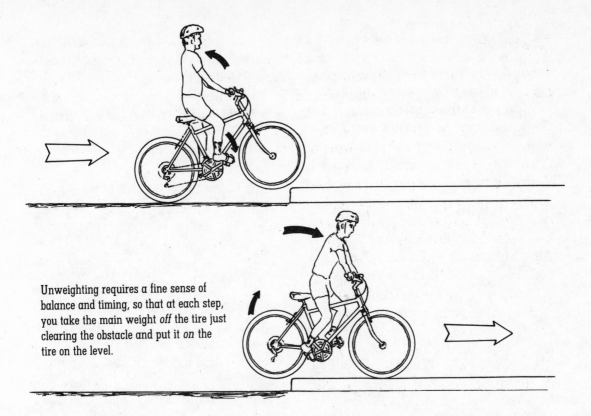

Unweighting requires a fine sense of balance and timing, so that at each step, you take the main weight *off* the tire just clearing the obstacle and put it *on* the tire on the level.

- To ride over a curb, approach it head on, select a low gear and move your weight onto the front wheel just before contact with the curb. Then swiftly pull up on the handlebars while applying power on the pedal downstroke to help lift the front wheel. Get the cranks horizontal quickly and lean forward again to take weight off the rear wheel, pulling up on the pedals—you need toe clips for this—as it mounts the curb.
- Perfect your landing technique by riding off a sidewalk edge. Stop pedaling before liftoff, keep the cranks horizontal and stand on the pedals with your weight biased to the rear wheel, which should land first. Keep your knees bent and legs loose and flex them as you land to act like shock absorbers.
- Work at keeping your arms loose and relaxed to absorb shock, and see that the brake levers are positioned for easy fingertip operation; rotate them on the handlebars if they're not.
- Practice braking with the emphasis on the rear brake, but also maintain speed control with pressure on the front brake, especially on steep descents.
- To practice turning by shifting your body weight—as opposed to steering with the handlebars—ride with one hand at slow speed and move your shoulders and hips in the required direction.
- Practice skid turns by riding slowly over a flat area—it's much easier on wet grass. Stand on the pedals with your weight to the rear, turn the front wheel in the desired direction, then apply the rear-brake lever and slide the bike out sideways, putting your inside foot down on the ground for support if necessary. To skid right, apply more pressure on the right pedal. More pressure on the left pedal helps induce a left turn.

- Experiment with tire pressures. Lower—up to 15 pounds per square inch—than the manufacturer's recommendations on the sidewalls is usually better, as more rubber is put down, making for better traction.
- As you venture into rougher terrain, learn to analyze ground conditions so that you're familiar with the traction afforded by loose gravel, rock, grass and so on.

Maintenance

Though they're built to take extra punishment, bikes used regularly in off-road situations need more maintenance than road bikes, beginning with a thorough cleaning and lubrication.

Start by spraying or splashing off mud or dirt, so as not to scratch the paint. Using a solvent or degreasing compound, remove grease and grime from the chain, chainwheels, derailleurs and wherever else it may have accumulated. Use brushes for stubborn areas, and apply soap and water to the non-greasy areas.

Dry the bike, then lubricate those parts that were degreased. Keep the adjustable seat post cleaned and lubricated. Once in a while, sealed bearings should be cleaned and repacked with grease.

Inspect your bike closely after heavy rides, checking it over as you would a road bike, but looking especially for such items as frame alignment, cracks in the frame, bent wheels and loose spokes. Also highly stressed are the chain and derailleurs, and the brake shoes are used much more frequently than in road riding. Generally check over the cables for excessive wear, and the bottom bracket and headset for looseness.

Commuting

Riding a bike is my job, but how about riding your bike *to and from* your job? If you tend to view cycling more as a leisure pursuit and less as a practical means of conveyance, it might pay you to consider commuting to work on your bike. That way you can extend the pleasures of cycling into the workaday world—imagine enjoying the trip to the office!—and the two-wheeled approach also enables you to take advantage of many other benefits. Strong cases can be made to show that traveling by bicycle to your place of work can be good for your body, mind, productivity and bank account.

Your body benefits through improved fitness obtained by regular cycling. Your mind reaps the rewards of an improved self-image—the result of better fitness—and the exercise helps relieve stress. Beyond that, the exercise-induced byproducts of greater self-confidence, an improved sense of well-being and feeling of extra energy contribute to improved productivity and greater accomplishment, both in your job and in your private life.

In the workplace commuting cyclists tend to be more alert, less accident prone, have less absentee-ism, and are more productive. These factors, which benefit employers, can lead to improved rates of pay and faster promotions. Corporate executives tend to sport the lean and hungry look these days, and for the upwardly mobile the bicycle can be a shortcut up the ladder of success.

After you pay for your bike your transportation costs are practically nil, since you've eliminated the costs of operating a car (insurance, gas, maintenance, depreciation), parking (including fines), or public transit. Your schedule benefits through more efficient use of time, as well as time-saving: bikes are usually as fast, sometimes faster, than cars or public transportation in heavier traffic, plus you can save, or eliminate, the time you might normally set aside for taking exercise.

Commuting by bicycle is also an unselfish act, since at the very least it harms no one while benefiting others. Environmentally speaking, bikes have it all over motorized vehicles. They're nonpolluting, from both a toxic-fumes and noise point of view, they don't consume valuable resources, and they take up minimal space.

With so much going for it you'd wonder why more people don't cycle to work. In fact, many cities around the world already feature a high proportion of bike commuters—Amsterdam in rush hour is a marvelous sight—almost every enlightened urban area encourages it, and the numbers are increasing nearly everywhere.

Let's look at some of the practical considerations of cycle commuting.

Efficiency

If your place of work is about 10 kilometers (6.2 miles) or less away from home, most studies show that the door-to-door time in major urban areas is at least about the same for a bike and a car, with bikes often being quicker in rush hours. Over longer distances, particularly where roads allow higher speeds, a car will be faster. But every car trip means time lost in varying degrees through starting it up, backing it out of a driveway, struggling through mainstream traffic—where a bike can often remain in constant motion—looking for a parking space, dealing with parking-lot attendants, and so on.

Over shorter distances a bike can also compete on fairly even terms with public transport, particularly in crowded rush-hour situations. When the nearest bus, streetcar or subway stop is some distance from your place of work, the fact you can cycle to the door gives you another advantage over public-transit commuters.

Routing

You can further outdistance regular commuters by bringing creative route choices into play. In urban areas your mobility on a bike is much less restricted than with other vehicles, which must stick to certain arteries. You can wheel through quieter streets, parks, alleys, parking lots, bike paths and the like, taking shortcuts and maintaining more constant mobility, while those in motorized vehicles are stopping and starting. The options open to cyclists mean that it's possible to vary the route to and from work to avoid repetition and boredom.

The starting point for route planning is a detailed map, one that shows every possibility and preferably is prepared specifically for cyclists, showing bike routes and all the safer, faster streets. Many urban centers now publish maps of this type, which can be obtained from bike shops, clubs and cycling organizations. One of the best ways to arrive at your choice of route is to talk to coworkers and others who already commute on bicycles. They'll have sorted out all the possibilities and can recommend routes.

Before trying route options on your bike, you can make reconnaissance missions in a car or on foot. Traffic density, pavement surfaces, road hazards (sewer gratings!), street widths, one-way streets, intersections, stop signs and lights, hills, the aesthetic appeal of neighborhoods—these are some of the factors to be considered when choosing your route.

Your first bike trip can be taken in off-peak periods to evaluate the practicalities of your selected route, checking the distance and generally getting the feel of the road. If you've chosen an unfamiliar path of travel look for such landmarks as prominent buildings, intersections and parks to navigate by. Time your trial run so you'll know how much time to allot for commuting.

Mixed Methods

You might also consider choosing a route that allows mixing your cycling with other methods of transportation, in order to extend your bike-commuting range, make it more practical, or simply add variety. You can cycle part way, then park your bike and hop on board a car, bus, train, or ferry.

When bike-parking facilities are provided a short distance from your work it might be easier to leave your bike there and walk the rest of the way. If you live in suburban areas, even out in the country, you can cycle to a rail, subway or bus station, and use those methods of transport to complete your journey. This is one way of eliminating rides through heavy traffic, and your morning and evening commutes can be more like relaxing bike tours. The process can be reversed by bringing your bike on the public transit into the city and finishing your journey by cycling.

Combining cycling with public transportation is highly organized in some places. In England and Holland, for instance, most rural rail stations provide protected bike-storage areas, and some stations have more bikes than cars in the parking lots. In waterfront cities such as San Francisco and Toronto (those who live on the Toronto Islands), cycle commuters use ferries to complement their two-wheeled travel.

With a bike rack on your car you can drive one way and cycle the other. You might drive to work, leave your car there overnight and ride home. The next day you can reverse the process. This direct comparison is one way to test the efficiency of bike commuting, as well as providing a solution to inclement weather.

A variation on the car/bike theme is to drive your car within cycling distance of your work, park it—at a lot, a friend's home, or on a street—and ride your bike the rest of the way, in order to avoid traffic jams and parking hassles. Bike/car pools extend these possibilities even further, with one car fitted with bike racks serving the needs of several commuters.

Bikes

Bikes intended for regular commuting and city riding need to be maneuverable, comfortable, fairly rugged, and reliable. Wheels, rims and tires should be able to withstand the rigors of city streets, where you're often less able to avoid bumps and road debris because of the close proximity of traffic. Efficient brakes are a vital necessity, gear-selection importance increases with more varied terrain and distance traveled, and corrosion-resistant and/or sealed components are a more important consideration than on a bike ridden only on fine days.

A good touring road bike commutes very well, its longer wheelbase, less acute geometry and touring saddle contributing to greater stability and riding comfort. Touring wheels and tires are built to take punishment, a rear bike rack is often standard equipment, and the frame can accommodate more weight.

For those more concerned with making their commuting pay off in terms of exercise, a sports-oriented road bike is a good choice, providing everything necessary for getting from A to B, with the accent on a simultaneous workout.

Two of my mountain-bike models are designed specifically for city/ commuting use, and many people believe that a citified ATB is the only way to go. For proof of this you need only look at the proliferation of bike couriers, most of whom seem to ride mountain bikes. The ruggedness inherent in a mountain-bike frame and the touring-type geometry provide the foundation for a city bike. Smoother, somewhat narrower tires, fewer wall-climbing gears, higher handlebars and less expensive pedals are features. Advantages include braking power that is generally better than that of other bike types, greater acceleration from the longer cranks, a better grip on the road with the wider tires, controls always right at your fingertips, and an upright seating position, which gives you a better view of the traffic action.

Besides the customary tire and tool kit, pump and water bottle, accessories for a commuting bike might include a mirror, a chainguard to protect clothing from oil and grease, fenders for bad weather, lighting and reflectors for night riding, detachable bags or packs you can take with you when you park your bike, and the best lock you can buy.

Clothing

If your commuting distance is short you can ride in the clothes you wear at work. For this reason some women prefer using a ladies' bike, with its mixte frame, so they can pedal easily in skirts and dresses. Problems of flapping trouser legs for men can be kept in check with a pant clip or chainguard.

But a proper cycle journey requires wearing a helmet, cycle clothing and shoes, which necessitates having a change of clothing for work. You can carry your civilian gear in panniers on your bike or in a backpack. Some people plan ahead and deliver, by car or coworker, several days' wardrobe to their place of work. It helps if you have an enlightened employer who provides a place to shower and change.

The problem of dealing with a sweat worked up while cycling is a deterrent for some would-be commuters. It is reassuring to know that sweat by itself has no odor, but bacteria in dried perspiration and clothing does. So if you wipe away the sweat and change your clothes you should have no problems. You can perform your ablutions with a washcloth and towel in a washroom, finishing up with a deodorant and the application of makeup, if that's part of your normal routine. Another solution, which I have used on occasion where water wasn't handy, is to wipe yourself down with a wet cloth doused with alcohol or eau de cologne, or an airline-type towelette.

Security

When your faithful bike has brought you to work, the problem of where to leave it during the day remains. Once again, a cyclewise employer can solve this by providing a safe and secure storage area.

The best solution is to bring your bike into your place of work. This might entail negotiating stairs, escalators or elevators. On stairs you can roll your bike up the steps, steering it with one hand on the handlebars and the other on the seat tube, or you can carry it by resting the top tube on your shoulder or grasping it lower on the seat tube just above the bottom bracket. On an escalator you should turn the front wheel sideways to prevent the bike from rolling. In crowded elevators you can stand the bike vertically on its rear wheel and hold it by the handlebars. You can also roll it this way in tight spots by standing behind it and pushing it along on the rear wheel. In these public situations a well-cleaned, degreased bike is an asset, to avoid unfriendly stares from the meticulously dressed.

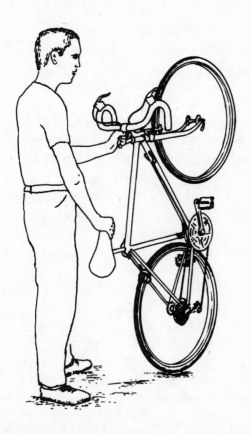

Carrying a bicycle: put the top tube on the soft, fleshy part of your shoulder and hold the handlebars with the hand on the same side. To roll a bike upright, grasp the top of the stem in one hand, and hold the seat with the other. This makes it easy to go around sharp, narrow corners.

If you can't keep an eye on your bike during the day, here are some other suggestions. (See the Theft and Locks sections as well.)

- Park your bike in a prominent place where any act of pilfering can be witnessed by others. It helps to establish a rapport with security guards and parking-lot attendants. They might be happy to keep an eye on your bike.
- If your place of work has some unused storage area (mailroom, janitorial room, etc.) you might get permission to use it for daytime indoor parking.
- Buy the best lock you can find—the U-shaped types are best—and secure the frame, front wheel (if it's a quick-release type) and everything detachable (perhaps your helmet, too) to a bike rack or some other immovable object.
- Bring anything not bolted to the frame with you. This includes the pump, water bottle, panniers, bags and packs, battery lights, even the seat if it's a quick-release type, and any other accessories.
- Mark your bike frame with some personal identification (your social security number, for instance) using some sort of engraving tool. Record the serial number, keep a written description and take a color photograph of your bike to help police identify it should it be stolen.
- For commuting, some people use a nondescript, battered old rattletrap that makes a less-attractive target for a thief, and save their good bike for other times. Trouble is you'd miss out on all the advantages, pleasures and rewards of riding a better bike daily.
- Home storage for a bike in daily use, especially if you live in a small apartment, can be more easily managed with hooks, from which you can hang your bike on a wall. Purchased at bike shops, they also provide a good solution for off-season storage, and you should choose a warm, dry place to discourage rust or corrosion.

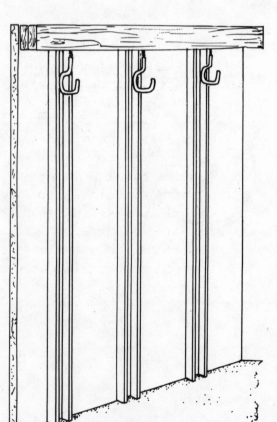

A simple J-hook, available in any hardware store, is one way to hang a bike. Stand the bike up (as in the previous illustration), and lift it up so the front wheel hooks over the "J". Other, more sophisticated racks are also available, with slots to hold the wheels, and flanges that hinge over the rims so you can lock the bike in.

Tips

If you're going to become a regular commuter your cycling concerns must have a broader scope than for casual urban riding, particularly in matters of safety. You need to master all the bike-handling skills so that you're fully in charge of your bike and know how to operate it in traffic flow alongside city buses, gravel trucks, fire engines, and so on. You must be fully aware of all the traffic laws, rules and regulations, know how to ride defensively, the prevailing attitudes to cyclists among local motorists, and so on.

I've already covered the essential cycling-survival techniques, but before you venture into full-fledged commuting, I recommend you take every opportunity to learn everything you can about safe riding in traffic and gradually build up your confidence. Read books, watch videos, take lessons, ride with experts... See Cycle Sources.

Beyond the safety aspect, cycling clubs and organizations can often provide invaluable practical information. In many areas these groups are highly organized and efficient, often working closely with local governments to improve conditions for cycle commuting and to establish signed bicycle paths or routes on city streets.

Unless you're a fair-weather cyclist you'll have to polish your all-weather capabilities to get full value from your commitment to commuting. This calls for the proper clothing for warm- and cold-weather conditions, as well as the necessary bike skills and riding adjustments for wet pavement, snow and such. No matter where you live it's almost a sure thing that there are bike commuters on the road year round, including winter's worst in countries like Canada. Talk to these people—eccentrics, some of them, but always interesting—to find out whether you're a likely candidate for year-round commuting.

When I was attending the University of Waterloo in southwestern Ontario, I rode to class nearly every day, the exception being one or two days during really severe blizzards. In the worst of winter my bike would be the only one on the rack, and since I also rode it between classes, I was usually the first one on hand for lectures.

One useful piece of advice from veteran commuters and bike educators is to take your first venture into serious traffic with someone who knows their way around. The noise and confusion, the cut and thrust of aggressive motorists, and sheer density of vehicles can be an intimidating experience for first-time commuters. Riding with an expert will get you safely through hassles until you feel confident enough to tackle the world of city cycling by yourself.

Competition

Bicycles were raced almost from the day they were invented, and to a considerable degree they evolved the way they did through developments pioneered and proven in competition. The recent breakthroughs of click-shifting and pedal systems, for instance, come from the proving grounds of racing. I also use competition to get my bike-design ideas into gear, but beyond that—if racing improves the breed—it also improves the cyclist.

At least 40 times a year I take to the roads on my racing bike to put all my cycling skills and fitness to the ultimate test—in competition with other riders, myself and the clock. The races last from less than an hour to as long as three weeks. They're held in cities, towns, villages and the open countryside, over every kind of terrain and in all kinds of weather. In short, racing covers the full spectrum of the cycling experience, with the added dimension of meeting personal challenges and achieving goals while engaging in the sheer excitement of the chase.

Competition is attractive not only to riders who wish to test themselves but also to enormous numbers of people who want to watch them do it. In western Europe and South America, bike racing has always vied with soccer and motor racing as the most popular spectator sport. An estimated 30-million people line the meandering route of the annual Tour de France, and the global television audience multiplies that number into a potential of one-quarter of the world's population. As the good word spreads to North America, where the bike boom is pushing racing more into the public consciousness, cycling competition is now the fastest-growing sport, in terms of both those who view it and those who do it.

The main forms of bicycle racing can be broken down into the three areas where the competitions take place: off-road, track and road.

Off-Road Events

As we saw in the Off-Road section mountain bikes were created for competition, and that branch of the sport is flourishing as never before. Most of the action is in North America where the main events are sanctioned by the National Off-Road Bicycle Association (NORBA), which was founded in 1983 and is the governing body that wrote the original rules, and continually adapts them to keep pace with new developments.

The emphasis in off-road competition is on having fun while putting mountain-bike riding skills to the test. The sport is less rigidly structured than other bike racing, with more of the event details left up to the imagination of the organizers. The main types include cross-country races (mostly through rough stuff), uphill and downhill races (the originals), orienteering (like car rallying where map and compass reading is involved), observed trials (where slow and steady wins the race) and stage races (longer events that may include any of the above, plus stretches of pavement).

One major difference between mountain-bike events and road or track competition is that the rough terrain keeps speeds down; wind resistance is less of a factor and slipstreaming doesn't come into play. Once the pack has sorted itself out from the start, the competitors tend to become separated and find themselves in an individual battle against the course rather than with each other. But speed is not always the name of the game.

Observed Trials are the most curious form of off-road competition and have been described as a combination of golf, ballet, equestrianism, slalom skiing and tightrope walking. The object of the exercise is to ride over a short course marked with flagging and gates, and laden with obstacles and hazards—called traps, and consisting of mudholes, logs, barrels, even wrecked cars!—without putting your feet down. Each time a foot touches the ground—called a dab—or a gate is missed, or a rider goes off course, or falls, points are given. A perfectly clean run, which requires great agility, concentration and bike control, scores zero points and wins the event.

That form of competition is based on an import from Europe where it began as an offshoot of motorcycle observed trials. Another type of off-road competition with European roots and related to motocross—riding motorcycles off-road—is cyclo-cross. It began as a form of winter recreation for road racers, and the bikes are modified road machines (longer wheelbase, lower saddle, knobby tires) that take competitors out into typical off-road circumstances. There are professional cyclo-cross racers in Europe who compete in the Netherlands, Belgium and Switzerland, and there is an annual World Championship event. One of my teammates, Pascal Richard, won the World Championship of Cyclo-cross a couple of years ago. The races are short —about an hour—and these hardy souls spend a good deal of time running through nature's worst terrain with their bikes on their shoulders.

Track Events

In track racing, the track is called a velodrome. A banked oval made of wood (indoors) or harder surfaces like concrete (outdoors), it can measure in circumference from about 150 meters (indoors) to 500 meters (outdoors) with 333 meters, or one-third of a kilometer (one-fifth of a mile), being the most common size. Track races are held over varying distances according to the type of event, usually 1,000 meters for time trials or sprints and 4,000 meters for pursuit races. These are Olympic events and that's when most people see track racing, the most highly specialized version of cycling competition, and one where all the action can readily be seen, though some of it is not so readily understood.

Time trials are the most basic form of track racing, and the most grueling, since they demand that contestants pedal as hard as they possibly can over the required distance or time, as in one-hour time trials. Individual racers battle only the stopwatch, but team trials involve tactics and precision where teams of four riders take turns leading and towing each other along to greater speeds.

Sprint races are more subtle and involve psychology, as well as sprinting ability. Speed counts only near the end, and before then a sprint resembles a chess game as the opponents feel each other out. The two, sometimes three, riders usually cycle slowly around the track, sometimes hardly moving at all, not wanting to give the game away by taking the lead, until the last lap when one will make a break, accelerating madly for the final 200 meters, trying to hold off the pursuer from passing.

Pursuit racing is similar to a time trial yet more complicated, because while the opponents are on the track at the same time, they start on opposite sides of the track. In individual pursuits the winning rider is the one who completes the distance first, or catches up to his opponent. Team pursuits, with two, more often four, racers per team, are like team time trials—each team uses slipstreaming techniques to gain speed. This calls for very disciplined teamwork, refined strategy—knowing when to attack and when to follow—and precision—being able to position their bikes exactly—from well-matched riders.

Other types of track racing include: points races, a mass participation event where points are awarded for winning sprints at designated laps; scratch races, all-out races for larger groups of riders; devil-take-the-hindmost or miss-and-out, where the last rider on each lap is eliminated; madisons, marathon events related to the six-day races of yesteryear; and motor-paced races, time-trialing behind motorcycles.

Purpose-built track bikes are a special breed, with extra-light frames, short wheelbases, higher bottom brackets (so the pedals don't hit the banking), a fixed single gear (with no freewheel cog), and no brakes. New technology is creeping into this branch of the sport in the form of carbon-fiber frames with flattened tubing, disc wheels, smaller front wheels and so on, all in the interest of less weight, more efficient riding position, and improved aerodynamics. Riders, too, are changing traditional gear for teardrop-shaped helmets and skintight suits.

Some of my earliest competitive cycling was in track racing, and these days this branch of the sport, though it depends on the existence of velodromes, has never been more intense or as popular.

Road Racing

Called the King of Sports, its riders
the Kings of the Road, road racing is
the type of competition most people
associate with cycling. It began in
Europe and still reigns supreme
there, while it also flourishes in South
America; the USSR, too, supports a
thriving road-racing series. In recent
years the tradition has been imported
to North America with great success,
and there are more and more
well-organized races contested by
well-funded amateur and professional riders.

One of the main reasons road
racing is reaching out to a larger
audience all the time is that more
non-European riders are climbing to
the top of the profession. The success
of my buddies Phil Anderson (ranked
among the world's best for several
years) and Greg LeMond (1983 World
Champion and 1986 Tour de France
winner) helped popularize the sport
in Australia and the United States
respectively, and I suppose my
achievements in Europe have con-
tributed to increased awareness in
Canada. For some time road races
were banned in Britain—deemed a
safety hazard on public roads—but
that has changed, and the British
Isles can now claim several of the
world's best riders, including Scots-
man Robert Millar and Irishmen
Sean Kelly and Stephen Roche.

But continental Europe is still the
pinnacle. It's where the prestige and
money are, though we have to work
very hard to get our share, since
Europe is also where the greatest
competition is. Every major road race
there is an epic event steeped in history and tradition and watched by
throngs of knowledgeable spectators
who regard the racers as heroic
gladiators.

From February to October, more
than 40 professional teams, composed of some 600 riders from nearly
two dozen countries, compete in up to
180 major events, and many lesser
ones, all over western Europe. The
sport is governed by the Union
Cycliste Internationale (UCI), head-
quartered in France, and there are
three main categories of road racing
on the professional circuit: criteriums,
classics, and stage races.

Criteriums

In criteriums, one-day events held in
larger urban centers, riders do laps
around inner-city circuits composed
of cordoned-off streets for up to 100
kilometers (62 miles). Criteriums are
easier on the spectators since they
can usually see all the action, and we
get over 100,000 fans at some criteriums in Europe; in the past two or
three years we've had crowds
approaching that in Canada. But it's
tough on those of us who have to perform, since there's virtually no letup
in the pace. To encourage the competitors, organizers throw out incen-
tives called *primes* (pronounced
preems), which are usually cash
prizes awarded to riders who happen
to be leading across the finish line

on certain laps—announced by loudspeaker only a few minutes ahead of time.

Criterium riding calls for sprinting ability, constant aggression and the courage and precision to hold your own in dense traffic. Bikes designed especially for criteriums have higher bottom brackets for cornering and extra-stiff frames for instantly responsive handling.

Classics

Classics, the most prestigious types of shorter road races, are one-day, point-to-point events, usually between major cities. There are about 16 long-established ones on the European tour, each with its own special character and challenge. A typical classic is Paris to Brussels, founded in 1893, an arduous journey of around 300 kilometers (180 miles) that takes us about seven hours to complete.

An untypical classic is Paris-Roubaix (founded in 1896), the most infamous of them all. It's known as the Hell of the North, a term that aptly describes riding for many hours on muddy—if it isn't raining, it's snowing—cobblestoned country lanes, and it's an achievement just to finish.

There are spring and fall classics, and about a dozen of the major ones are designated World Cup events with points awarded to teams and riders, and overall winners determined at the end of the season.

One of the most exciting new developments for North Americans is the inclusion of a Montreal race, the Grand Prix Cycliste des Ameriques, in the newly organized World Cup tour, which is patterned after skiing's World Cup. Though the race only began in 1988—I, ahem, happened to win it—it was very well organized and now paves the way for a truly international World Cup.

World Championship

The most important one-day road race is the World Championship, usually held in a different country each year in late August on a longer closed circuit over a distance of about 250 kilometers (155 miles). In the World's (as it's called), which also includes track events and other races for pros and amateurs, the top three finishers are awarded medals, and the sense of pride and accomplishment one feels while standing on the victory podium is terrific. The winner gets to wear the very prestigious Rainbow Jersey until the next year.

Team affiliations are forgotten in this race, and we ride for our countries. I sported the Maple Leaf when I competed in my first World Professional Road Racing Championship in Barcelona in 1984. The competition included 118 riders from 21 countries and hot weather—34 degrees in brilliant Spanish sunshine.

I was fortunate enough to win a

bronze medal there, in a seven-hour race consisting of 19 laps on a hilly circuit. It was just a couple of weeks since I'd won a silver medal for Canada in the Los Angeles Olympics, and had turned professional to compete in this event. I was a mighty tired, but very happy, rider after that effort. But in 1988 my World Championship had a less-happy ending when a rider attempting to pass me crashed. I almost fell, too, but recovered to finish second. Then I was unjustly, I feel, disqualified, and I lost my silver medal.

Stage Races

Cycling's glamor events, the most grueling, dramatic and well-publicized, are the stage races. The longer stage races are called tours, and each country in western Europe has at least one major tour: the Vuelta d'Espana, the Giro d'Italia, the Tour of Switzerland, the Tour of Holland, and of course the original—the Tour de France.

Stage races are really a series of road races held over consecutive days. Besides covering long distances over open roads, they include a prologue—a short sprint on the first day, mainly to publicize the start of the event—criteriums and time trials, which are similar in format to those held in velodromes except these are staged on roads.

Each daily stage is like a separate race, with a massed start—except for the time trials where the riders depart individually, and often use special time-trial bikes—and covering a distance of between 150 and 300 kilometers. Prize money is awarded to teams and individual riders for each stage competition. Individual times are recorded and the total time accumulated for the complete event, and this is called the General Classification. He, or she, with the least time is the winner.

The leaders in various categories during a stage race are awarded colored jerseys which they wear until overtaken by other riders. The colors vary in certain races, but in the Tour de France the overall leader wears the Yellow Jersey, the Green Jersey is based on points given for best finishing positions for sprinters, the white-and-red Polka Dot Jersey is worn by the leading climber, and the White Jersey is given to the top rookie rider.

In my first Tour de France, in 1985, I wore the White Jersey for 17 days and was classified tenth overall at the finish, and in 1988—when I was fourth overall at the end of the 3,300 kilometers (2046 miles)—I won the first stage and wore the Yellow Jersey for five stages.

Those Tour highlights brought me more publicity than any of my accomplishments in other races, including wins, mainly because the Tour de France is covered by something like 140 TV stations in 72 countries for a total audience estimated at one billion people. So, we road racers don't ride alone. In fact, this is very much a team sport.

Team Tactics

Road-racing teams in Europe have as many as 25 members (though only 14 per team are allowed in the Tour de France), and the majority of the team riders are there to serve the few "protected riders" who pursue the glory. The two or three protected riders, sometimes up to half a dozen on a strong team, are those whose extra skills and strengths are thought to give them a better chance of success, and the best one of them is usually appointed as team leader. Often, there is also a team captain who works closely with the team manager—the *directeur sportif* who follows the peloton in a car—to keep track of the race and assign the *domestiques* their tasks.

The *domestiques* are paid to give their protected teammates every possible opportunity to gain the advantage over the opposition. Some riders are career *domestiques*, playing second fiddle to the stars, while others, myself included, start as *domestiques* and work their way up to protected status. When I first turned professional I worked to help Bernard Hinault and Greg LeMond win races and learned firsthand that, no matter how talented a rider is, a great deal of credit for his success must go to his teammates.

Besides performing such mundane tasks as dropping back to the following team vehicles to pick up clothing or food and drink for the protected riders—and even help to push them along as they relieve themselves while riding!—*domestiques* work hard to help conserve their teammates' energy in other ways. When a leader gets a puncture or suffers a mechanical problem he might commandeer a *domestique*'s bike until his own can be repaired. If a leader drops back in the peloton for any reason (a puncture or crash, for instance), the *domestiques* help to haul him back into contention by taking turns pacing him.

Much of the *domestiques*' work involves riding in front of their protected teammates to block the wind, but also includes such activities as chasing after breaks to "haul back" escaping opponents, wearing them down by engaging them in dummy attacks, blocking them by setting a slow pace in front, sitting on them and refusing to help in the drafting process and so on. These tactics are usually under the guidance of the *directeur sportif* or the team captain, or both; and it is another duty of the *domestiques* to relay their instructions verbally to the protected riders.

In the final sprint, the faster *domestiques* will lead out the protected riders to give them a flying start to the finish line. Occasionally a *domestique* will find himself in front at this point and will win a stage—sometimes against team orders—but for the most part they must sweat it out behind the scenes, unheralded and unrecognized except by their teammates and knowledgeable enthusiasts. With the *domestiques* providing such valuable services it's no wonder that most protected riders who achieve success share the wealth with the whole team.

Most of the ebb and flow of a road race is based on the wind-resistance factor, which dictates that two people taking turns to break the wind will travel further and faster than one. Three riders working in relays are faster still, and the more the merrier, up to about a dozen riders, until the leapfrogging advantage begins to wear a bit thin as the distance to the front lengthens. At that point those at the tail end of the peloton are more likely to be wheelsuckers (also called parasites, limpets, and other epithets applied to those who won't do their share of work), who are just along for the ride.

A high-speed peloton is a phenom-enon to behold as it whizzes over the ground like a mini-cyclone, and the vacuum caused by the air displace-ment can actually be felt. A flying pe-loton can sustain a pace of upwards of 60 kilometers per hour (37 mph) for up to an hour, a speed something like 10 kph faster than the record for an individual rider in a time trial. A peloton in a stage race is a beehive of activity and a highly volatile mo-bile platform from which individual riders will launch themselves to exer-cise their particular skills in certain disciplines.

Sprinting

Sprinting sends the peloton into a pandemonium of pumping thighs, churning cranksets and whizzing tubulars as the riders jockey madly for position. It can happen at any time during a race, but most certainly within attacking distance of the finish line. It's always exciting for the spec-tators, as it is for the riders, though we're much too busy to appreciate the spectacle. All-out pedaling and just gutting it out aren't enough in a sprint. You also have to fight for a strategic position, and that often involves extremely tight racing and the risk of bumping.

My sprinting ability was one of my greater strengths as an amateur, though as a pro I've had to balance my skills more. In sprinting you first of all have to save your strength until you need it by biding your time back in the peloton, but staying near enough to the front so as not to lose touch. Then when the time is right to strike, you stand up and pump.

I use my upper body like a fulcrum, keeping my back arched like a rain-bow and as still as possible, using it as brace for my legwork while letting the bike sway from side to side with each pedal stroke. I keep my shoul-ders only as far forward as the front axle and my head up for better for-ward vision. Thus, less of my weight is over the front wheel—too much weight there can cause instability—and my hips are in the best position for more leverage against the pedals. I pull on the bars of the bike in a row-ing motion to counteract the leg movements. This puts more power directly into the pedals and prevents my bike from flopping around in wasted motion, which can also be dangerous for nearby riders.

Climbing

The peloton begins to play less of a role when steeper hills have to be negotiated and speeds drop. The steeper things get, the more work riders have to do alone, and so the pack tends to fall apart as those with climbing strengths surge upward and onward in a solitary struggle demanding great strength and endurance. Spectators know this and, liking to see us suffer, tend to concentrate on the heights in races like the Tour de France. The panting pack climbing a high Alpine pass is an inspiring sight, very emotional for the spectators and terrifically painful for us on the bikes.

Great climbers are said to be born, that they have extra lung capacity to suck in and process more oxygen under extreme effort. Riders who live and train in mountains tend to be better climbers, and a notable example is Luis Herrara from Colombia, who has lots of Andean experience behind him. I had a reputation for faltering on the hills, but I've changed that with more mountain training. Some of my best performances in the Tour have been in the mountain stages, and I look forward to improving on them in the future.

The uphill struggle is only half the story, since the return journey can be very dangerous and frightening. The European Alps tend to corkscrew downhill, and so you're often faced with sheer drops on one side as you fly around tight bends. But he who hesitates—brakes—is lost. You have to throw caution to the wind.

Time Trialing

Like those in track events, time trials on the road pit individual riders against the clock, and the peloton plays no part in the results. It's simply up to the solitary rider—who increasingly makes use of special streamlined trials bikes, teardrop helmets and so on—to marshall his energies and portion out his endurance over a set distance.

In the Tour de France a time trial might be held on a stretch of road up to 80 kilometers (50 miles) long, and covering it quickly demands the ability to gobble up ground in higher gears. It also requires the ability to endure suffering, because it hurts; much of the time you can't gasp in all the air your body needs, and you'll often see a trialist who's given his all fall off his bike at the finish.

This discipline of road racing is less appreciated by spectators, but it really is a trial for the rider. It's a struggle against the clock, and the rider faces the loneliness of the long-distance runner while engaging in the type of exhaustive effort put out by a sprinter.

Road-Racing Tips

Besides putting a premium on your bike-handling skills and physical fitness, racing requires a great deal of mental input and strength of character.

A race is often a battle of wits that you have to try to keep about you while you're experiencing a wide range of emotions: despair (at getting left behind in a break, for instance); elation (at catching up or leading); fear (on a high-speed descent); apprehension (at what might lie ahead on an unfamiliar road); aggression (as you push yourself to beat rivals); and relief (at being able to cruise for a moment after an all-out effort).

All those peaks and valleys are accompanied by varying degrees of fatigue and discomfort, ranging from dull aches and pains to pure torture, times you feel as though your lungs might burst and steel rods are being driven through your legs.

But the negatives are offset by the chance of success and, beyond the tactics employed by your team, there are ways to improve your chances of doing well.

- Conserve your energy. Always have something in reserve to counteract sudden surges and to sprint at the finish. Don't lead unnecessarily. Ride in the easiest gears for as long as possible.
- Stay alert. Ride near the front where the race is happening. Concentrate on watching how the race is developing. Know where you are and how far there is to go in the race. Be on the lookout for breakaways.
- Evaluate the competition. Watch for strengths and weaknesses, see who looks strong, who seems flagging, particularly near the finish. Focus on those likely to break and keep them within your range.
- Stay near the front as you get close to the finish—among the first-dozen riders is best. Here you can more easily keep track of developments and respond to them.
- Move up through the middle of the pack, not the sides—there's less wind resistance inside. But often it's crowded there, and a teammate can help you move up outside. Move into a gap in front of you as quickly as it appears.
- Know your strengths and weaknesses and plan accordingly. If you're a poor climber move up before the hill, try to stay in contact during the climb, and speed up on the descent.
- Use the element of surprise. Make your attack at a moment when no one expects it.
- Use psychology. Feign strength and stamina if necessary. Do the reverse by implying you're too exhausted to work, so that others will have to do the pulling. All's fair in love, war and racing!

Starting Competitive Cycling

It wasn't really very long ago that I decided to try competitive cycling for the first time. If the idea appeals to you, you'll find, as I did, that it's only a relatively short step, and a very rewarding one, from recreational cycling to testing yourself in competition.

Cycling competition is one of the most democratic and accessible of sports, probably because the necessary skills are more easily acquired by more people. It's no simple thing to learn to stickhandle while skating fast, hit a tennis ball properly time after time, slug a baseball over the fence or flatten a gigantic lineman. Granted, the top bike racers need to be exceptional athletes, but anyone can pedal a bike, and whatever their sex—women's racing is one of cycling's major growth areas—age, skill level, degree of competitive intensity, or kind of bike, some form of competition exists.

Besides the types of races I've talked about here, there are BMX and freestyle events for younger people, marathon races (such as the annual Race Across America, or RAAM), endurance events (for periods of 24 hours and more), triathlons (cycling, swimming and running), and various others.

The best place to start is by joining a local bike club. That's how it all began for me, and the enthusiastic people I met in the St. Catharine's Cycling Club played a major role in helping me get where I am now. A good club will provide you with the camaraderie, support, expertise and coaching to help you get wherever you want to go, and the group effort makes it more fun.

See the Cycle Sources section for the various organizations who can put you in contact with a club. Your bike shop can often help, too, and when you investigate competitive cycling you'll see just how well organized and how broad the field is.

See you at the races!

Fitness Riding

I ride about 25,000 kilometers (15,500 miles) a year on bicycles. Only about one-quarter of that total is accumulated in races. The rest is logged in training rides when I work on improving my skills and, more particularly, my fitness.

I have to do this to keep up with the demands of the profession, but a great many recreational riders do it voluntarily, using cycling as a short-cut to improved fitness. In fact, fitness is one of the prime reasons for the current cycling boom, and the sports/fitness models in my line of bikes are among the best-sellers.

People who take up cycling for fitness reasons have chosen well. We racers are said to be among the best-conditioned athletes in the world, but for any rider, the benefits of cycling are right there for the pedaling.

Some Benefits

As I noted back in The Cycling Body section, cycling can satisfy most of the requirements of an exercise program, particularly in the area of cardiovascular fitness.

Cycling gives the heart, lungs and circulatory system a thorough workout and conditions them to function more efficiently. The heart is actually enlarged—doctors have been astonished at the size of some cyclists' hearts—and strengthened so that it pumps more blood, and lung capacity is increased so that it delivers more oxygen. Both organs do their job with less effort, supplying more blood and oxygen to the muscles, so they can do their work better. In the process the arteries and veins are flushed out and cleansed of impurities such as fat and cholesterol, while the increased activity makes blood less prone to clotting and reduces blood pressure.

With the way cleared for it to work more efficiently the heart in a trained athlete works much less harder than the heart in an unfit person. The average heart beats at a rate of about 70 times a minute while at rest. The resting heart rate—one of the main measures of fitness—of a well-conditioned cyclist can be in the low 40s, which saves a great deal of wear and tear on the most important muscle in the body.

Weight control is another attractive byproduct of cycling exercise, which burns off calories at a healthy rate. A person weighing 68 kilos (150 pounds) can sweat off calories in a game of racquetball at a rate of 650 per hour, roll away about 190 per hour while bowling, or walk off calories at a rate of between 200 and 300 per hour.

Depending on the amount of effort expended (a function of what gear is used, wind conditions and terrain), the same person cycling at 20 kilometers per hour (12 mph) will use up between 300 and 600 calories per hour. Speeding up to 30 kph (18 mph) consumes calories at a rate of 600 to 900 per hour. Therefore, regular cycling, combined with a close watch on food intake, can be a very effective weight-control measure.

But in order for cycling, or any form of exercise, to work best you have to subject your body to a certain amount of stress.

Exercise More Caution

I already mentioned this back in The Cycling Body, but it's even more important in this section, which concerns more vigorous physical activity. Before embarking on any fitness program I recommend that you have a thorough examination by your doctor. This is particularly vital if you are older or your present state of fitness is not high. Ideally your examination should include a stress test and an electrocardiogram.

Riding a bike slowly is no harder on your body—perhaps even less so—than going for a leisurely stroll. But just as running is more stressful than walking, so is hard pedaling more stressful than cruising. You should get your doctor's approval before you start to ride your bicycle hard enough to get a thorough workout. When you embark on a training program, keep it within reasonable bounds so that you don't overtrain.

The Training Effect

Exercise physiologists use the term "training effect" to describe the exercise necessary for maximum improvement of cardiovascular fitness. The training effect consists of two components: aerobic and anaerobic activity. In order for your bicycle to work as a fitness machine, you have to ride it in two different ways: easier and more slowly over longer distances in aerobic activity (for greater endurance), and harder and more quickly over shorter distances for an anaerobic effect (for more cardiovascular capacity).

Aerobic exercise, which increases the oxygen intake capability—a main factor in endurance—is best achieved by riding at a moderately stressful pace, which makes the heart and lungs work somewhat harder than normal. But the effort expended should stop short of oxygen debt so that the pace can be maintained for longer periods; the increased workload can gradually build up cardiovascular endurance. To borrow a term from running, this means long, slow distance (LSD) training; in cycling circles it's sometimes called steady state training. However, the speed is relative, and as you get more fit, your long-distance riding will be faster and at a higher intensity in order to achieve the training effect.

Anaerobic activity, wherein the physical effort requires more oxygen than the cardiovascular system can supply, pushes the training effect even higher. The body is thus conditioned to produce greater muscular effort on demand—as in sprinting—but is only capable of doing so for a short time, until oxygen starvation brings on fatigue. The accumulation of lactic acid, an anaerobic byproduct, in the muscles leaves them sore and unable to perform until they are rested, the oxygen supply replenished and the lactic acid flushed out. The type of riding required here is called interval training—short bursts of effort, followed by brief recovery periods.

To achieve and maintain minimum cardiovascular fitness you need to exercise aerobically for at least 20 minutes, three times a week, working vigorously enough to get your heart rate up within the prescribed target zones according to your age. As you improve your fitness your cardiovascular workout will be of longer duration. The goal in fitness riding is to keep your heart rate up near the top of the range—about 80 percent of its maximum—during your fast-paced (anaerobic) interval workouts, and lower—about 70 percent of the maximum—for longer periods of time in steady, slower distance (aerobic) training. If you're training to become a racer you'll need to up the workload to nearly 100 percent. Working your heart at anything less than 65 percent of the prescribed rates provides very little cardiovascular benefit.

Your fitness riding, including both aerobic and anaerobic components—LSD and interval training—can be closely monitored by keeping track of your heart rate. You can use the table listed in the Frequency and Intensity section, or calculate your own heart-rate range using a simple formula: subtract your age from 220—the upper limit the heart is capable of—and take a percentage of that to arrive at your target heart rates during workouts. Thus, the maximum rate for a 40-year-old would be 180 beats per minute. An interval workout rate (80 percent of the maximum) would be 144; an LSD workout (70 percent) would be 126 beats per minute.

Your pulse rate will also tell you when you've overdone it or pushed yourself too far. Anything over ten beats per minute above your normal resting rate (taken first thing in the morning before you get up) may mean you haven't fully recuperated from your previous workout. Go out for an easy ride then—I believe "active rest" is better than not riding at all.

By monitoring your heart rate you can chart your progress, a great way to keep up your motivation.

Motivation

Obviously the harder you train the more fit you'll become. But the extra work involved can sometimes turn your cycling into a chore unless you take steps to keep it enjoyable. Here are some suggestions for keeping boredom out of your fitness riding.

- Take a systematic approach by establishing goals, long- and short-term (increasing your distances, preparing for competitions and so on), and keeping track of your progress.
- Keep your goals realistic so you won't be disappointed. Don't expect to become fit enough overnight to win the Tour de France. Slow and steady wins the fitness race.
- Keep a training diary, noting the details of your training rides: distance, type of workout, difficulty experienced, weather, and so on.
- As a motivator, a bike computer is a good investment, especially if it has a pulse monitor. You can also use it to calculate your pace, prompt your cadence and keep track of your time and distance during your training rides.
- Establish regular training routes so that you can more easily compare and record times and distances using known landmarks. And distances seem less over familiar terrain.
- Join a fitness-oriented cycling club. The people there can help steer you in the right direction, keep up your morale, provide inspiration, and often coaching.

- Get more detailed information on training from pamphlets, books and magazines (see Cycle Sources). The more literature you consume, the more likely you'll be consumed with the desire to train.
- Buy the best-quality sports/fitness bike you can afford. Besides the fact that the right bicycle is designed for you to get the most out of your training, any extra financial investment you make helps motivate you to get your money's worth, because you'll ride more often!

A fitness bicycle will keep you in shape during the winter. Some can be fitted with louvers on the back wheel to create "wind resistance" for a more strenuous workout.

Training Rides

It's really quite simple to turn your recreational cycling into fitness riding: you just have to work harder. You can do this most easily by riding regularly farther and faster, by using the pedaling resistance available in the gears on your bike, riding a fixed-gear track bike if you have access to one, climbing more hills, tackling more serious off-road terrain on a mountain bike—in short, pushing yourself, with better conditioning and improved fitness as your goals.

Before you get serious about fitness riding you should establish a training base through regular riding and plan on very gradually building yourself up, a day and a week and a month at a time. This gradual approach is necessary over the long run, as well as on individual fitness rides. You should ride slowly at first to warm up, then gradually ride harder, and finally end each session by cooling down, both of which can be accomplished by simply pedaling easier.

Refer back to The Cycling Body section for more details on this aspect of training, and for suggestions about how to combine fitness riding with other exercises and activities to maximize your training benefits. Remember, you should work out at least three times a week, but days of rest are vital components of training, more so as you work harder.

Long, Slow Distances

For LSD or steady state training, you should strive for a cadence of between 80 and 100 rpms in a gear high enough to keep your heart ticking over at around 70 percent of its maximum. You should build yourself up until you can work at this rate for a minimum of 20 minutes at first. Work at that level for a while, then extend yourself gradually beyond it, increasing your time/distance according to your goals. My longer training rides are from five to seven hours, which should be within striking distance of a highly motivated and well-conditioned rider.

As a rough guide, a beginning fitness rider should strive for an LSD workout of about 30 kilometers (18.6 miles) at a stretch, and do it at least three times a week. You'll find that regular riding over this distance will become easier as your endurance improves, which will also serve to speed up the journey. Eventually you'll cover the distance faster and likely want to extend yourself more.

After you've established a base of, say, 2,000 kilometers (1,240 miles) of long, slow distance riding, you should be ready to tackle more intense, shorter-distance training. Here, with the intensity increasing and the distance decreasing, you're closer to anaerobic-type work.

Interval Training

This is pretty serious stuff, elevating your heart rate to its maximum allowable rate for a short period, resting for a brief interval, then revving up again. It's hard on the body and you're likely to feel muscular pain. Recovery periods are very important, and when you start interval training you should add more stretching to your training routine (see The Cycling Body).

Beginning fitness riders should confine their interval workouts to once a week. After a month or two of this, two interval sessions a week, separated by two or three days of rest or LSD riding, are within reason.

Interval training can vary from short exertions of up to 30 seconds, longer periods of up to two minutes, or up to five minutes for maximum anaerobic power.

A typical interval training ride might begin with a 10- to 15-minute warmup of pedaling at an easy rate (maintaining a cadence of at least 90 rpm), then one minute of hard riding (in a higher gear), followed by one minute of easier pedaling (in a lower gear at an LSD pace), with the intervals repeated up to 10 times and followed by a 10- to 15-minute cooling-down ride to help flush away lactic acid in the muscles. Seasoned riders in good condition might throw in another set of 10 repetitions after their cooling-down period.

During the peak interval of all-out effort the heart rate should be up near 80 percent of maximum, possibly over it. During the recovery interval the heart rate should fall to the bottom of the target zone, preferably below 70 percent.

Interval training needn't be as rigidly structured as this. You can improvise as you ride, throwing in your intervals at random by sprinting for landmarks (a telephone pole, a rider ahead of you, for instance) or whenever or wherever the mood strikes you—including inside your home.

Indoor Training

Until recently inclement weather could provide a good excuse to suspend training rides. Students of the game of avoidance could point out that stationary exercise bikes, with adjustable pedal tension, don't really duplicate the training effect obtainable on the open road. And using rollers—on which you can mount your road bike—requires a constant balancing effort and also doesn't provide the necessary resistance to work the heart, lungs and muscles enough for a proper training effect.

The invention of the wind trainer changed all that. You can now train indoors with the kind of wind resistance encountered during roadwork, while eliminating such negatives as road shocks and traffic hassles.

On most models you remove the front wheel of your road bike and clamp the front forks onto a stand. As you pedal, the rear wheel drives fan blades, which create a wind resistance that increases with your speed, and some models have a rolling resistance—similar to your bike tires on pavement—mathematically built in. You can change gears, work on your cadence, stand up in the saddle and so on, in a very close approximation of the workout you would get outdoors.

During indoor training you can make the time fly while listening to headphones (no traffic to beware of now), watching television (there's even a video on the market that simulates riding outdoors), reading a cycling magazine (reading stands that clip on the handlebars are available)—or thinking about racing.

Race Fitness

Racing is a logical extension of riding for fitness, and when you start doing that you need to think about training the way I do. In fact, if you become serious about amateur racing, you'll probably have to train more than I do, since we pros tend to use races for training purposes. And racing is an excellent way of keeping fit.

As an amateur I did lots of weight training in the off-season to build up my muscles, particularly those in the legs. About half my weight-training effort went into building power and strength in my legs with squat lifts, while the other half was devoted to work on upper-body development. In the winter I combined that with playing hockey, cross-country skiing and some running, the idea being to develop all-round fitness and provide a change of pace from constant riding.

As a professional or amateur, even if you're just a fitness rider interested in training in the racing manner, an important thing is to avoid stagnation, which can happen by riding continually in one mode, doing three hours at the same tempo, or two hours on the same route, day after day. To be a fit all-round cyclist or racer you should simulate race conditions by varying the terrain from flats to hills, and riding in hot and cold and wet and dry weather to toughen yourself. You should also learn to change your rhythm during your rides, alternating between fast and slow, and practice changing from mode to mode quickly, to prepare yourself for the abrupt transitions from relaxed riding to intense effort in a race. You have to be able to adapt quickly, because a bike race has many moods.

Nowadays I ride mountain bikes as much as I can in the winter, then switch to my road bikes in the early spring, about a month before the racing season begins. I gradually build up intensity and distance, trying not to do much overdistance work—longer than race distances—so as not to overtrain, but remain fresh for the first races.

As the season starts, racing takes over the bulk of my training, and my season-long competition program is structured around certain events. I enter some races to get in shape and develop more power and stamina for the more important races. To prepare for the spring classics I will do a stage race like the Tour d'Adriatico, then usually follow that with a couple of days of motor-paced training—riding behind a car, often driven by Elayne—to polish my form.

To get ready for the Tour de France in July, I use June events like the eight-stage Dauphine Libéré and the ten-day Tour de Suisse as training races. Though my goal in them is improved fitness, I always strive to do well, and a win is quite acceptable! In the remaining week before the Tour de France I might do some longer intervals to prepare for the time trials in the Tour, some more intense motor-pacing, and some sprinting to keep sharp.

The period after the Tour de France is a difficult one, as I have only a short time to recuperate for important one-day races like the World Cup event in Montreal, which is only about a week after the Tour. By now I've got all the distance and endurance work in the world and only need maintainance training. If I have the energy I might do some intervals or shorter intense workouts, plus a longer ride once a week. I always put a lot of training effort into preparing for the World Championships in late August, throwing in a short stage race or two…and so goes the racing life.

PART FIVE

Cycle Sources and Cyclespeak

Organizations

I first got into the sport of cycling by joining a club, and I recommend that as the way to get the most out of cycling. National, regional and local associations, committees and affiliated clubs offer membership to all age groups and cycling preferences. They are sources of everything you need to know about cycling, and they teach skills and safety, hold seminars and workshops, offer riding courses, provide information, literature and maps, conduct tours, issue racing licenses, conduct competitions, and much more.

(*Note*: the following source addresses were correct at the time of writing. Check with major cycling associations, bike shops and libraries, for any changes.)

Canadian Organizations

Canadian Cycling Association
1600 James Naismith Drive
Gloucester, Ontario
K1B 5N4

Provincial Associations

Alberta Cycling Association
11759 Groad Road-Percy Page Ct.
Edmonton, Alberta
T5M 3K6

Bicycle Association of British Columbia
1367 West Broadway
Vancouver, British Columbia
V6H 4A9

Manitoba Cycling Association
1700 Ellice Avenue
Winnipeg, Manitoba
R3H 0B1

New Brunswick Cycling Association
141 Ryan Court
Fredericton, New Brunswick
E3A 2Y9

Newfoundland Cycling Association
P.O. Box 2127, Station C
St. John's, Newfoundland
A1C 5R6

Bicycle Nova Scotia
P.O. Box 3010 South
Halifax, Nova Scotia
B3J 3G6

Ontario Cycling Association
1220 Sheppard Avenue East
Willowdale, Ontario
M2K 2X1

P.E.I. Cycling Association
Box 840
Montague, Prince Edward Island
C0A 1T0

F.Q.S.C
4545 avenue Pierre-de-Coubertin
Montreal, Quebec
H1V 3R2

Saskatchewan Cycling Association
2205 Victoria Avenue
Regina, Saskatchewan
S4P 0S4

Other Canadian Contacts

Steve Bauer Bicycles
Niagara Bicycle Corporation
7 Meadowlark Crescent
St. Catharines, Ontario
L2W 2M6

Toronto City Cycling Committee
8th Floor, East Tower
City Hall
Toronto, Ontario
M5H 2N2

International Organizations

Alliance Internationale de Tourisme
  (AIT)
2 Quai Gustave-Ador
1207 Geneva
Switzerland
(International touring information)

Bikecentennial
Box 8308
Missoula MT 59807
U.S.A.
(American touring information)

Cyclists' Touring Club (CTC)
69 Meadrow
Godalming Surrey GU7 3HS
England
(United Kingdom touring information)

National Off-Road Bicycle Association
  (NORBA)
Box 1901
Chandler AZ 85244
U.S.A.
(Mountain bike Competition)

Books

Bicycles have inspired a lot of people to write about them, and you'll find quite a large selection relating to the subject in libraries and better bookstores (look under travel and fiction too). Here's a sample of some of them, as sources of further information and entertainment.

The Bicycle Touring Manual, Rob Van der Plas (Bicycle Books Inc, 1987). Very thorough and detailed, including a camping section.

The Complete Book of Bicycle Commuting, John S. Allen (Rodale Press, 1981). Comprehensive, though somewhat dated.

The Complete Book of Bicycling, Eugene A. Sloane (Simon & Schuster Inc., 1988). Strong on the mechanical side with lots of how-to photographs.

The Complete Guide to Bicycling in Canada, Elliot Katz (Doubleday Canada Limited, 1987). Touring destinations from sea to sea.

Cyclecraft, John Franklin (Unwin Hyman Limited, 1988). Well organized and informative; strong on safety and handling traffic.

Cycling in Europe, Nicholas Crane (Pan Books, 1984). Detailed information on every country.

Delong's Guide to Bicycles & Bicycling, Fred DeLong (Chilton Book Company, 1978). Thoroughly illustrated, large format.

Fat Man on a Bicycle, Tom Vernon (Collins, 1982). Very entertaining account of a mainly gastronomic tour through France via cycle.

Full Tilt, Dervla Murphy (John Murray, 1965). A well-written autobiography of this lady's cycle trip, alone, from Ireland to India.

Freewheeling, William Humber (The Boston Mills Press, 1986). A comprehensive history of bicycling in Canada.

Glenn's Complete Bicycle Manual, Harold Glenn and Clarence Coles (Crown Publishers, 1973, since updated). One of the best on maintenance and repairs.

Kings of The Road, Robin Magowan and Graham Watson (Springfield Books Limited, 1988). A portrait of road racers and racing.

The Penguin Book of the Bicycle, Roderick Watson & Martin Gray (Penguin Books, 1984). Strong on history.

Richard's Mountain Bike Book, Charles Kelly and Nick Crane (Ballantine Books, 1988). Includes a section on expeditions.

Richard's New Bicycle Book, Richard Ballantine (Ballantine Books, 1987). An update of a highly opinionated classic; excellent on maintenance and repairs, using many exploded diagrams.

The Woman Cyclist, Elaine Mariolle and Michael Shermer (Contemporary Books, 1988). All about the sport from a woman's point of view.

Magazines

Bicycling: Rodale Press, 33 E. Minor St., Emmaus PA 18098, USA

Cyclist: P.O. Box 907, Farmingdale, New York 11737-0001, USA

Mountain Bike: Rodale Press, 33 E. Minor St., Emmaus, PA 18098, USA

Pedal: 710 Spadina Avenue, Suite 709, Toronto, Ontario, M5S 2J3, Canada

Winning (North American edition): 1127 Hamilton Street, Allantown PA 18101-9959, USA

Winning (European edition): Offpress Ltd., 22 rue de la Concorde, 1050 Brussels, Belgium

Cyclespeak

For a first-time cyclist the jargon of the sport can be bewildering, particularly since different words may be used to describe the same thing in different areas. The words used reflect the long history and evolution of bicycles and the international background of the sport, plus such related fields as fitness. The vocabulary is also spiced with the inclusion of more modern slang and terminology, and the linguistic changes seem to be ongoing.

Here's a glossary of the terms you're likely to hear most frequently:

aerobic—with oxygen, as in aerobic exercise in which the cardiovascular system works to supply oxygen for muscular effort.

anaerobic—without oxygen, as in intense exercise in which the cardiovascular system is unable to keep pace with the work.

attack—a sudden surge to break away from a racing group.

bonk—suddenly running out of energy. Also known as hitting the wall.

bidon—the French word for the drinking bottle on a bike.

bottom bracket—the part of the frame where the down tube and seat tube meet and the crankset is located.

BMX—an abbreviation of bicycle motocross. Also refers to a type of bicycle.

breakaway—a rider or group of riders escaping from the pack.

cadence—the rate of pedaling measured by the number of time a pedal is turned in one minute.

calipers—the arms on the brake that press the brake shoes against the wheel rim to provide stopping power.

cantilever brakes—type of brake with the cables pulling directly on each caliper, found most often on mountain bikes.

carbohydrates—starches and sugars found in some foods, which provide the main source of muscle energy.

cardiovascular—pertaining to the heart, lungs and circulatory system.

casquette—peaked cotton racing cap.

century—a ride of 100 kilometers or miles.

chainstays—the two horizontal tubes at the bottom rear of the frame that hold the rear wheel.

chainwheel—(a.k.a. chainring) the large-toothed wheels moved by the pedals to turn the chain.

classic—traditional prestigious and historic one-day race.

clinchers—(a.k.a. wired-ons) tires with a separate inner tube, similar to car tires.

clunker—heavy, old bike used in the early off-road days.

coaster—less-sophisticated bicycle with (coaster) brakes activated by pedaling backwards.

components—those parts attached to the bicycle frame.

computers—electronic devices for measuring cycling speed, cadence, distance, time and pulse rate.

cranks—the arms that connect the pedals to the chainwheels.

crankset—the unit that comprises the two or three chainwheels, crankarms and pedals.

criterium—shorter race consisting of laps around a circuit of closed-off streets.

cog—the cluster of gears on the rear freewheel.

cyclo-cross—a competition wherein road bikes are taken off-road and into rough terrain.

derailleur—front and rear devices that shift the chain from one chainring, or freewheel cog, to the other, to provide a different gear ratio.

directeur sportif—racing-team manager.

domestique—racer who works to help protected riders on a team.

down tube—the frame tube running from the head tube to the bottom bracket.

drafting (also called pacing or slipstreaming)—following closely in the wake of another rider.

drops—type of handlebars; also lower sections of road-type handlebars that run parallel to the ground.

dropouts—metal lugs that accommodate the front (on the forks) and rear (on the chainstays) wheels.

echelon—line of cyclists riding in single file and slightly to one side of each other to lessen the effect of a crosswind.

feeding—eating and/or drinking while riding (usually racing).

fieldsprint—a mass sprint for the finish line by a group of racers.

forks—the front part of the frame that fits into the head tube and holds the front wheel.

frame—the skeleton of the bicycle consisting of all the tubes, minus the wheels and components.

freewheel—the set of five, six or seven cogs (toothed rings) on the rear wheel hub that the chain engages to provide the gearing.

gear block—another term for the freewheel.

glycogen—chemical for the elements derived from starches, which provide the fuel for muscular work.

hammer—to pedal hard.

headset—the ball bearings inside the head tube that allow steering.

head tube—the short tube on the front of the frame that holds the handlebars and forks.

hub—central part of the wheel to which the spokes are attached; contains the axle and bearings.

hoods—coverings over the brake levels on drop handlebars.

indexed shifting—(a.k.a. clink shifting) a more precise system of shifting gears that produces an audible click as each gear is engaged by moving the shift lever for the rear derailleur.

knobbies—off-road tires with pronounced tread patterns.

lead out—a race tactic wherein one rider sprints away towing another behind, then the second rider overtakes at a greater speed (afforded by slipstreaming).

lug—hollow pieces of metal that join the various tubes together in the frame.

mixte—a bicycle frame without a top tube designed for women wearing skirts.

motorpacing—riding closely behind a car or motorcycle that breaks the wind for the cyclist.

musette—bag with shoulder strap containing food or drink for racers.

observed trials—off-road competition where the idea is to keep pedaling, come what may, over various obstacles.

pace line—a group of riders riding in single file or formation and taking turns leading so as to break the wind.

panniers—front and rear packs for carrying items on bicycles.

peloton—(a.k.a. bunch, pack and field) the main group of riders in a race.

prime (pronounced preem)—a prize awarded to the leader at pre-selected intervals during a race.

pull—to ride at the front of a pack facing into the wind.

quadriceps—the large muscles on the front of the thighs, used a great deal in cycling.

road rash—skin abrasions caused by falling on pavement.

seat stays—two tubes at the rear of the frame connected to the top tube and the chainstays, and containing the dropouts for the rear wheel.

seat tube—the tube on the frame running from the top tube to the bottom bracket in which the seat post sits; its length is used to determine frame size.

sew-ups—another name for tubular tires, which have the tubes sewn inside the tires.

side-pull brakes—type of brakes with the cables pulling from one side—as opposed to center-pulls that pull from a central location.

sitting in (or sitting on)—riding behind someone who is facing the wind.

slipstream—the vacuum behind a rider, which makes pedaling easier for following riders.

soft pedal—to turn the pedals without applying pressure.

spinning—a fast, fluid rate of pedaling, or cadence.

sprint—short burst of speed, usually near the finish line of a race.

stages—sections within longer races that are held over several days (the Tour de France is a stage race); stages can be in the form of criteriums, time trials, or road races.

time trial—a race in which riders compete individually against the clock.

toe clips—the metal cages and straps that fit over the toes of shoes to secure the feet to the pedals.

top tube—the horizontal tube on the frame running from the handlebars to the seat.

tubulars—(a.k.a. sew-ups) lightweight tires, with the inner tubes sewn inside them, that are glued to the rims.

velodrome—a closed-circuit racing track with banked corners.

wheelbase—the distance between the front and rear hubs.

wheelsucker—term of disparagement for a rider who refuses to share the workload of riding at the front during a race.